THE QUICK-REFERENCE GUIDE TO
COUNSELING
TEENAGERS

The Quick-Reference Guide to

COUNSELING TEENAGERS

TIM CLINTON
AND CHAP CLARK
WITH JOSHUA STRAUB

BakerBooks

a division of Baker Publishing Group
Grand Rapids, Michigan

Published by Baker Books
a division of Baker Publishing Group
P.O. Box 6287, Grand Rapids, MI 49516-6287
www.bakerbooks.com

Printed in the United States of America

Library of Congress Cataloging-in-Publication Data
Clinton, Timothy E., 1960–
    The quick-reference guide to counseling teenagers / Tim Clinton, Chap Clark,
with Joshua Straub.
      p.   cm.
    Includes bibliographical references (p.   ).
    ISBN 978-0-8010-7235-2 (pbk.)
    1. Christian teenagers—Pastoral counseling of—Handbooks, manuals, etc. I.
Clark, Chap, 1954– II. Straub, Joshua. III. Title.
    BV4447.C546 2010
    259'.23—dc22   2010011714

10   11   12   13   14   15   16   7 6 5 4 3 2 1

Contents

Introduction

Developmental psychologist Erik Erikson observed that the "identity crisis" of adolescence is the most significant conflict a person faces throughout life. During these crucial years, young people have to answer the question, *Who am I?* For many, the question seems overwhelming. The pressures of peers, the new drives of emerging hormones, and the expanding opportunities to experiment with behaviors can combine to create a perfect storm of temptation and self-doubt. Some seek help from mature adults, and many find forgiveness and direction in life through Christ, but some teens try to cope by resorting to self-destructive behaviors.

In today's world of adolescence, *cutting, dusting, choking,* and *salvia* don't refer to cutting vegetables, cleaning your house, or choking on a burger. These terms refer to practices that are more serious—much more serious. Five years ago you wouldn't have heard these words used with the meanings that are now common in youth culture vernacular. They reveal how desperate for healing many of our youth are. *Cutting* refers to cutting oneself in a desperate attempt to relieve internal pain and depression. *Dust Off* is an aerosol computer keyboard cleaner that contains compressed gas and can be used to get high. *Choking* oneself can cause a euphoric state. And *salvia* is a hallucinogenic herb that is banned in eight states and is more powerful than and considered to be the next marijuana. These new fads among teens are leading to many deaths.

Teens are crying out for connection and looking anywhere to find it. "Rave" parties—large-scale gatherings with fast, electronic music and free-form crowd dancing, often coupled with the use of illegal drugs—have taken the place of family night at home. *Sexual morality* is as broad and relative a term as ever, reckless relationships abound, and parents have never before been so uninvolved or unsure about what to do. Ministering to teens has never been more difficult.

THE TEARS OF A GENERATION

With technological advances and community networks like Twitter and Facebook and immediate communication through text and instant messaging, you'd think we'd be more connected than ever before, have healthier relationships, and be less concerned with issues of self-esteem, drug abuse, alcoholism, and loneliness. But the reality is quite the contrary. The relational pain and social isolation cuts deeper today than in the past twenty-five years.[1]

Take self-esteem. Today 75 percent of girls have wished they could surgically change something about their body.[2] Twenty years ago models weighed 8 percent less than the average woman; today they weigh 23 percent less.[3] The overwhelming messages from television, billboard marketing, the internet, and mainstream magazines have taken a toll. Eighty-one percent of ten-year-olds now worry they're too fat.[4]

And relational gluttony flourishes. Chat rooms, web pages, and "EMO"—the latest music fad with confessional lyrics that invite young people to "be real" and express themselves—have teenagers giving more than they should emotionally and physically to others, even strangers. Gone are the days of courting and dating. Today, teenagers live in a culture of "hooking up," which could include anything from innocent kissing to oral sex or intercourse, depending on whom you ask. Thirty percent have admitted to hooking up with someone they just met that day. Sixty-four percent have hooked up with someone they considered a friend.[5] When a generation is taught to do what *feels good*, it seems preposterous to them to think of guarding the heart, as we're taught in Proverbs 4:23.

With meaningless, superficial relationships come increased loneliness, hurt, hopelessness, and tears. Teens are left relationally empty over and over again, and the adults who watch don't know what to do. Teen suicide has become the third-leading cause of death among the age group.[6] And eight thousand teens a day will contract a sexually transmitted disease.[7] Relational gluttony is not the answer to emotional emptiness. It only perpetuates it.

The cries of this generation are real. The genesis of the problem, we believe, is found in the breakdown of healthy, meaningful relationships that promise stability and wisdom. Consider that three thousand kids a day will see their parents divorce.[8] Worse yet, by age eighteen, 33 percent of girls and 17 percent of boys have been sexually abused by someone they loved or trusted.[9]

That's not all. Nearly 40 percent of America's kids do not live with their biological father—and more than half of them haven't seen their dad in the past year.[10] Sixty-three percent of youth suicides occur in homes where there is no father. The same is true of the homes of 90 percent of homeless/runaway children, 85 percent of children with behavior problems, 71 percent of high school dropouts, 85 percent of youths in prison, and well over 50 percent of teen mothers.[11] Nearly 73 percent of the U.S. population believes homes without fathers is the most significant family or social problem facing America.[12]

The hole in the hearts of our teens is deep. And it has left them searching for and accepting nearly anything to fill it.

A SEARCHING GENERATION

When you look at what modern kids believe, the confusion is startling.

More than any other generation, the present-day culture reflects a postmodern belief in which, generally speaking, a relativistic mindset takes precedence over any absolutes. In fact, Ron Luce, president and founder of Teen Mania, reported that 91 percent of teens today do not believe in absolute truth.[13] In another survey, George Barna found that only 6 percent of teens believe in absolute truth. And by the way, these are teens who define themselves as "born-again Christians."[14]

Barna also found that only 22 percent of born-again adults believe in moral absolutes and 64 percent believe truth is relative to a particular situation. Their beliefs will, of course, influence their children, so it's not surprising that an alarming 83 percent of teens believe moral truth is dependent on a given situation.

Josh McDowell, who has worked extensively with teens, asserts:

> Seventy-five percent of all kids coming to Christ today are not coming to Jesus because He's the way, the truth, and the life. They are coming to Christ because He is the best thing that's come along so far, that they've filtered through their experience. And as soon as something better to them comes along, they're gone.[15]

It's interesting that in separate surveys both Barna and McDowell found that Christian teenagers are most likely to make moral decisions based on what feels right in the moment. Teenagers today are making decisions out of feeling, not because of an objective truth outside of themselves.

Contrary to what many adults believe about them, teens are usually not "bad kids"; they're young people searching fervently for something real, something authentic, something divine. All they need is somebody to lead them, someone they can trust.

SEEING THE NEED

Christians are called "to proclaim freedom for the prisoners and recovery of sight for the blind" (Luke 4:18), and this includes breaking the relational and spiritual bondage our youth are often enslaved to and helping them see through the cultural lies to the truth of the Word. This *Quick-Reference Guide* is designed to assist professional counselors, pastors, and lay counselors in doing just that!

If you are a professional counselor, you are already very familiar with the topics in this guide. This book will help you:

- accurately determine the client's problems by using the assessment questions in each section
- see a client's problem and solutions from a biblical perspective
- give clear guidance to your clients so they can take strong steps forward
- be more aware of resources that can help your client stimulate right thinking, processing, and action

If you are a pastor or lay counselor, we recommend that you take time to read through the entire book, marking key points in each section that stand out to you. As you become familiar with the topics, symptoms, approaches, and resources, you will want to make a list of referral resources in your community. The guide will help you:

- gain information about the nature of teen stresses, problems, and disorders
- assist you in compiling a list of competent referral resources
- assess the nature and severity of the teen's problem
- remind you that there are limits to a lay caregiver's role
- assist you in making the proper referral to a physician, a professional counselor, or an agency

HOW TO USE THIS GUIDE

This *Quick-Reference Guide* provides insights and resources to help you assess problems and offer effective solutions. The elements in each section are:

1. **Portraits.** Each topic begins with a number of counseling vignettes that tell a common story about teens struggling with the issue at hand. The portraits show how a specific topic surfaces in an individual's life and relationships. We provide several portraits for each topic because one issue can present itself in different ways in different individuals' lives.

2. **Definitions and Key Thoughts.** This section covers some of the most current statistical findings and clinical insights for each issue. The research will help you understand the nuances of the problem and provide direction for your conversations with the teen, and perhaps the teen's parents.

3. **Assessment Interview.** The interview for each topic provides important, probing questions you can use to assess the person's needs and situation. In many cases, you'll need to ask follow-up questions or say to the person, "Tell me more about that." Some of the topics include a separate set of questions for parents.

4. **Wise Counsel.** This section provides additional insights into the presenting problem, the biblical perspective, the process of healing and restoration, or another issue related to your care for the teen client. Sometimes the insights in this section are clinical, and sometimes they are pastoral, but in every case, they give added perspective to help you meet needs.

5. **Action Steps.** This is one of the most important sections in the guide because it helps you move the conversation from assessment and problem identification to creating a map and plan for healing, recovery, and growth. Without an action plan, clients are often confused and drift without making progress toward some concrete goals for change. Most Action Steps will be directed to the counselee. In some cases there are Action Steps for the parents as well. Those addressed to the counselor will be in italics.

6. **Biblical Insights.** Here we provide passages of Scripture that relate to the topic, and we've explained the significance of each one with several important points. You may want to explain the Scripture to the teen or you may choose to study it by yourself to enrich your understanding of how God works to change lives. Many of the passages and insights can be used for virtually all of the topics.

Take some time to look over the insights in each chapter to find passages that apply to the people who come to you for counseling.

7. **Prayer Starter.** Many Christians welcome—and even expect—prayer as an integral part of the counseling process, but prayer is not an appropriate intervention with every person you see. If a person isn't a believer or has shown resistance to God, you can pray silently during the session or after the appointment is over and the person has left. We realize individual preferences about prayer and the needs of those we help differ greatly, but we recognize that prayer is an essential element in biblical counseling. The Prayer Starter sections provide a few simple lines to begin a prayer that is said out loud or silently, during or after an appointment.

8. **Recommended Resources.** This guide is not meant to provide an exhaustive look at any of the topics. In each case we provide an overview and a brief template for addressing the needs. Continuing education is very important, so each Recommended Resources section lists a few books and/or multimedia programs we have found to be useful and trustworthy.

One additional note: to avoid the cumbersome use of "he or she" throughout this guide, we have chosen to alternate the use of the male and female pronouns, using only one in a chapter. In most cases these are alternated from one chapter to the next, unless the topic of a chapter is gender specific.

A VARIETY OF NEEDS

A quick glance at the table of contents shows that some of the problems clients face are primarily *medical* (such as eating disorders or attention deficit hyperactivity disorder); some are *psychological* and are the result of traumatic events, addictions, compulsions, or inordinate fears; and some deal with *communication* between teens and family members. In many (if not most) cases, the problem is actually a combination of these causes.

If there is any question about a medical condition causing or contributing to the problem, the client should be referred to a physician. A wide array of therapeutic approaches have proven effective for teens, from rational emotive therapy, which helps clients identify and replace destructive thought patterns, to behavior therapy and support groups for abuse or addiction.

We appreciate your desire to help people walk with God. Christian counseling is a strong, effective form of discipleship and is often the door to breaking through years of pain, misperceptions, and destructive habits that have kept people from being fully alive to God. We are honored to be partners with you in your work, and we trust that God will continue to use you in powerful ways to touch people's lives.

ADDITIONAL RESOURCES

The American Association of Christian Counselors (AACC) provides training, curricula, books, workshops, and other resources to equip people to care for others. At the end of each topic in this guide, you'll find specific resources for greater understanding of the issue, and we recommend additional materials and online help for those who want broader input on counseling topics and skills. These include:

The Bible for Hope: Caring for People God's Way by Dr. Tim Clinton and many other leading contributors (Thomas Nelson, 2006).

Caring for People God's Way: Personal and Emotional Issues, Addictions, Grief, and Trauma by Tim Clinton, Arch Hart, and George Ohlschlager (Thomas Nelson, 2005).

Other valuable training resources are offered through the AACC's Light University. Courses include:

Breaking Free

Caring for Teens God's Way

Extraordinary Women

Healthy Sexuality

Marriage Works

In addition, the AACC offers many more resources and training on three websites:

www.aacc.net

www.ecounseling.com

www.lightuniversity.com

Continue to sharpen your skills and deepen your understanding of issues that affect the people God puts in your path. These resources can help.

The American Association of Christian Counselors has nearly fifty thousand members throughout the country and around the world. The AACC is dedicated to providing the finest resources to help professional counselors, pastors, and lay counselors care for hurting people. Outstanding training, books, and events augment membership benefits that include the magazine *Christian Counseling Today*. For more information about the AACC, go to www.aacc.net.

Abortion

PORTRAITS : 1

- Kate is in trouble—big time. She's a senior in high school, and on the surface, her life looks terrific. She received a scholarship to college, she has a handsome boyfriend, and she's a leader in her church youth group. But recently she took an at-home pregnancy test and it was positive. She can't give up her dreams for this one mistake. Besides, it's such a simple procedure, and no one needs to know.
- *I have been forgiven, I know it, but why can't I get over this?* Nancy kept repeating the words to herself as she glanced at her friends sitting with her in church. They have been asking, "What's been up with you? You're acting different." Her teachers have also been concerned as her grades have plummeted. Nancy tried to concentrate on the sermon, but the Right to Life announcement in the bulletin claimed all of her attention. *I didn't realize what I was doing,* she mumbled.

DEFINITIONS AND KEY THOUGHTS : 2

- The term *abortion* refers to the premature exit of a human fetus. It is most commonly understood today as an *artificially induced expulsion* by either surgical or chemical means, which is the primary focus of this chapter.
- A young woman with an unplanned pregnancy needs to understand that the *"quick and easy" choice is neither quick nor easy* but can carry long-term repercussions.
- Often a woman chooses to keep an abortion a secret, especially if she is a part of a Christian or pro-life community or family that she perceives might be judgmental or condemning. If her family members don't know, the *grief and loss* surrounding an abortion may remain unprocessed for years.
- An abortion can be *experienced as a loss*, sometimes to the point of *trauma*. Some of the possible side effects are a tendency to *reexperience the event* with dreams or flashbacks, as well as a tendency to avoid all thoughts or feelings associated with the abortion.
- Other *possible side effects* from an abortion are emotional numbing, sleep disorders, difficulty concentrating, hypervigilance, depression, guilt, and an inability to forgive oneself.

- Trying to cope alone with the reality of an abortion is often *isolating* and *may reinforce a woman's sense of shame.* Self-destructive behaviors, such as substance abuse, may also be present.

- If someone confides in you that she has had an abortion, realize that in sharing this experience, she has decided to trust you. *Be careful with any verbal or nonverbal behaviors* that might increase her guilt and shame or drive her away from the support and care she needs.

- Consider the findings from a survey of 252 women who joined a post-abortion support group:

  — 70 percent had a prior negative moral view of abortion.
  — More than 80 percent would have carried to term with better circumstances or more support from loved ones.
  — 53 percent felt "forced" to have the abortion by people in their lives.
  — 64 percent felt "forced" to have the abortion by circumstances in their lives.
  — Almost 40 percent were still hoping to learn of some alternative to abortion when they sat down for counseling at the abortion clinic.[1]

3 : ASSESSMENT INTERVIEW

For the Teen Contemplating Abortion

1. How do you know that you are pregnant? Have you had a medical examination? (*These gentle questions about the pregnancy will help the counselee feel comfortable and take responsibility.*)
2. How far along are you in your pregnancy?
3. What are your current financial circumstances?
4. What do you expect will be your family's response to your pregnancy? Is it possible to invite them to help you make decisions about what to do?
5. Do you have adequate social support (healthy, genuine relationships with family, friends, youth group leaders, mentors, teachers, and/or others)?
6. Who is the baby's father? What kind of relationship do you have with him? Does he know what you are planning?
7. Have you considered any other options besides abortion? Have you thought about carrying the baby to term? What are your hopes and fears about this option?
8. What do you see happening in your life if you have an abortion? What do you see happening if you make a different choice? (*Often abortion is chosen because no other option looks even possible. Sometimes the decision to have an abortion is made quickly to "solve the problem." Communicate with your counselee that she has some time to make her decision. Help her see that her life will be different, but not "ruined" if she carries her baby to term. See Action Steps below to help her process other options, such as placing the baby for adoption.*)

9. Do you have any questions about pregnancy and abortion? (*Do not assume that she is fully informed about either.*)

For the Teen Who Has Had an Abortion

1. What is the reason you came in today? Can you name the source of anxiety or distress in your life?
2. Take me back to that time in your life and tell me what happened. (*Listen for any signs of post-traumatic stress, such as disturbing dreams or triggers that bring back the event. By choosing to begin to tell you her story, she is breaking her silence, which is the beginning of the healing process but also potentially disturbing, as denial of the event is no longer possible.*)
3. What were the main reasons, at the time, for your making the choice you made?
4. Do you feel depressed, down, or sad most of the time? Do you have difficulty eating or sleeping?
5. Have you ever contemplated suicide? If so, do you have a plan? (*If it is discovered that the teen has a plan and means of carrying out the act of suicide, you must seek immediate help and ensure that the teen is not left alone. For more information, please refer to the section Suicide.*)
6. Are you currently using drugs or alcohol? Does this help with the anxiety? (*If the teen is using drugs and/or alcohol, please refer to the section Drugs and Alcohol for more information.*)
7. How are you managing life now? Can you identify the triggers of your pain?
8. Have you considered how this decision affects other relationships—with your parents, your friend(s), God?
9. Do you feel that you need forgiveness? Why or why not? If so, can you forgive yourself?

Throughout the interview, practice active listening by appropriately reflecting the teen's feelings and by clarifying thoughts. Active listening is essential in building trust, uncovering hidden feelings and thoughts, and connecting with genuine empathy and love.

In 2005, 1.21 million abortions were performed, down from 1.31 million in 2000. From 1973 through 2005, more than 45 million legal abortions occurred.

Rachel K. Jones in Perspectives on Sexual and Reproductive Health, 2008

WISE COUNSEL 4

For the Teen Contemplating Abortion

If the client desires it, be sure to provide her with *adequate practical support* to encourage her to carry her baby to term. Have on hand information about agencies that provide medical care and a home to stay in for pregnant women. Discuss *how to deal with the father of the baby and her family.* Explore with her places and people from whom she can expect the most support. Emphasize to her that she is making *a decision for both her life and her baby's life.*

If the client is not already able to see the *longer perspective*, encourage her to do so, rather than fixating on her immediate situation. Recent research on brain imaging has found that the prefrontal cortex, or the part of the brain used for problem solving and understanding consequences, is the last part of the brain to fully develop and does not do so until a person is in her midtwenties. Therefore teenagers are more likely to *figure out ways to survive the present* rather than think about the *long-term benefits and consequences* of their actions.[2]

Address *any behaviors that endanger your counselee's safety*, such as suicidal behavior or substance abuse.

For the Teen Who Has Had an Abortion

Encourage your client to talk about what she has felt and experienced emotionally and physically since the abortion. Many times, postabortive women are so horrified by what they have done that they cannot even put their inner pain into words. *Practice unconditional positive regard and reflective listening.* Take some time to explore her emotions, and give her the freedom to express any anger, fear, frustration, hatred, and shame.

Be very careful to *model God's grace and forgiveness* as you speak with the teen, realizing that she is already struggling with a heavy weight of guilt and shame. Remind her of the truth of Scripture: "If we confess our sins, he is faithful and just and will forgive us our sins and purify us from all unrighteousness" (1 John 1:9).

Communicate clearly to her that this decision, while taken seriously in God's eyes, has not doomed her for life. If she has accepted Christ, *His blood has covered every sin in her life*—including the decision to have an abortion. As you dialogue about her feelings and shame, help her to see that *Jesus will forgive her* and wants to set her free from self-hatred and guilt. Remind her that sometimes it's hard to forgive ourselves, but God's grace is always bigger than our mistakes.

Help the teen realize that, while she cannot change the past, she can decide how she will go about living today. Work with her to find ways to *avoid isolating herself by getting involved* in her community, through her church, friendships, or a local support group.

5 ACTION STEPS

For the Teen Contemplating Abortion

1. Consider Options

- You may feel that your only option is an abortion, but there are other choices you can make. Your counselor will help you explore alternative choices. Throughout the United States there are nearly three thousand crisis pregnancy centers staffed by volunteers who are able to provide true alternatives and who will lovingly help educate expecting mothers about what options are available.
- Look in the Yellow Pages under the heading "Abortion Alternatives," or call, toll-free, 1-800-848-LOVE.

- *Determine if there is any level of risk, emotionally and/or physically from the teen's boyfriend or her family, related to her choice about the child.*

2. Communicate

- You will need to communicate with family members about your situation.
- *Work with the client on a suitable strategy and plan. Assess how to do that (depending on what you know of the family members). You may need to be involved as a third party in such a conversation.*

3. Get Help

- *Encourage the teen and her parents to contact the crisis pregnancy center together.*
- If you have a church, find ways the church can help you care for your future.
- Most important, look to God for help. He promises never to leave or forsake you, and His love for you never runs out.

4. Follow Up

- *Be sure to follow up with the client by setting another appointment.*
- Although you may regret your pregnancy, you can begin immediately to make some wise choices regarding the future of your baby.
- *Work with her and her family and boyfriend, if possible, to create a social support network around her and her baby.*

For the Teen Who Has Had an Abortion

1. Tell Your Story

- Continue to tell your story through future counseling sessions and journaling. This will help you face the reality and move on.

2. Get Help

- Several organizations and materials exist to facilitate healing after an abortion. Some possible organizations are A Time to Speak, Project Rachael, and Victims of Choice. *Know which ones exist in your area for a referral.*

3. Find Support

- *If there is a confidential grief support group in your area, encourage your counselee to attend with a family member or friend.*

4. Focus on Forgiveness

- *Be sure to communicate both verbally and nonverbally your acceptance of your counselee and God's forgiveness of her.*

- Healing from an abortion is a process and certainly cannot be accomplished in one session; however, healing is possible. Forgiveness, including an ability to accept God's forgiveness and to forgive yourself, is possible through God's grace.
- Remember that abortion isn't the unforgivable sin.

6 BIBLICAL INSIGHTS

If men fight, and hurt a woman with child, so that she gives birth prematurely, yet no harm follows, he shall surely be punished accordingly as the woman's husband imposes on him; and he shall pay as the judges determine.

Exodus 21:22 NKJV

God is the champion of life and has always protected women, children, and the weakest members of society.

Your eyes saw my substance, being yet unformed. And in Your book they all were written, the days fashioned for me, when as yet there were none of them.

Psalm 139:16 NKJV

God knows each person from the moment of conception. His eyes see the unformed body in the mother's womb.

Many claim that a child in the womb is no more than a mass of tissue, but the Bible makes it clear that God sees the tiny embryo as a new life with a future already prepared.

To abort a child is to end a human life unjustly.

Before I formed you in the womb I knew you; before you were born I sanctified you; I ordained you a prophet to the nations.

Jeremiah 1:5 NKJV

God is well acquainted with every individual from before time began. He cares for and values each one of us.

7 PRAYER STARTER

Lord, we pray for Your grace and wisdom to overflow into this young woman's life. She is worried and scared, and she needs a touch from You . . .

RECOMMENDED RESOURCES 8

Florczak-Seeman, Yvonne. *A Time to Speak: A Healing Journal for Post-Abortive Women.* Love From Above, 2005. Books can be purchased at www.lovefromaboveinc. com.

Focus on the Family. *Post-Abortion Kit: Resources for Those Suffering from the After-math of Abortion.* Includes audio, several booklets, and other helpful resources. Available at www.family.org/resources/itempg.cfm?itemid=2326.

Freed, Luci, and Penny Yvonne Salazar. *A Season to Heal: Help and Hope for Those Working through Post-Abortion Stress.* Cumberland House, 1996.

Reardon, David C. *Aborted Women—Silent No More.* Acorn Books, 2002.

Websites

Ecounseling: www.ecounseling.com

Focus on the Family: www.family.org

Justice for All: www.jfaweb.org

National Organizations for Teens Contemplating or Recovering from Abortion

1-800-395-HELP—www.pregnancycenters.org

1-800-BETHANY—Bethany Christian Services

Adoption

1 PORTRAITS

- Philip is a junior in high school. He loves his adoptive mother and father, but he can't seem to shake the nagging feeling that somewhere out there is his "real" mother, a woman who for some reason didn't want him. He can't seem to resolve the sense of hurt and anger, and he feels guilty that his adoptive parents know he feels this way.

- After overhearing some neighborhood gossip, thirteen-year-old Jean asked her parents a terrifying question: "Is it true—was I adopted?" After learning the truth, she was brokenhearted and felt that her world was falling apart. In contrast, Brian's parents told him the truth before he could say the word *adoption*. His very first memories are of sitting on his dad's lap, flipping through a scrapbook about the adoption process. His mom and dad told him how they prayed God would send them a little boy to love, and he was the answer to their prayer.

2 DEFINITIONS AND KEY THOUGHTS

- *Adoption* is when a person takes a child who isn't his biological offspring and *legally makes that child his son or daughter.*

- Adoption is more than providing a bed and three square meals. Persons who adopt *bring the adopted child into their family to provide love and care,* just as if the child were biological kin.

- Though it isn't a popular topic, due to genetic factors, there is a greater chance that *an adopted child will be more dissimilar to a parent in terms of temperament, intelligence, and physical type than a person's biological children.*

- In addition to dealing with the typical issues that arise during the adolescent years, teenagers who were adopted as infants or as very young children are likely to experience *other emotional struggles* related to being adopted. The physical and emotional conditions of the teenage years tend to function as *a catalyst for teens to explore a series of emotional issues related to their adoption.*

- Specifically, a teen who has been adopted may be overwhelmed by *feelings of grief, loss, abandonment, rejection, and perhaps guilt or shame because of being adopted,* even if previously he seemed well adjusted and unaffected by the fact of his adoption. These new emotions of the teen can be difficult for both the teenage child and the *adoptive parents, who often find these emotions a shock.*

- *Grief and loss* are a fundamental part of coping with the adoption process. For those adopted as young children, the *process of dealing with the adoption* may not begin until the teenage years—when the teen *begins to ask questions* related to who he is and where he came from. Sometimes the teen may not be aware of the source of his anger or anxiety.
- Parents of adopted children—even well-intentioned, caring parents—*sometimes feel that their children don't appreciate them* or are being dramatic when they begin to express mourning or grief over the fact that they were adopted.
- In addition to feelings of grief or shame, *some teens express anger and rejection* as they deal with the sense of being abandoned by their birth parents.[1]

ASSESSMENT INTERVIEW :3

The following questions will help you determine the adopted teen's desires and needs.

1. When and how did you learn that you were adopted?
2. Tell me about your relationship with your adoptive parents. What do you appreciate about them? What are some causes of tension?
3. In general, how does it feel to be adopted?
4. Tell me why you came to see me today. How can I help?
5. Most teens your age are trying to "find themselves" and define their sense of identity. How is this process coming along for you?

Throughout the interview, practice active listening by appropriately reflecting the teen's feelings and clarifying thoughts. Active listening is essential in building trust, uncovering hidden feelings and thoughts, and connecting with genuine empathy and love.

WISE COUNSEL :4

Counseling the Adopted Teen

Adolescence is a time when all young people shape and define their sense of identity, so it is entirely normal for an adopted child to wrestle even more with this crucial issue.

Strong, sometimes conflicting emotions can characterize a teen who has been adopted. He may *feel betrayed* by his biological parents yet guilty for his *anger and hurt*. He *desperately wants to belong*, but he knows he must eventually face the fact that his birth parents gave him up. Encourage the teen to *share his feelings and insights about his identity, security, and desire to belong*.

Some teens want to take steps to find their birth parents. Recognize this need and respect the child's desires. If there is some reason this might prove detrimental to the teen's safety and well-being, *be honest about the risk*. Make sure to *involve the adoptive parents* in this discussion if at all possible, so they can hear their child's desires and understand the situation. If the teen and his adoptive parents decide to move ahead with contacting the birth parents, be a partner not an adversary.

Counseling the Adoptive Parents

Generally the way a child understands and perceives his adoption depends on *the way the parents talk about it* during the early years, as well as in adolescence. Parents are advised to *find examples of adoptions that convey respect and dignity to the adopted child*. One such example is the story of Moses, who was adopted by Pharaoh's daughter and chosen by God to do great things for the nation of Israel. Other examples could be persons the parents know, such as a friend of the family or a respected person in the community who was adopted. The more the child knows about good, successful people who were adopted, the less he will see being adopted as a disadvantage.

Adoptive parents should *never approach the subject of adoption sadly or negatively*. The adoption is *something to be thankful for and celebrate*.

The child should not be constantly reminded of his uniqueness as an adopted child. Instead, parents should stress how similar their family is to all other healthy and happy families. Similarities abound, especially with the increasing commonality of blended families.

Just like parenting biological children, *adopting and caring for an adopted child, of any age, is hard work*. And as with having biological children, adoption should be seen as *a lifelong commitment*.

5 : ACTION STEPS

For the Adopted Teen

1. Recognize Your Struggle as Normal

- Virtually all adolescents struggle with their identity and try very hard to find a place where they belong. Understand that some, perhaps most, of the inner tension you are feeling is entirely normal and universal for teenagers.

2. Express Your Need

- Talk with people you trust about your feelings of confusion, depression, ambivalence, and/or anger.
- Talk with your parents and your counselor about your desire for a relationship with your birth parents if you have that desire.

3. Depend on God

- When you think about the fact that you are adopted, remember that before you were even born, God knew you intimately. He put you together, and by His grace, He placed you in an adoptive family.
- Talk to God about how you are feeling—your anger, frustration, fears, anything. He promises never to leave you or forsake you. Whether or not a relationship

is possible with your birth parents, God is your heavenly Father, and you can always count on Him.

4. Accept Support and Direction

- Your counselor will provide insight and direction about how to talk with your parents about your emotional struggles.
- If you want to contact your birth parents, enlist the participation and assistance of your parents so the whole family is part of the pursuit.
- *You may need to meet with the adoptive parents to address any fears they may have of their child becoming more loyal to the birth parents than to them.*

For the Couple with an Adopted Child

1. Tell the Truth

- *Many adoptive parents want to know when the right time is to tell their child he is adopted. The answer is always the same—right now.*
- If the child you adopted is now older and still does not know he is adopted, begin praying about how you will share this information. You want to be sure you do it before the child discovers the truth through somebody else. Sit down with your spouse and write out the conversation you will have with your child before you talk to him. You may want to go over it with your counselor, your pastor, or a trusted confidant before the conversation to be sure your words are ordered correctly and the message comes across in a positive manner. Your child needs to hear a message of love and acceptance, not that he is different or somehow does not belong. You may need to ask for forgiveness or at least offer an explanation as to why you waited so long to tell him.

2. Affirm Your Child

- Sometimes adopted children feel out of place in a family unit, especially if there are siblings who are biological children. No matter how accepted into the family the adopted children are, they realize they are different—their genes are not the same as those of the rest of the family. Physically they may be much different—they don't have Mom's fair skin; they don't have Dad's eyes.
- Try to balance the scales by reframing the adoption in an extra-special way. Some parents have said to their adopted child:

   — "We prayed to God for a little boy, and He sent us you. You are a wonderful answer to our prayers!"
   — "Other parents, when they have kids, have no clue what they're going to get. But we were able to choose you specially."

- You may want to honor the child's adopted status by celebrating two birthdays each year. The first is the child's biological birth. The second is the day of the child's adoption. It may seem trivial, but this practice really helps children associate their adoption with something good from the beginning. Dialogue with

Adoption has been a blessing to many needy children. And the need persists. The United Nations estimates there are 143 million orphaned kids around the world.

www. hopeoftheorphan.org

23

your teen to find creative and unique ways to celebrate his adoptive birthday—maybe a special weekend trip, a sleepover, going to the movies or a sports event, or a dessert night out. Help your teen see that his adoption is something to be proud of, not something to hide.

3. Stay Actively Involved in Your Teen's Life

- The teenage years can be a time of "testing the waters," especially for adopted children. As your child begins to push for independence, look for ways that he can develop a healthy sense of self, rather than unrealistically restricting the rules. Help your teen discover what he enjoys doing—perhaps sports, music, outdoor activities, drama. Help him get involved.

- Don't expect your adopted teen to be consistently compliant or as stable as biological children. Even though the child may be an answer to prayer, this does not mean God has given you a child who will not offer challenges. He might bring with him a series of problems—from emotional trauma to physical or psychological issues—that may need professional attention. Handle your adoptive teen with care and offer unconditional love, even when he fails. Get professional help if you are overwhelmed or do not know how to deal with your teen's behavior.

4. Rely on God's Strength, Not Your Own

- Parenting teens can be difficult, and when a child is adopted, this only adds to the complex factors involved in guiding a child on the journey to adulthood. Realize that despite your best efforts, you cannot love, discipline, and shape the life of your adoptive teen without the continual grace and strength of God.

- Talk to God. Pray for your teen every day, even when you are frustrated or upset with him. Remember, God loves this child dearly and has given him to you as a gift.

6 BIBLICAL INSIGHTS

Oh, the depth of the riches of the wisdom and knowledge of God! How unsearchable his judgments, and his paths beyond tracing out!

Romans 11:33

People make choices, but God's love and purposes are sovereign over all of creation. Teens who have been adopted need to understand that they aren't in their new family by accident. Their new family isn't perfect, and it may not be all they want it to be, but they can rest in the fact that God has sovereignly placed them there. It is their responsibility to navigate adolescence and their family relationships, just as it is for any teen in any family.

When he was placed outside, Pharaoh's daughter took him and brought him up as her own son.

Acts 7:21

Probably the most famous adopted person in the Bible is Moses. Born an Israelite, Moses was raised in the house of Pharaoh. God used Moses to bring the Israelites to freedom, as told in the book of Exodus.

Mordecai had a cousin named Hadassah, whom he had brought up because she had neither father nor mother. This girl, who was also known as Esther, was lovely in form and features, and Mordecai had taken her as his own daughter when her father and mother died.

Esther 2:7

Esther is another notable example of an adopted person in the Bible. Esther's beauty was so great she was chosen to be King Xerxes's queen.

Esther was a woman of great piety, faith, and courage. As queen she served to help and protect the Jewish people.

PRAYER STARTER 7

For the Adopted Teen

Lord, thank You for Your goodness. Thank You for the life of this person. We come to You today because we are grateful for him and ask You to bless his life. Help him to grow up to know and love You . . .

For the Adoptive Parents

Thank You for these parents, Lord. Please give them wisdom as they train and discipline their child. Help them know how to talk with him about his adoption . . .

RECOMMENDED RESOURCES 8

Eldridge, Sherrie. *Twenty Things Adopted Kids Wish Their Adoptive Parents Knew.* Dell, 1999.

Gianetti, Charlene C. *Who Am I? And Other Questions of Adopted Kids.* Price Stern Sloan, 1999.

Keck, Gregory C. *Parenting Adopted Adolescents: Understanding and Appreciating their Journeys.* NavPress, 2009.

Keefer, Betsy, and Jayne Schooler. *Telling the Truth to your Adopted or Foster Child: Making Sense of the Past.* Greenwood, 2000.

Meeks, John, and Debbie Riley. *Beneath the Mask: Understanding Adopted Teens.* C.A.S.E., 2005.

Slade, Suzanne. *Adopted: The Ultimate Teen Guide.* Scarecrow Press, 2007.

Verrier, Nancy. *The Primal Wound: Understanding the Adopted Child.* Gateway Press, 1993.

Alcoholic
and Abusive Parents

1 PORTRAITS

- Rachel was very active in her youth group even though her family was rarely involved in church. She attended regularly, including the evening meetings and services. One Sunday evening Rachel's friends saw that she was distraught. She explained, "My dad wigged out again in his drunken stupor and tried to hurt me. He's done it before lots of times, but tonight I thought he was going to kill me!"

- A.J., a thirteen-year-old seventh grader, has always been a little shy. More recently at school he has completely withdrawn. His biology teacher goes to his church, knows his youth pastor, and has discussed with him his concern about A.J.'s declining grades. As the two adults talk together in the foyer before the service on Sunday, they see A.J. approach the church with his grandmother. After walking over to greet him, they discover that A.J.'s dad was arrested the night before for beating his mother, as A.J. watched helplessly in horror.

2 DEFINITIONS AND KEY THOUGHTS

- Children and teenagers of alcoholics (COA) or substance abusers (COSA) are *children and teenagers affected by an alcoholic parent or caregiver.* Some of the most common characteristics of these children are:

  — unresolved *hurt, anger, and fear*
  — a *distorted sense of responsibility* (too much about some things, too little about others)
  — *trusting untrustworthy people or refusing to trust* even those who have proven to be trustworthy
  — *manipulating and being manipulated* instead of enjoying respectful relationships
  — pervasive *insecurity* and a desperate desire to be accepted

- Even if the child is no longer living with the alcoholic or substance-abusing parent because of separation, divorce, abandonment, incarceration, or death, or even if the parent is not currently abusing the substance, *the child can still feel the residual effects of the instability or abuse.*

- Quite often children and teens who grow up in these families *become addicts and abusers* themselves. For more information about teens who are abusing drugs or alcohol, see the section Drugs and Alcohol.
- Often alcoholic and drug-abusing parents exhibit these characteristics:

  — *a pattern of out-of-control alcohol usage or drug addiction for a year or more*
  — *mood swings*
  — feelings of *shame or worthlessness*
  — *impulse control problems* regarding alcohol or drug use
  — using alcohol or drugs to *reduce anxiety*
  — *obsessing* about alcohol or drug use
  — *failed efforts to control* the use of alcohol or drugs
  — *negative consequences* at home or work

- For children and teenagers who witness substance abuse and domestic violence in the home, symptoms are very similar to those who have been the target of physical abuse. *Feelings of anger, guilt, shame, fear, confusion, and helplessness are common* in these teens. They may experience *a variety of emotional, behavioral, and physical symptoms*, such as bed-wetting, insomnia, diarrhea, lowered immune system, nightmares, aggressive behaviors, regressive behaviors, low self-worth, and emotional withdrawal. Learning disabilities are also linked to teenagers living in an abusive environment.

- For teenagers who have grown up in homes where abuse and domestic violence are prevalent, *unpredictability is completely predictable*, and routine is rarely the norm. In fact most teenagers in these circumstances have been moved around with the parent who leaves the abuser. They have been in and out of numerous schools, pulled out of peer groups and forced to enter new ones, and likely living with limited finances. These factors *multiply the existing stress* in the teen's life.

- Often a teen's behavior is shaped by the beliefs she develops about the victim and abuser, those in authority, and even herself. Often children older than *six lose respect for the victim and begin to respect and defend the abuser*. When this happens, the child learns that anger and violence are effective weapons to control others. Research has shown that most adult abusers have either been abused or witnessed abuse as a child.

- Aggression in teenagers who have witnessed domestic violence is *a key predictor of future aggression* in their own intimate relationships.

Roughly 1 in 8 American adult drinkers is alcoholic or experiences problems due to the use of alcohol. The cost to society is estimated to be in excess of 166 billion dollars each year.

National Center for Health Statistics and the National Institute on Alcohol Abuse and Alcoholism

ASSESSMENT INTERVIEW 3

1. What is your relationship like with your father/stepfather/male caregiver? Describe your best experiences together. When are/were they? What do you like best about your dad? What is it you have the most trouble with?

27

2. What is your relationship like with your mother/stepmother/female caregiver? Describe your best experiences together. When are/were they? What do you like best about your mom? What is it you have the most trouble with?

3. Tell me about what is going on at home. You can choose to start from the most recent event that made you decide to come talk to me or you can start from your earliest memory.

   Give the teenager an opportunity to tell her story. Ask clarifying questions and help her process what it is like to live the way she does. Just listen to her. Hear her vantage point. Use common mirroring techniques to repeat back to her what she says so she can hear herself as well. This is important for children who have experienced such trauma.

4. How often do you see your father [mother] drunk? Have you ever seen him [her] high on drugs? How often? Describe your parent's behavior during this time.

5. Has your father [mother] ever physically abused you? Was he [she] sober or drunk? When did this happen?

Note: *If physical abuse is taking place now, you have a duty to report it. Every state has a hotline for reporting abuse or neglect. Under the Child Abuse Prevention and Treatment Act, child abuse is "any recent act or failure to act: resulting in imminent risk of serious harm, death, serious physical, or emotional harm, sexual abuse, or exploitation of a child (usually a person under the age of eighteen, but a younger age may be specified in cases not involving sexual abuse), by a parent or caretaker who is responsible for the child's welfare."*

4 : WISE COUNSEL

One of the tragedies of counseling a teen who has been the victim of a strained relationship with an alcoholic or abusive parent is that *the parents often refuse to get help for their problems.* If they are willing to take steps toward sobriety and peace, the whole family can experience love and rebuild trust. If they aren't willing, *the teen needs to be supported and equipped to deal with the painful reality of the family.*

Consider an intervention but don't try it without a competent professional to guide the process. Often the family members have been intimidated by the addict or abuser for so long they have given up hope that change is possible. Perhaps the other parent is willing to take courageous steps. Work with this parent, other authority figures, and the teen children to *create an intervention* requiring the addicted or abusive parent to get help.

Helping the Teen Deal with Emotions

Invite the teen to express deep, sometimes explosive feelings. Often teens in these families are like volcanoes: they keep the lid on for a long time, but sooner or later *the internal pressure is so great that they explode.* In the first conversations about their family, they may seem completely numb, but the emotions are there. *When they feel safe, they'll take the risk of sharing a little of their fear, hurt, and anger.* Often male teens are able to communicate their anger most easily, but under the anger is a reservoir of hurt and fear that they may not have admitted to themselves.

To make progress, teens (and anyone in relationships like these) need to *learn to forgive, grieve, and acquire new relational skills.* These are the traits learned in a healthy home environment, but these teens will have to learn them in spite of their home environment. *Forgiveness and grief go together* because they both focus on the loss the teen has experienced.

Forgiveness is a choice and must include *emotional forgiving,* the process of letting go of deep, internal pain and allowing God to heal your heart. Emotional forgiveness does not happen overnight and requires social support and genuine, caring relationships. The process won't be rapid because often it involves *the progressive realization of how deep the wounds have been inflicted.* Each realization of wounds requires the *grieving of losses.*

Helping the Teen Acquire New Skills

The teen needs plenty of insight and support during these difficult times of healing and growth. In addition, *the teen will need to acquire new skills* of speaking truth, resolving conflict, being strong in the face of manipulation, and setting healthy boundaries.

Teens need to understand that *healthy conflict resolution never involves violence.* Because the teenager has grown up seeing violence used to deal with anger and conflict, she must learn *alternative ways* of dealing with the abuse and violence she experiences.

Help teens establish a sense of stability by helping them *develop a routine for their lives.* Teens who can drive and have access to a car can escape when they need to leave the house. They can also create a stable routine for school, youth group activities, studying at the library, sports activities, and work to ensure some sense of predictability.

Create *a list of resources* for the teen, including:

- professional counselors
- support groups
- treatment centers
- women's shelters

Establish a "safe house" that the teen can go to should a crisis arise. Communicate that if the teen feels endangered at any time, she should leave her parents' home, go to the safe location (friend's house, school, or other safe place), and call 911. Help the teen realize that *it is okay to leave for her protection*—this is not running away or being a bad kid.

Teens with addicted or abusive parents must realize that wishful thinking or excuses about their parents only further enable their parents' problems. *Excusing, minimizing, and denying the reality of the problem hasn't worked* in the past and it won't work in the future. Teens desperately need *your support and patience* for them to take steps toward emotional healing and developing new relational skills.

They need to learn not to blame themselves for their parents' addictions but, rather, realize that they cannot change their parents or magically "fix" their family. *Teens from abusive families need to be provided opportunities to discover who they are as individuals and develop a healthy sense of self-esteem.*

5 ACTION STEPS

The following steps are to be taken by the counselor in an effort to help the teen victim of abuse and/or violence.

1. Be a Safe Haven

- The most important role for a caregiver working with troubled teens is to be a safe person—perhaps the only safe person in the teen's life. Provide empathy, but don't overreact emotionally to the teen's problems. Invite honesty, and when appropriate, share your own story of hurt, hope, and healing.
- The teen is under tremendous pressure to remain quiet and compliant and not to take bold steps of change. Realize the enormity of the teen's challenge and provide the encouragement the teen needs to move forward.

2. Invite the Teen to Begin Grieving, Forgiving, and Learning New Skills

- Help the teen understand the connection between grieving and forgiving, as well as the process of both. Quite often people in deeply troubled families don't have any context for grief and forgiveness, so you'll have to start at the beginning.
- When we mention forgiveness, many teens react in anger, refusing to forgive the ones who have hurt them so much. Explain that forgiveness isn't excusing the offense and it doesn't condone the offender's behavior. It is a way of unhooking from the wounds of the past and is accompanied by the process of grieving those wounds.
- Help the teen develop new relational skills to avoid manipulation and carve out healthy ways of relating to others.

3. Help the Teen Regain a Sense of Stability

- Teens in addictive or abusive homes feel that their lives are out of control. Help the teen develop a sense of stability by implementing a routine and escaping the most destructive times in the family.

4. Consider an Intervention

- A teen's cry for help may be the beginning of change for the whole family. Quite often at least one of the parents is willing to come in and start the process, but the family system won't progress until the primary addict or abuser is willing to participate.

- Interventions always include an element of risk and should never be done without the help of a competent professional. It first requires all involved to make a commitment to change and severe consequences for refusal. When used effectively, interventions offer a clear path forward for the most hardened addict or abuser. Whatever the outcome, they clarify the truth for the whole family when they see the addict or abuser's response.

5. Enlist Support

- A teen in an addictive or abusive family needs plenty of support and encouragement. With the teen's permission, talk to those who can offer help in this pivotal time. Consider a teacher, principal, pastor, youth leader, or relative such as an aunt or uncle.

6. Watch for the Risk of Suicide

- Some teens assume they are the reason their parent drinks or abuses, and they may conclude that they shouldn't go on living. Be alert to any assertions the teen makes of hopelessness and/or plans to end her life. Take immediate action to get the help the teen needs. (For more information, see the section Suicide.)

7. Remind the Teen of God's Love

- Help the teen look to God for protection and guidance.
- Recommend that she join a youth group or other small group that will encourage her to trust God for her needs.
- Show her Scriptures that speak of God's great love for us and His ability to protect us (see Biblical Insights in this chapter).

8. Take Care of Yourself

- Caring for teens and children of addicts or those who witness domestic violence is stressful and exhausting for caregivers. Caregivers may suffer "compassion fatigue," a persistent emotional strain that comes from working with traumatized people. In fact this strain can cause caregivers to acquire symptoms much like the ones the teens experience, such as despair, isolation, anger, sadness, and difficulty sleeping and eating.

- Caregivers need to be aware of the stress they experience so they can actively seek the support they need. They may want to meet regularly with peers who also help families in crisis. Too often compassionate caregivers become consumed with the enormity of the pain in their clients' lives. They need to find emotional outlets and maintain their physical health so they can continue to work effectively with teens and their families. They need plenty of rest, good nutrition, exercise, and hobbies to give them a sense of balance.[1]

6 BIBLICAL INSIGHTS

The LORD is close to the brokenhearted and saves those who are crushed in spirit.

Psalm 34:18

Deeply wounded people can feel helpless, hopeless, and alone, but the Lord assures them that He understands, He cares, and He is near to them. As we trust in God's goodness and grace, He revives our crushed spirits.

So do not fear, for I am with you; do not be dismayed, for I am your God. I will strengthen you and help you; I will uphold you with my righteous right hand.

Isaiah 41:10

Even when we feel most helpless, without hope and without strength, God reminds us that He will give us the support we need.

Get rid of all bitterness, rage and anger, brawling and slander, along with every form of malice. Be kind and compassionate to one another, forgiving each other, just as in Christ God forgave you.

Ephesians 4:31–32

Unresolved anger inevitably turns to bitterness, which poisons every desire, goal, and relationship we have. We can choose to forgive those who hurt us. Our forgiveness of others is based on our own deep experience of God's cleansing of our hearts.

7 PRAYER STARTER

Gracious Father, You aren't surprised that my friend is suffering at home. You understand completely, and You care deeply. And Jesus, You know what it's like to be abandoned and abused. I pray that You will convince my young friend that You are there every step of the way, and You will lead her down a path toward hope and peace. Give wisdom, Lord, about how to handle all the turmoil in the home and all of the confusion, hurt, and anger in my friend's heart. Thank You that You will give peace and a new way of handling the problems. Others in the family may not ever change, but my friend is committed to learn, grow, and change through all of this . . .

RECOMMENDED RESOURCES 8

Benda, Brent, and Thomas McGovern, eds. *Spirituality and Religiousness and Alcohol/Other Drug Problems: Treatment and Recovery Perspectives.* Haworth Press, 2006.

Chase, E. P. *Help! My Family's Messed Up.* Kregel, 2008.

Howver, J. and M. Hutchinson. *Secret Survivors: Real Life Stories to Give You Hope for Healing.* Youth Specialties, 2008.

Leehan, J. *Defiant Hope: Spirituality for Survivors of Family Abuse.* Westminster John Knox Press, 1993.

Murphey, Cecil. *When Someone You Love Abuses Drugs or Alcohol.* Beacon Hill Press, 2009.

Nelson, James B. *Thirst: God and the Alcoholic Experience.* Westminster John Knox Press, 2004.

Quick, Daryl E. *The Healing Journey for Adult Children of Alcoholics.* InterVarsity Press, 1990.

Spickard, Anderson, and Barbara R. Thompson. *Dying for a Drink: What You and Your Family Should Know about Alcoholism.* Thomas Nelson, 2005.

Anger

1 PORTRAITS

- David and his parents fight constantly. Last week David got so angry that he smashed a glass vase against the wall.
- At sixteen Sarah feels she is just a burden to her busy mom. So Sarah locks herself in her bedroom with the stereo at maximum volume.
- Brian's coach has been pushing him all week. In a bid to shut out the world, he goes home and drinks himself into a stupor.
- Jenny has had it with her sister who has once again left the room they share in disarray. This time she is throwing all of her sister's belongings out into the yard.

2 DEFINITIONS AND KEY THOUGHTS

- Anger is a *powerful emotion* with intensity that ranges from frustration to severe rage. It can last from a few seconds to a lifetime. *The feeling of anger isn't a sin*; however, what we *do* in our anger determines whether or not we sin.
- Anger is best understood as *a state of readiness*. It is a natural response to a real or perceived threat or injustice, inspiring a *powerful alertness that heightens our emotions*. Even Jesus experienced and expressed anger (see Mark 3:5).
- Anger is *mentioned more than five hundred times in the Bible*. In fact the only emotion cited more often is love. Anger first appears in Genesis 4:5 and last appears in Revelation 19:15.
- Anger can *lead to healthy or unhealthy behavior*. *Assertiveness* that involves problem solving and compassion is a healthy response to anger. Aggression that involves hurting or controlling others, revenge, or hatred is an *unhealthy response* to anger.
- When anger is an automatic response to a situation, it is considered a *primary emotion*. Anger can also be a secondary emotion as a reaction to another feeling, such as fear, hurt, or sadness.
- During adolescence a wide range of *social and hormonal changes* may contribute to a teen's moodiness or short temper. In many ways this is normal, in the same way that the "terrible twos" are a normal phase of development. *Setting strong*

boundaries, while maintaining understanding and flexibility, helps when dealing with an adolescent struggling with anger.

- A *deep sense of anger* is often at the core of many of our most violent and prevalent social problems, like rape, domestic violence, substance abuse, and suicide.

Reasons We Get Angry

Anger is *a response* . . .

- to a person, situation, or event; to an imaginary or anticipated event; or to memories of traumatic or enraging situations
- to a real or perceived injustice or hurt—in the form of frustration, betrayal, deprivation, injustice, exploitation, manipulation, criticism, violence, disapproval, humiliation, intimidation, threats, and so on
- when someone has violated a boundary in our lives and invaded our physical or emotional space

How We Handle Anger

Anger always finds a way out. Teens, like adults, handle anger in one of three ways:

- *Repression*—denying anger's presence. This is *unhealthy* because even though it may not be observable, the anger is still present—turned inward on the teen. Repressed anger can lead to numerous emotional and physical problems, including volcanic outbursts of hostility, depression, anxiety, headaches, and gastrointestinal problems.
- *Suppression*—acknowledging anger and then stuffing it. With this approach to coping, the person redirects anger-driven energy into activity that *may be healthy or unhealthy*.
- *Expression*—ventilating the angry feeling. *Healthy expression* of anger generally involves gentle and/or respectful assertiveness; *unhealthy expression* can involve an aggressiveness that hurts others. Teens expressing anger with aggression might be seeking revenge. They might say, "At least you know where I'm coming from!" yet, they may be too emotionally engaged to acknowledge the potential destructive force of their expression.

Levels of Anger

- *Irritation*—a feeling of discomfort that someone or something has caused
- *Indignation*—a sometimes powerful feeling that something must be answered; some wrong must be corrected
- *Wrath*—a strong desire to avenge a wrong
- *Fury*—the partial loss of emotional control
- *Rage*—a loss of control involving aggression or an act of violence

35

- *Hostility*—a persistent form of anger and enmity toward others that becomes deeply ingrained in the individual's personality and affects his entire outlook on the world and life

Causes of Anger

- *External causes*—anger can be *a response to harm that someone has inflicted* (a physical attack, insult, abandonment) or to *a circumstance where there is no person at fault* (100-degree days, physical illness, highway traffic).
- *Internal causes*—anger is sometimes caused exclusively by *an individual's misperceptions of reality or destructive thinking* about normal life issues ("I should not have to take this test!"), memories of traumatic past events, medications, or health issues.

3 ASSESSMENT INTERVIEW

The nature of your questions will be tailored to fit the teen's demeanor at the beginning of the interview. Some are quick to express their anger, but many feel dragged to the meeting by a parent or school counselor, and the last thing they want to do is disclose their true feelings and perceptions. They may be defensive, so it will take your best efforts to create an environment of trust and warmth.

1. Tell me what brings you in today. How can I help?
2. What are some situations (or people) that bother you?
3. When you are bothered or annoyed, what are your initial feelings and reactions?
4. What do you do with those feelings? Do you express them, stuff them down, or redirect them in some way?
5. Do your feelings affect you in other ways, like keeping you awake at night, causing stomach problems, causing you to eat too much or not enough, and things like that?
6. How do your feelings affect your relationships at home, with your friends, and at work (*if appropriate*)?
7. Who are some people who understand what really bothers you? How do they help you deal with your anger?
8. Do you think your feelings of anger might be connected to other feelings, like hurt or fear? If they are, tell me about those feelings and what might cause them.
9. How would your life be different if you could resolve some of the issues that bother you?
10. Are you willing to work with me to find some solutions to the problem situations, relationships, and feelings?

WISE COUNSEL : 4

The emotion of *anger isn't sin*. However, this emotion needs to be expressed and dealt with in constructive ways. *Unresolved anger* can lead to a host of personal and inter-personal problems. Often those who repress their anger are depressed, anxious, or hostile or they have other psychological and biological problems. Those who express their anger in unhelpful ways will devastate their relationships with others. Usually *anger leads to resentment* (resentment is anger with a history), which, left unresolved, turns to *bitterness or hostility*.

> Fools vent their anger, but the wise quietly hold it back.
> *Proverbs 29:11 NLT*

Help the teen understand what makes him mad. There is a difference between inconveniences and genuine reasons for anger, such as the betrayal of a friend or somebody gossiping about you. Identifying what triggers angry reactions will help the teen recognize right away how he needs to respond and control it.

If the person gets *physiologically worked up* over minor annoyances, he needs to step back from the situation and ask himself what's going on inside. Sometimes these small triggers can be the signal that something deeper is involved. Teach the teen to do a *quick self-check of recent situations* with loved ones or others who may have angered him.

Explain to the teen the practice of *self-talk*. Many times a person can calm himself down with simple and truthful statements about a situation. Phrases like "calm down," "respond; don't react," "get a grip," or "in your anger, do not sin," can *remind him to slow down when anger has been triggered*.

Exercise is another way to reduce anger. Many teens and adults admit that going to the gym, working out, running, or playing a sport helps them reduce feelings of anger. Exercising also gives a person *time away from the situation* when he can properly think it through.

Relaxation techniques, such as rhythmic deep breathing, counting, or stretching, can help calm emotional and physiological arousal.

Making a habit of time in solitude and prayer is helpful. Memorizing Bible verses to use in self-talk can also provide an important filter for anger.

ACTION STEPS : 5

For any of us, the goal isn't to be anger free but to control our response to the powerful feelings of anger.

1. See It

- Focus on the source of the anger:
  - — List the triggers
  - — Until you can control the anger, avoid the triggers as much as possible.
  - — With your counselor, explore your history of anger (and suppressed anger) and how you typically express your anger. You may begin to see patterns in your behavior.

Note: *It is possible that the anger a person feels today isn't due to a "trigger" but is instead rooted in anger from past experiences. For example, a teen may become angry at a teacher for being demanding. He might be thinking, This man is heartless—the same as my dad. Such anger is misdirected toward the teacher, who may not be heartless at all.*

- Learn to identify anger before it is out of control. Identify how you feel physically when experiencing anger:

  — Identify angry feelings while they are still minor.
  — State out loud, "I'm feeling angry right now."
  — Learn to become aware of the first warning signs of anger, which may be physical changes. Anger promotes a sympathetic nervous-system response (a physical state of readiness) and biological changes, such as rising heart rate and blood pressure, amplified alertness, tensed muscles, dilated pupils, digestion problems, clenched fists, flared nostrils, and bulging veins.

2. Delay It

- *Brainstorm ways to delay the expression of anger. You and the teen will think of several, but you might offer some suggestions, such as:*

  — Take a "time-out"; temporarily disengage from the situation if possible (a minimum of twenty minutes).
  — Do light exercise until the intensity of anger is manageable.
  — "Write, don't fight"; jot down troubling thoughts. This exercise is personal and writings should be kept private, possibly destroyed, not sent to anyone.

- Talk with a trusted friend who is unrelated to the anger-provoking situation. Don't just vent—ask for constructive advice.
- Pray about the anger and ask God to give you insight.
- Learn the value of calming. A teen in a state of fury isn't equipped to deal appropriately with an anger-provoking situation. Calming will help you let some of your angry feelings subside before expressing anger in a healthy way.

3. Control It

- *Brainstorm some ways to express anger in a healthy way and offer suggestions, such as:*

  — Respond, don't react.
  — Maintain a healthy distance until you can speak constructively (see James 1:19).
  — Confront to restore, not to destroy.
  — Empathize (yelling is a failure to empathize). Speak slowly and quietly (makes yelling difficult).
  — Surrender the right to seek revenge (see Rom. 12:19).

- If anger begins to escalate to rage, don't interact with others. Instead, temporarily redirect your energy to solo activities or reestablish calm in some other way before confronting others.

4. Own It

- *Help the teen develop a plan of action:*

  — Find an accountability partner.
  — Join an anger-management group.
  — Consider follow-up with a professional counselor.

Note: *Underlying issues such as deep emotional wounds that have been identified in counseling need to be considered. Make plans to work on such issues through additional counseling (with you or by referral to another professional) and/or support group.*

BIBLICAL INSIGHTS 6

If you do well, will you not be accepted? And if you do not do well, sin lies at the door. And its desire is for you, but you should rule over it.

Genesis 4:7 NKJV

Cain's problem with anger wasn't that he became angry. It was that he remained angry and acted out of his anger. Cain's anger could have led him to insights about himself and his situation, but it missed the mark. Instead, Cain's anger turned to deadly jealousy.

Anger must be ruled or it will rule. Uncontrolled anger quickly becomes destructive. When we invite God to help us identify our anger and we take positive action, anger becomes a servant rather than a master.

"Be angry, and do not sin": do not let the sun go down on your wrath, nor give place to the devil.

Ephesians 4:26–27 NKJV

It's interesting that this passage doesn't say, "Never be angry." Anger is a natural emotion—it's part of being human. No matter how "perfect" life may seem, feelings of frustration and anger can pop up in an instant when a person feels his rights have been violated. Actually, anger is only the sign of a much deeper issue—usually when someone feels betrayed, unvalued, or belittled. Feelings of anger show that an individual has hope that things *can* get better. If handled properly, anger can actually lead to positive change.

When you are angry, it's important to take a step back from the situation and ask why. Rather than lashing out in hurtful ways or stuffing the anger inside and pretending everything is fine, learn to confront your feelings honestly

Better to be patient than powerful; better to have self-control than to conquer a city.

Proverbs 16:32 NLT

and seek to resolve differences with others in loving, respectful ways, as God would want.

Satan loves nothing more than using anger to divide and destroy relationships. That's the reason the Bible emphasizes the importance of confronting the cause of anger, rather than being ruled by our changing emotions.

And I became very angry when I heard their outcry and these words.

Nehemiah 5:6 NKJV

Nehemiah's anger was righteous indignation because many Jews were suffering at the hands of rich countrymen who had lent them money. Expressing his anger in a healthy way, Nehemiah called a meeting of the moneylenders, who agreed to his firm requests.

When we feel anger burning beneath the surface, we can ask God to guide us toward a productive way of resolving the conflict.

Do not make friends with a hot-tempered man, do not associate with one easily angered, or you may learn his ways and get yourself ensnared.

Proverbs 22:24–25

People may not be able to change the anger others express, but they can avoid close ties with "furious" people. Such people are ready to explode, and anyone around will either catch the brunt of their fury or become similarly furious.

Choose carefully those who will be your closest friends, business partners, and spouse.

God said to Jonah, "Do you have a right to be angry about the vine?"
"I do," he said. "I am angry enough to die."

Jonah 4:9

When Jonah learned that God would spare the Ninevites, instead of rejoicing in their repentance, Jonah became angry. His anger at Nineveh's sinfulness was justified, though his selfish anger at God's mercy was not.

Perhaps, with selfish motivation, Jonah was concerned that his reputation had been ruined with the false forecast of the city's destruction. Or he may have desired a front-row seat at Nineveh's demise—after all, Assyria was Israel's enemy.

We must consider honestly the source of our anger.

PRAYER STARTER 7

Lord, we all get angry. Anger is a powerful emotion that You have given us, and Your Word teaches us clearly about the constructive and destructive force that anger is. Help us to follow Your Word, Lord, by teaching us to control our anger when we have been threatened and wronged. Bless this young person, God. Help him control his anger and not hurt others . . .

RECOMMENDED RESOURCES 8

Anderson, Neil T., and Rich Miller. *Getting Anger under Control.* Harvest House, 2002.

Carter, Les. *Getting the Best of Your Anger: Before It Gets the Best of You.* 2nd ed. Revell, 2007.

Carter, Les, and Dr. Frank Minirth. *The Anger Workbook.* Thomas Nelson, 1992.

Chapman, Gary. *Anger: Handling a Powerful Emotion in a Healthy Way.* Northfield, 2007.

Anxiety and Phobias

1 : PORTRAITS

- Carol was always on the alert. Her timid voice and shy manner indicated she was on constant watch for potential hazards.

- As an only child of a single mother, Janice feels she was born to be her mother's scapegoat. She can remember times as a young child when her whole body became tense at the time her mother was expected to come home. She became anxious because she never knew what would happen when her mother returned. As a teen, Janice is always wary of potential harm. She becomes tense even when there is nothing to be anxious about.

- Nadine is considered a "loner." Little does anyone know that this facade masks a deep fear of being around people. She becomes overwhelmed with panic when she is in the cafeteria at school eating with her classmates. Even though it seems irrational, she is afraid of saying something foolish, spilling food on her shirt, or beginning to stutter. When she is alone with one person, she's fine; but as soon as she's in a group, even making eye contact with someone feels painful. She avoids such situations like the plague!

2 : DEFINITIONS AND KEY THOUGHTS

- *Anxiety disorder* is a general term used to describe debilitating feelings of fear, which may be exhibited in a number of different ways, including generalized anxiety disorder, panic disorder, obsessive-compulsive disorder, post-traumatic stress disorder, and phobias of all kinds.

Fear

- *Fear* is an emotion that *draws someone into a self-protective mode.*

- Fear becomes a *problem* for a teen when she becomes *afraid of things that aren't real or when the feeling of fear is out of proportion* to what she is actually experiencing.

- More often than not, fears are related to what a teen perceives as *threats to her safety and security.* She may fear being ridiculed, left out of a group she values, looking foolish, or being considered a loser in any way.

- While most people experience fear as a negative emotion, fear also has a *positive component*. If you find that you have turned down a one-way street and see a car heading directly at you, fear triggers an autonomic response that sends a signal to your brain to "flee" the potentially dangerous situation.

Anxiety

- *Anxiety* is a *constant fearful state*, accompanied by a feeling of unrest, dread, or worry, but the teen may not be aware of what is creating the feeling of fear.
- Anxiety can be aroused by a number of factors:
  - *external situations* (changing schools, changing peer groups, experiencing rejection)
  - *lack of physical well-being* (lack of sleep, blood sugar imbalance, and other chronic physiological problems)
  - *learned responses* (imitating parents who are highly anxious)
  - *trauma* (experiences that cause great pain and the memories of those experiences)
- Many teens experience *a sense of not belonging or a lack of purpose*. The complexities and stresses of adolescence are fertile breeding ground for "*existential angst*" or anxiety.
- A diagnosis of generalized anxiety disorder is associated with three or more of the following symptoms present for more days than not for the past six months:
  - restlessness or feeling on edge
  - being easily fatigued
  - irritability
  - muscle tension
  - difficulty falling or staying asleep
  - difficulty concentrating
- In addition, anxiety's symptoms can include:
  - inability to relax
  - tense feelings
  - rapid heartbeat
  - dry mouth
  - increased blood pressure
  - jumpiness or feeling faint
  - excessive perspiring
  - skin feeling clammy
  - constant anticipation of trouble
  - constant feeling of uneasiness

Anxiety disorders are one of the most common forms of mental illness in the United States. In 2005 approximately 40 million American adults suffered from some form of an anxiety disorder (18.1% of adults).

Archives of General Psychiatry, 2005

43

Phobias

- A *phobia* is a fear of a specific thing or event, and the fear is *out of proportion to the threat* that the object, situation, or activity actually poses. For example, a teen may have a fear of spiders. She exhibits a phobia when seeing a small spider on the ceiling of a room and refuses to enter the room again until she is assured the spider is gone.

Panic Attacks

- A panic attack is a *sudden, overwhelming, fearful reaction* to a situation, accompanied by the feeling of impending doom. In a panic attack, the teen feels out of control. *Symptoms* include:

  — being paralyzed and unable to have the normal flight-or-fight response
  — shortness of breath
  — racing heartbeat
  — sweating
  — dizziness
  — nausea
  — diarrhea
  — ringing ears
  — choking
  — vertigo
  — being homebound for fear of another attack

- The teen generally has no clear idea what prompted the reaction and then becomes afraid of another episode. *The sufferer may feel as though she is going insane or having a heart attack.*
- Note: More than three attacks in a month or a teen's refusing to go out of the house indicate the need for professional treatment.

Relational Fears

- There are *four major relational fears* people experience that can significantly alter the quality of a person's life:

  — fear of failure
  — fear of rejection
  — fear of abandonment
  — fear of death or dying

- To some degree these fears are commonly experienced by virtually all people, but often the *inherent changes and pressures of adolescence magnify these fears.*

ASSESSMENT INTERVIEW :3

1. When do you feel afraid or anxious? Tell me what happens and how you feel.
2. How long and to what extent has your fear or anxiety occurred?
3. As you look at your experiences of fear or anxiety, what are the recurring triggers (circumstances, people, things)?
4. When are you more fearful or anxious? How do these times affect you (your attitude, your relationships, your activities)?
5. Of the things that cause fear or anxiety, which ones seem reasonable and which ones seem unreasonable? *(It is important to determine if the fears are based in reality.)*
6. What causes the fears or anxiety to subside?
7. How have you tried to cope with these feelings?
8. Do you have any health problems or are you on any medication that might contribute to your feelings of fear or anxiety?
9. How would your life be different if you were able to cope more effectively with your feelings of fear or anxiety?

WISE COUNSEL :4

Anxiety and fear are *automatic physiological responses* to real or perceived danger. While it is unrealistic to expect your client to just get over her feelings of apprehension, fear and anxiety are many times *defused by knowledge*. As a general rule, the more a teen can defuse the perceived threat, the less anxiety she will experience.

A teen battling anxiety or fear may establish an *irrational belief system* that is creating her anxiety. Often, unrealistic fears stem from negative or traumatic experiences in the past.

Most anxiety reactions are *learned behavior*—the body's way of trying to cope with uncertainty or mistreatment of some kind. Help the counselee think about whom she may have seen react to experiences with fear or anxiety and take some time to explore the complaints of anxiety or fear with the teen, looking for possible triggers that may be activating a learned behavior system. For example, if a teen experiences extreme anxiety over test taking, probe possible feelings of inadequacy or failure, unrealistic expectations, and negative past experiences with tests.

Anxiety can be contagious. Those who experience strong anxiety tend to elicit anxiety reactions in those who are around them. People need to be aware of their anxiety level (encourage the teen to rate her feelings of anxiety on a scale of 1 to 10) and how to cope with anxiety when it occurs so that it doesn't become debilitating. Dialogue with your client about healthy ways to cope with anxiety and fear. Many times teens become overwhelmed and simply "shut down" rather than actively work through the anxiety. For some teens, anti-stressors might include sports, running, playing an instrument, reading, or watching a movie. Encourage the teen to *do something* when she feels anxiety coming on, rather than acting as a victim of present emotions.

Automatic responses of anxiety and fear can be relearned in a healthy environment in which the client is encouraged to confront the object of her fear within the safety of the counseling relationship. In this process, the client learns to view the object of anxiety (such as test taking) in a new, less-threatening light, rather than being crippled by feelings of powerlessness.

Those who suffer from fear or anxiety need to be *patient with themselves*. Changing long-established patterns takes time. Encourage the teen to be intentional in her efforts to be positive and to have confidence that she will be able to overcome her anxiety or fears.

Avoid pat or simplistic answers like "Just trust God" or "All you need to do is give it to God." These solutions sound pious, but they don't address the profound and complex issues that the teen is experiencing.

Note: Refer the teen to a professional if you suspect she may be *clinically diagnosed with an anxiety disorder*. This diagnosis would consist of excessive or unrealistic anxiety for at least six months with at least four of the following criteria:

- excessive or unrealistic worry about future events
- excessive or unrealistic concern about the appropriateness of past behavior
- excessive or unrealistic concern about competence in one or more skills, such as athletic, academic, or social
- somatic complaints, such as headaches or stomachaches, for which no physical basis can be established
- marked self-consciousness
- excessive need for reassurance about a variety of concerns
- marked feelings of tension or inability to relax[1]

5 ACTION STEPS

1. Change Your Thought Patterns

- It is important to confront negative thoughts and irrational beliefs and focus on what is real. God has people who care about you and who can help keep you safe.
- Become familiar with Scripture verses, such as Philippians 4:6–7 and 1 Peter 5:7, that will remind you of God's provision of comfort and peace.

2. Focus on God

- Try to move your focus from fear to the character of God (see Ps. 32:10; Prov. 18:10; Eph. 1:18–21).
- God wants you to entrust your fears to him and to trust his people to help you. That doesn't mean your fears will suddenly vanish, but in God and the church you can find wisdom and strength to face your fears.

3. Watch for Triggers

- Learn to identify recurring triggers and try to minimize activities and input that induce anxiety.

4. Move Forward

- Consider setbacks learning experiences and resolve to continue to face your fears.
- Be willing to take risks as you work on your ability to face fear and anxiety.
- When you are feeling afraid, try to move your thoughts to the external world and others rather than on the internal feelings of anxiety.
- Keep your attention on the solution—letting God help you with your fears—and not on the problem.

5. Develop Relationships

- It is important for you to develop supportive, positive relationships.

6. Be Patient

- The more you commit yourself to relying on God and not dwelling on your fears, the more progress you will make.
- God is working to help you overcome the anxiety that is keeping you from living life to the fullest.

BIBLICAL INSIGHTS 6

If you should say in your heart, "These nations are greater than I; how can I dispossess them?"—you shall not be afraid of them, but you shall remember well what the LORD your God did to Pharaoh and to all Egypt: the great trials which your eyes saw, the signs and the wonders, the mighty hand and the outstretched arm, by which the LORD your God brought you out. . . . You shall not be terrified of them; for the LORD your God, the great and awesome God, is among you.

Deuteronomy 7:17–21 NKJV

The Christian life isn't easy. Believers face difficulties, pain, suffering, and sorrow. In situations that seem impossible, we sometimes become afraid. God told Israel not to be afraid when the battle seemed too great. Instead, they were to remember what He had done for them in the past and take heart. We can do the same and look at our fearful situations in the light of what God has already done for us, remembering that "the great and awesome God" will guide and protect us.

Trust in the LORD. . . . Delight yourself also in the LORD. . . . Commit your way to the LORD. . . . Rest in the LORD, and wait patiently for Him; do not fret because of him who prospers in his way, because of the man who brings wicked schemes to pass.

Psalm 37:3–7 NKJV

David encouraged God's people to trust in the Lord, delight themselves in Him, commit their way to Him, and wait patiently for Him to act. Trusting focuses our faith in God and helps us see Him at work in our lives.

Delighting in God means we experience pleasure in His presence.

Committing our way to God means entrusting everything in our lives to His guidance and control.

Waiting patiently is sometimes difficult, but waiting on God is the ultimate hope of our faith.

Surely He shall deliver you from the snare of the fowler and from the perilous pestilence. He shall cover you with His feathers, and under His wings you shall take refuge; His truth shall be your shield and buckler. You shall not be afraid of the terror by night, nor of the arrow that flies by day, nor of the pestilence that walks in darkness, nor of the destruction that lays waste at noonday.

Psalm 91:3–6 NKJV

When believers are afraid, they can run to a refuge and fortress—God Himself. No place could be safer than with Him!

Believers can trust that God will protect them in their times of fear. This does not imply that God's people will never suffer or face difficulty, but it does mean that we need not be afraid because we are in God's hands.

The Lord is near. Do not be anxious about anything, but in everything, by prayer and petition, with thanksgiving, present your requests to God. And the peace of God, which transcends all understanding, will guard your hearts and your minds in Christ Jesus.

Philippians 4:5–7

Knowing that the Lord is near is a comforting thought! Once we understand the constant presence of the Lord in circumstances, in the world, and in our lives, we can turn to Him, no matter the situation, for safety and protection.

Trust in the LORD with all your heart, and lean not on your own understanding; in all your ways acknowledge Him, and He shall direct your paths.

Proverbs 3:5–6 NKJV

It's one thing for people to trust God with their eternal destiny; it is quite another for them to trust God to handle the challenges and difficulties of daily life.

God promises to direct, or straighten, our paths. We need to trust God to help us handle the difficult situations we face, even in cases where we can't begin to see how He could.

If we really want to know God's will for our lives, or even for our actions in a particular situation, we must begin by trusting that God cares about every aspect of living and that He always will provide what we need.

PRAYER STARTER 7

Today, Father, a child of Yours is frightened. Fear has taken hold of her life and left her feeling helpless and hopeless. She wants to serve You, Lord, but this anxiety is debilitating and she can barely function. She needs the healing touch of Your hand, Lord, and wisdom to handle this anxiety . . .

RECOMMENDED RESOURCES 8

DeMoss, Nancy Leigh, and Dannah Gresh. *Lies Young Women Believe: And the Truth That Sets Them Free.* Moody, 2008.

Hart, Archibald D. *The Anxiety Cure: A Proven Method for Dealing with Worry, Stress, and Panic Attacks.* Thomas Nelson, 2001.

Hart, Archibald D., and Catherine Hart Weber. *Stressed or Depressed: A Practical and Inspirational Guide for Parents of Hurting Teens.* Thomas Nelson, 2005.

Rhodes, David, and Chad Norris. *Dismantled: An Honest Look at Some of Our Biggest Fears.* Following God Series. AMG, 2003.

Russo, Steve. *Fear No Evil? Shining God's Light on the Forces of Darkness.* Bethany House, 2007.

Sanford, Timothy L. *Losing Control and Liking It: How to Set Your Teen (and Yourself) Free.* Focus on the Family, 2008.

Schab, Lisa M. *The Anxiety Workbook for Teens: Activities to Help You Deal with Anxiety and Worry.* 2nd ed., rev. New Harbinger, 2008.

Attention Deficit Hyperactivity Disorder

1 : PORTRAITS

- Chris tries harder than everyone else in his class but he keeps falling short. He makes the silliest mistakes, forgets his homework, daydreams in class, and finishes only half of the exam before the timer buzzes.

  His teacher calls a conference with his parents. "I've seen this before. Chris is a very bright boy; that's not the problem. It's something else," his teacher begins to explain.

- "Julie, sit still," her mother barks. "What's the matter with you? Why do you keep jiggling your foot and tapping the table?"

  Julie tries to respond. "I don't know. I just feel like doing it."

2 : DEFINITIONS AND KEY THOUGHTS

- Adolescents suffering from *attention deficit hyperactivity disorder* (ADHD) exhibit *impaired functioning in multiple environments* (school, work, friendships) in three main areas: impulsiveness, hyperactivity, and inattention. Individuals with ADHD often act without thinking, have a hard time sitting still and/or being quiet, and are easily distracted from the task at hand.

- *Attention deficit hyperactivity disorder* is one of the *most common and yet least understood childhood disorders*. The American Psychiatric Association estimates that between 3 and 7 percent of children suffer from ADHD, and many other children who don't actually qualify for the diagnosis still struggle with significant symptoms.

- Although ADHD *begins in childhood* and is often diagnosed by the second or third grade, *some children remain undiagnosed* into the teen years, and some go undiagnosed until they reach adulthood.

- Teens with ADHD are *chronically inattentive, hyperactive,* or both—so much so that their daily life is disrupted. They have trouble focusing in class, doing their homework, finishing their chores, and adjusting their behavior to meet the demands of a situation. As a result, they *struggle in their friendships, family relationships, and school performance.*

- Teens with ADHD are not necessarily more active than their peers, but they do have trouble *calming down after activities.*

- Adolescents and adults with ADHD tend to develop *methods of coping* to deal with any impairments of normal functioning the disorder causes. However, for some, many aspects of daily life can be very difficult.
- ADHD symptoms can create *behavioral problems* in teenagers. For instance, they may become *defiant* with adults and develop *anger, resentment, or overt disrespect* toward authority. Fortunately, there are both medical treatments and behavioral steps that can help teens with ADHD.
- *Left untreated, ADHD can affect the growth and development of a teenager.* Often teens with this disorder are not involved in after-school or recreational activities. Their parents are half as likely to say that their ADHD teens have a lot of good friends and more than twice as likely to report that their teenagers are picked on at school or have trouble getting along with their peers. These *social problems* can put teens *at increased risk for anxiety, behavior and mood disorders, substance abuse, and teen delinquency.*
- If you suspect the teen is suffering from ADHD, use the following checklist to evaluate the symptoms, but remember that ADHD can be easily misdiagnosed. The American Academy of Child and Adolescent Psychiatry (AACAP) considers it necessary that *the following be present before diagnosing a child with ADHD*:

  — The behaviors must appear before age seven.
  — They must continue for at least six months.
  — The symptoms must also create a real handicap in at least two of the following areas of the child's life:

    in the classroom
    on the playground
    at home
    in the community
    in social settings[1]

- There are some circumstances in which a child or adolescent's behavior might seem like ADHD but is actually not. *Many other conditions and situations can trigger behavior that resembles ADHD.* For example, a child might exhibit behavior similar to ADHD symptoms when experiencing:

  — a death or divorce in the family, a parent's job loss, or other sudden change
  — undetected seizures
  — an ear infection that causes temporary hearing problems
  — problems with schoolwork caused by a learning disability
  — anxiety or depression
  — insufficient or poor quality sleep
  — poor nutrition

- ADHD can be described in *three categories*: inattentive type, hyperactive-impulsive type, and combined type.

The Inattentive Type

- Teens with the inattentive type of ADHD (formerly called simply attention deficit disorder) have *problems paying attention*, especially with difficult learning tasks such as memorizing and reading assignments, or with *sitting still* through monologues or lectures. Other characteristics of inattentive teens may include:

  — lack of organization
  — difficulty finishing tasks
  — lack of attention to detail
  — tendency to get distracted
  — withdrawn or shy behavior
  — difficulty with social conversations

The Hyperactive-Impulsive Type

- Teens suffering from the hyperactive-impulsive type of ADHD *can't sit still and have trouble controlling their outbursts.* They *disrupt* the rest of their classmates with their *loud voices* and *boisterous activity.* Also they have difficulty delaying gratification. Renowned ADHD expert Russell Barkley describes these teenagers as being "creatures of the moment." Hyperactive-impulsive kids may also display:

  — frequent fidgeting
  — over-talkativeness
  — difficulty sitting or standing still
  — overactivity (running, jumping, climbing)
  — impulsiveness
  — restlessness
  — aggressive behavior
  — inappropriate social behavior (such as grabbing things and speaking out of turn)

The Combined Type

- Teens with the combined type of ADHD can display *both inattentive and hyperactive-impulsive behaviors.* Because the combined type of ADHD is a broad category that manifests in different ways (*affecting attention, activity, and impulsivity*), people will exhibit a variety of behaviors. Some include:

  — difficulty paying attention
  — difficulty staying focused on a task or activity
  — difficulty finishing assignments at school or home
  — jumping from one activity to another
  — difficulty focusing on instructions
  — losing or forgetting things such as homework
  — becoming easily distracted, even during recreational activities

— difficulty paying close attention to details
— making careless or obvious mistakes
— difficulty organizing tasks and activities
— difficulty waiting one's turn
— interrupting or intruding on other people
— blurting out answers before questions have been completed
— fidgeting with hands or feet; squirming when seated
— difficulty engaging in activities quietly

ASSESSMENT INTERVIEW 3

For the Teenager and/or Parent

1. What is your reason for coming today?

   In most cases it may be the parent who has brought the teen to you for a variety of reasons—family conflict at home, low grades or behavior problems at school, inability to concentrate or sit still in public places, and so on. Be sure to understand and get a feel for what the teen wants to accomplish in the counseling relationship and what success would look like for him as well as for the parent. If the teen suspects you are siding with the parent and there has been a lot of conflict at home, rapport with the teenager may become difficult.

2. Have you [Has your teen] been to counseling before about this? If so, whom did you see? For how long? Are you currently taking or have you ever taken any medications for ADHD?

3. In the past six months to a year, have there been any major transitions in your [your teen's] life, illnesses you have had, or changes at school or in your eating or sleeping habits? If so, explain these changes. *Pay particular attention to behaviors that are described in the section above.*

4. Where have you [has your teen] experienced the most difficulty with what is happening (for example, at home, in the classroom, during extracurricular activities or sports, with peers, and so on)? *It is important to assess behavior across different contexts. ADHD will be present in multiple venues.*

   > The diagnosis of ADHD increased an average of 3% per year from 1997 to 2006.
   >
   > *Centers for Disease Control*

5. Do you [Does your teen] find that often you have a hard time concentrating when reading a book or listening to your teacher in the classroom? Does your mind wander and do you catch yourself daydreaming or thinking about other things than the task at hand?

6. Have you [Has your teen] been inconsistent at school—doing well one week and poorly the next?

7. Do you [Does your teen] often have a hard time following directions or paying attention to details? Do you make careless mistakes?

8. Do you [Does your teen] struggle following a routine, such as getting ready for school on time? Do you forget things or often misplace items?

9. Do you [Does your teen] get in trouble for being impulsive, talking out of turn,

being loud, or talking too much at school? Do you have a hard time waiting in line or for other people?

10. Do you [Does your teen] tend to become emotionally reactive to minor situations? If so, what does this look like?
11. Are you [Is your teen] bored a lot, looking for things to do?
12. Do you [Does your teen] find it difficult to sit still during a meal, in the classroom, at church, or during a social event?

Throughout the interview, practice active listening by appropriately reflecting the person's feelings and clarifying thoughts. Active listening is essential in building trust, uncovering hidden feelings and thoughts, and connecting with genuine empathy and love.

4 : WISE COUNSEL

It is normal for every teen to zone out in a boring biology class, leave their homework on the kitchen counter, and sometimes act in an excited, high-energy way. That's not a serious problem. *Teens with ADHD experience these issues to a degree that drastically and negatively impacts their performance in school and experiences in life.*

When helping someone with ADHD, a *multimodal approach* is often used. *Medication in combination with therapy* has been found effective in treatment. Informing teachers, coaches, and others is also important to ensure that *an appropriate approach to learning* is used with the teen with ADHD.

The teen's tendency to forget, be lethargic one moment and extremely energized the next, and be impulsive are most often not for oppositional or defiant reasons. It is important to inform the parent that *punishing such behaviors can actually do more harm than good* for the teenager with ADHD.

5 : ACTION STEPS

Below are several action steps for counselors and parents who are helping a teen with ADHD.

1. Medication

- Since ADHD has strong biological/neurological links, certain medicines can help people with ADHD by improving their focus and attention and reducing the impulsiveness and hyperactivity associated with the disorder. Ritalin, Adderall, and the newest drug, Concerta, are the three most popular medications for ADHD. *According to the* Military Personnel Procurement Manual, *the prescribed use of Ritalin is a "permanent disqualifier" for any who wish to join the military.*
- Prescription medication for the treatment of ADHD is still highly controversial. When medications are prescribed, consistent medical management is crucial. Some medicines may even have adverse effects as children age.

- Not all children need medication. Advise your client to consult his doctor and weigh the benefits versus the side effects of medication.
- Whenever a child or adult is prescribed medication for ADHD, it is vital that it be accompanied by some form of counseling therapy.

2. Counseling Therapy

- Counseling can be used to help the teen learn new strategies for coping with ADHD symptoms.
- Family counseling helps treat the disorder because it keeps parents informed and also shows them ways they can work with and help their teen.

3. Maintain Structure and Supervision

- One of the hardest parts of helping a teen with ADHD is that a higher level of structure will consistently be necessary. Often parents of ADHD teens wonder when they can finally relax the increased structure they have created to monitor their teen's school performance and home behavior. The reality is that usually parents should maintain the established structure until the teen leaves for college. This does not mean they have to be prison wardens, but maintaining structure and supervision will help the teen be happy and successful through the teen years.

4. Remember ADHD Is a Disorder with Opportunity

- Remind parents that their teen with ADHD has a neurologically based disorder, and that there is a "can't do" as well as a "won't do" component to the child's thinking and actions. When the disorder is harnessed, teens have as great a potential for lifelong success as a person without ADHD.
- Remind parents of a teen with ADHD how important it is to show grace, patience, and forgiveness to their teen.

5. Help the Teen Build on His Strengths

- Having ADHD isn't just practically difficult for a teen, it is also emotionally difficult. Parents and other adults should provide constant positive influence in his life.
- Help the teen find and build on his strengths. Personal strengths always overshadow the weaknesses caused by the disorder.[2]

6 : BIBLICAL INSIGHTS

I am fearfully and wonderfully made.

Psalm 139:14

God knit each of us together when we were in our mother's womb. Being diagnosed with ADHD does not diminish the wonder of God's creation.

I can do everything through him who gives me strength.

Philippians 4:13

The Lord is the source of wisdom and strength for every one of us. Teens with ADHD and their parents should be encouraged to remember that the gifts of wisdom and strength are as available to them as to anyone else.

God is our refuge and strength, an ever-present help in trouble.

Psalm 46:1

Neurological disorders are difficult for the person and often for every member of the family, but the teen and his family aren't alone. God loves to show His goodness and kindness to those who call out to Him.

Be patient with all.

1 Thessalonians 5:14 NKJV

When someone in the family has ADHD, the whole household can become tense. Instead of loving one another and trying to affirm each other, people can become critical and angry. Patience is a choice. When we realize how patient God is with us, we can extend that patience and love to others.

7 : PRAYER STARTER

Dear Lord, we come to You today because this young person is struggling with attention deficit hyperactivity disorder. Please help Your child find relief from this disorder. Please help him learn to deal with the symptoms. Please help his doctors find a medication that helps reduce the symptoms. And, Lord, give everyone involved a healthy dose of love and patience with each other . . .

RECOMMENDED RESOURCES 8

Angelotti, Maren. *Of Different Minds: Seeing Your ADHD Child through the Eyes of God.* Gospel Light, 2008.

Barkley, Russell A. *Taking Charge of ADHD: The Complete, Authoritative Guide for Parents.* Guilford, 2000.

Dendy, Chris A. Zeigler *Teaching Teens with ADD and ADHD: A Quick Reference Guide for Teachers and Parents.* Woodbine House, 2000.

Dobson, James. *The New Strong-Willed Child: Birth through Adolescence.* Tyndale House, 2007.

Larimore, Walt, Diane Passno, and Dennis Swanberg. *Why ADHD Doesn't Mean Disaster.* Tyndale House, 2006.

Richardson, Wendy. *When Too Much Isn't Enough: Ending the Destructive Cycle of ADHD and Addictive Behavior.* NavPress, 2005.

Thomas, M. Russell. *Turbo Charged Childhood: Fresh Hope for Raising Children with Attention Disorders.* Xulon Press, 2008.

Walker, Beth. *The Girls' Guide to AD/HD: Don't Lose This Book!* Woodbine House, 2004.

Warren, Paul, and Jody Capehart. *You and Your ADD Child: How to Understand and Help Kids with Attention Deficit Disorder.* Thomas Nelson, 1995.

Weiss, Lynn. *Give Your ADD Teen a Chance: A Guide for Parents of Teenagers with ADD.* NavPress, 1996.

Wender, Paul H. *ADHD—Attention Deficit Hyperactivity Disorder in Children, Adolescents, and Adults.* Oxford University Press, 2000.

Attitudes

1 PORTRAITS

- Josh is driving his parents crazy with his negativity and bad attitude. "They can tell me what to do," he barks, "but they can't make me do it!"
- Carrie's mom complains, "I can't even have a conversation with her anymore. All of my children are wonderful to be around, until they reach about fifteen years old; then they change. Should I just kiss my relationship with my daughter good-bye for the next few years?"

2 DEFINITIONS AND KEY THOUGHTS

- *Attitude* can be described as an individual's *disposition or current state of mind.* While everyone struggles with ups and downs in morale, teens often exhibit an "*attitude problem,*" that is, a persistent negative outlook on life, often evidenced by grumpiness, social detachment, and frequent complaining.
- When raising teens, many parents find that a teen's *behavior* can be acceptable, but the teen's *mood* seems to the parents to be *sulky, pessimistic, and negative.*
- An inappropriate *attitude* is difficult for many parents to address. *Behaviors* are much easier to define, and infractions are more easily addressed through conversation, adjusting boundaries, and discipline. Some teens declare, "You can tell me what to do but you can't make me happy about it."
- Often during the teenage years, *combinations of social and hormonal changes* lead to mood swings.
- *Respecting the thoughts and feelings of a teen* is important when beginning to help her change her attitude problem.
- An occasional negative attitude is normal for most teens. *Behavior disorders* such as *oppositional defiant disorder* and *conduct disorder* are more serious. If the teen's attitude and behavior seem significantly different from that of other teens, parents should seek a *professional consultation with a mental health professional.*
- *Parents of teens need to gain insight and learn skills to understand, guide, and nurture* their teen children. The world has changed so drastically since parents were adolescents. Today teens are under more pressure and stress than ever before. *Compassion, gentleness, and encouragement* must be the parent's first responses to a negative attitude.

ASSESSMENT INTERVIEW : 3

For Parents

First, help the parents determine if the teen has a behavior problem or an attitude problem. The two issues are often mistaken for one another, but there are some key differences. The following interview questions will help you distinguish between the two. (If the teen has a behavior problem, please see the section Discipline.)

To identify a behavior problem, ask the parent to indicate if these are common concerns:

1. The teen often bullies, threatens, or intimidates others.
2. The teen initiates physical fights.
3. The teen has been physically cruel to people or animals.
4. The teen has robbed or stolen from another person.
5. The teen commonly breaks rules.
6. The teen commonly breaks curfew.
7. The teen commonly lies to authorities.
8. The teen has destroyed or set fire to someone else's property.
9. The teen regularly ditches school.

To identify an attitude problem, ask the parent to indicate if these are common concerns:

1. The teen often loses her temper.
2. The teen often argues with adults or authorities.
3. The teen is persistently negative or pessimistic.
4. The teen often deliberately annoys or antagonizes people.
5. The teen states that she dislikes or hates others.
6. The teen often blames others for her conduct or misbehavior.
7. The teen is often touchy or easily annoyed by others.
8. The teen is often angry and resentful.
9. The teen is often vindictive or spiteful.

Teens are under enormous pressure, some caused by others, and some self-inflicted. Every 24 hours:
- 3,000 teens experience the divorce of their parents
- 1,629 teens are put in adult jails
- 3,288 teens run away from home
- 1,512 drop out of school
- 7,742 teenagers become sexually active

Dr. Archibald D. Hart

For the Teen

1. Tell me why you've come to see me today.
2. What are some things that bother you most at home, at school, and at work (if applicable)?
3. How would you describe your response to these things? What helps you cope with these difficulties? What drags you down and makes things worse?
4. When you try to express your feelings and concerns to your parents, how do they respond?
5. How would you like them to respond?
6. How do your friends relate to their parents? Do they relate better or worse to their parents than you do to yours?

7. What are some things that make you happy and give you relief? What do you enjoy?

8. What would it mean to you if you felt as though your parents were supportive instead of critical about your attitude?

4 WISE COUNSEL

When meeting with the family, assure them that *God has placed them together* and He will show them how to grow together as a family. Changes may need to be made and, while the *changes may be difficult* at first, the family will be able to accomplish them with the Lord's help.

Encourage the parents of a *defiant or strong-willed teen* to avoid panic when considering their child's future. Some of the most successful adults were difficult to handle when they were teenagers. Encourage parents to *envision a positive future* for the child and share that vision with the child.

Talk about the *importance of spending time together*. In our culture it can be quite difficult to get the whole family together unless there is a crisis. There are countless distractions and excuses, but making family time a priority is essential to *build trust and express affirmation*, which are especially important during the adolescent years.

Parents need to consider how *their behavior and attitudes might be affecting their teen's attitude*. Many parents experience considerable stress at home and at work, in relationships and with finances. *When the home environment is stressed during their children's teen years* (which are tremendously demanding and threatening to teens), it puts added pressure on the teens, and the parents may have little energy for offering love, discipline, and guidance. Parents must honestly analyze their own lives and how their reactions to life may contribute to their child's struggles.

> Everything can be taken from a man or a woman but one thing: the last of human freedoms to choose one's attitude in any given set of circumstances, to choose one's own way.
>
> *Viktor Frankl*

Unconditional Love

Parents must love their teens even when they don't deserve it. This doesn't mean they accept everything their children do. Love and acceptance are not synonymous. It does mean they remind them that they *love them even when they disagree* with or are heartbroken by their children's actions.

Teens need physical touch, words of encouragement and affirmation, and quality time—all of these *communicate love*. Expressing love also helps to break down invisible barriers that have come between parents and their children. Keep in mind that adolescents are very *aware of appearances* and may not want to be hugged in front of their peers.

Sometimes, especially in adolescence, teens can feel like our enemies but in reality they are simply learning how to think and act on their own. A *certain amount of "push back" is normal*.

Discipline

The quality of *the parent's relationship with the child determines the effectiveness of the parent's discipline strategies*. Show us a home where all that is going on is discipline, and we will show you a home where the parent/child relationship is most likely gone!

The Bible cautions fathers *not to discourage* their children (Col. 3:21) but it also says that those who love their children are careful to discipline them (Prov. 13:24). *Discipline, unlike punishment, always envisions a better future for the child.*

Balance is the key. Parents must discipline and train their teens, but their discipline does not mean they are running a boot camp.

Parents must follow through with consequences. If a parent threatens to take away a teen's driving privileges or not let a friend come over to visit, *the parent must follow through* if the teen misbehaves. *Consistency is king.* The actual discipline is less important than the consistency of following through on consequences when a teen disobeys.

Parents should be careful to establish *only the rules and discipline they are going to enforce*. There are *three rules* that can serve as guides in disciplining teens:

- *The KFC Rule.* KFC stands for kind, firm, and consistent.
- *Granny's Rule.* This simply means that first the child must do what the parent wants and then she gets to do what she wants. For instance, the parent might say, "If you want to go swimming, then first you must do these chores."
- *The Millennial Rule.* This rule says that if the parent allows the child to get away with something, it may take a thousand times of correction to retrain her.

Guidance

The job of the parent is to *teach their teen about life*, guiding her in all areas, especially in God's Word (see Deut. 6:4–9).

Guiding teens may also mean *allowing them to make mistakes*. When a child gets into trouble at school or with the police, the parent should understand that *they are about to walk through a crisis with their child*.

Parents should *be prepared for disappointment* with some of their child's choices and behaviors. They should not make the mistake of too readily helping their child get out of the difficulties she is experiencing because of her choices and behaviors. *More growth takes place through a crisis than at any other time.*

5 ACTION STEPS

For the Teen

1. Find the Root of Your Attitude

- Many times a negative attitude stems from selfishness. When life becomes "all about me," it's easy to develop a sour outlook on *everything*. Look for the "why" behind your negativity—are you overwhelmed, frustrated, hurt, stressed?
- Address these issues, and look for ways to change your habits to help remedy the root problem. (For example, if waiting until the night before your class project is due makes you frustrated and grumpy, change the way you approach schoolwork.)

2. Take Control of Your Thoughts

- People may do things that frustrate you, but, ultimately, you are the one who decides how you will respond.
- Rather than focusing on the negative things in your life, change your focus to look for the many ways that God is blessing you. It's easy to take for granted simple things like being alive, having food, the opportunity to go to school, a car or job, friendships, and other good things, but the truth is that none of these are guaranteed.

3. Talk—Don't Pout

- It's natural to withdraw when you feel belittled or attacked, but rather than griping, *do something*. If you are frustrated with your parents' rules, talk to them about it in a straightforward, respectful way. If you have a disagreement with a friend, sit down and talk about it—don't just cut them off.
- Part of maturing is learning to take responsibility for your own behavior—rather than blaming other people. Learn to express your frustrations in a healthy, beneficial way that leads to change. Don't use the silent treatment on people.

4. Help Someone Else

- Life is not about you or getting what you want. Rather than complaining or griping, reach out to someone else and look for ways to love and serve her. A classmate, teacher, neighbor, friend, or other acquaintance could use your help.
- The amazing thing is that when we reach out to others, God begins to work in our hearts to change our attitudes!

For the Parents

1. Take an Honest Look

- *Some parents blame themselves for every problem in their children's lives, but others fail to even look at themselves to see if their attitudes and actions might contribute in some way to a child's struggles. If parents have come for help, ask them to take an honest look at themselves, especially regarding the following areas.*

— What is the ratio of affirming statements to critical statements you speak to each other and to your teen?
— How do you handle difficulties you experience at work and at home? Do you complain and blame each other or trust God for wisdom and peace?
— Make time for regularly interacting as a family, not just watching TV or playing video games.
— Try to understand the transition of a child who is moving through adolescence toward adulthood. This process necessarily involves the teen in crafting her own opinions that might be different from yours.
— Learn to respect your teen's privacy, while requiring responsible behavior.

2. Focus on the Relationship

- Trust and respect are essential in any relationship. Adolescents are going through one of the most difficult and awkward stages of life. They need affirmation and understanding, which take time, attention, and intention. The quality of your relationship with your teen will determine the effectiveness of your attempts to communicate love and your discipline strategies.

3. Clarify Rules and Responsibilities

- If possible, work together with your teen to decide on appropriate rules and responsibilities.
- Develop a workable plan, possibly including the following:

  — the rules to be followed
  — how discipline will be handled for infractions of the rules
  — what is negotiable and what isn't (for example, curfews might be negotiable)
  — chores (who does what, what is required, when chores must be completed)
  — privileges and responsibilities, including allowance, use of the car, and handling finances

4. Develop a Plan

- Collaborate with your teen to develop a comprehensive and workable plan to help her navigate the turbulent waters of adolescence. This plan will help your teen understand what is expected and could list everything from chores to homework to curfew to involvement in the family.
- Include in the plan expectations, rewards, and consequences, taking into consideration the age of the teen and the issues involved.
- The point is to listen to your teen and set reasonable guidelines for behavior. Expect her to be involved in this process, rather than just slapping on rules.

5. Adjust the Plan as Needed

- *If you sense that the parents are immature enough that they won't even be able to develop a good plan (or that their kids will run over them), follow up after they have had their family meeting to look over the plan they developed. You may need to help them accept the parental role or be more realistic.*

- Work through the plan for a couple weeks and make tweaks as needed—always with a family meeting. (For example, if chores are still not getting done, you may need to add consequences that will get results.)

- The plan should reward desired behavior and specify consequences for undesired behavior.

6. Be Consistent

- Post the plan where your teen can see it.

- Mom and Dad must be 100 percent together on this. Your child must not think that she can get one to overrule the other or that she can pit you against each other.

7. Trust God to Guide

- Ask for God's leading in how to raise your teen to be a responsible adult.

8. Spend Time Together

- Try to have at least one meal a day together as a family. Depending on the circumstances of your family, it may be more feasible to eat breakfast together than to have dinner together.

- Most important, keep the relationship between you and your teen strong. To make times together meaningful, be careful to:

  — talk with your teen
  — listen to your teen
  — show your teen you love her
  — spend time playing games with your teen
  — remember that kids spell love T-I-M-E
  — encourage your teen
  — pray with your teen

6 BIBLICAL INSIGHTS

"For this child I prayed, and the LORD has granted me my petition which I asked of Him. Therefore I also have lent him to the LORD; as long as he lives he shall be lent to the LORD." So they worshiped the LORD there.

1 Samuel 1:27–28 NKJV

Parenting is demanding and rewarding. Many people prepare and study for years to enter a chosen profession, but for parenting we usually receive on-the-job training. The goal of parenting is to guide a child into healthy, secure, and productive adulthood.

Fathers, do not provoke your children to wrath.

Ephesians 6:4 NKJV

This is an important warning concerning the power parents hold over their children. They can build them up or tear them down.

But from everlasting to everlasting the Lord's love is with those who fear him, and his righteousness with their children's children—with those who keep his covenant and remember to obey his precepts.

Psalm 103:17–18

One of the great promises of the Bible is that the mercy of the Lord continues from one generation to the next, even to our children's children. This does not mean that the children of Christians will automatically believe in God but that God's mercy and goodness are available to each generation.

Parents must set the right example for their teens. They are living not merely for themselves; they are setting a precedent that will affect generations to come.

PRAYER STARTER 7

Lord, we ask You to work lovingly and powerfully in this young person's life, but first, we ask You to work in her parents' lives. Father, they need Your wisdom and strength and they need You to give them direction. We know that during the teenage years change occurs and is positive and needed but also that it can be a struggle for everyone to cope with this process—so please give the teen and her parents an extra measure of strength and encouragement . . .

RECOMMENDED RESOURCES 8

Clark, Chap. *Hurt: Inside the World of Today's Teenagers*. Baker Academic, 2004.

Clark, Chap, and Dee Clark. *Disconnected: Parenting Teens in a MySpace World*. Baker, 2007.

Elkind, David. *The Hurried Child*. Da Capo Press, 2006.

Hersch, Patricia. *A Tribe Apart: A Journey into the Heart of American Adolescence*. Ballantine Books, 1999.

Taffel, Ron, ed. *Breaking through to Teens: A New Psychotherapy for the New Adolescence*. Guilford Press, 2005.

Bullying

1 PORTRAITS

- James hates getting on the bus in the morning. Usually, the only seat left is next to Scott, and every time he sits down, Scott swears at him and elbows him repeatedly on the way to school.
- When Brian got back to his locker, he realized his socks had been stolen and the rest of his clothes were soaked in urine. The other guys in the locker room were laughing. This is nothing new for Brian.
- Alice never gets a moment's rest from the girls in her class. She had a single conversation with a boy and this offended his girlfriend. Now the girl is on an all-out campaign to terrorize Alice. Every day at school the other girls call her a "ho."

2 DEFINITIONS AND KEY THOUGHTS

- *Bullying* is any behavior that *belittles or is aggressive* toward another person. Bullying may be *verbal* (derogatory comments, calling names, telling lies about) or *physical* (kicking, hitting, shoving) but always stems from *an imbalance of power*. Other forms of bullying include social exclusion, cyber bullying, racial slurs, stealing, and threatening behavior.
- It is believed that bullying is much *more common among preteens and younger teens* than it is among older teens. Older teens tend to channel their anger toward others by aligning with groups that assert their identity and "power" through violence, sometimes to the point of criminal "gang" activity. Obviously this is a *more intense and dangerous form of bullying*.
- School bullying occurs *more frequently among boys than girls*; however female teen bullying does occur. *While male teens are more likely to be bullied physically* (hitting and pushing), *females are more likely to be bullied verbally through sexual comments and rumors or gossip.*[1]
- Teen bullying is a *warning sign*. The perpetrator is at risk of more severe antisocial or delinquent behavior in the future. For that reason, *intervention is needed both for the bullied and the bully.*
- While bullying is often considered to be simply "normal kid stuff," it can *severely damage the emotional health of the victim.* Bullied teens are often tense and afraid,

and in some cases they begin to avoid school or other places where they might be bullied.

- In one survey of junior high and high school students, more than 88 percent reported that they had witnessed bullying in their schools. Being *a witness to bullying* can lead bystanders to feel guilty for not standing up to a bully on behalf of the bullied person or for failing to report the incident to someone who could help. *Repeatedly avoiding getting involved to protect victims can leave bystanders feeling helpless and powerless.*[2]

- While bullying occurs in many settings and can happen in many different ways, *bullying behaviors* generally fall into *four major categories*:

  — *Visual bullying*: behaviors meant to intimidate the victim. This form includes violent gestures (such as the middle finger, or physical gestures that suggest a person is going to do physical harm), making faces, drawing offensive pictures about the victim, graffiti, or defacing a person's belongings.
  — *Verbal bullying*: verbal threats, name-calling, cruel jokes, gossip and rumors, and offensive sounds.
  — *Physical bullying*: any kind of hitting, throwing of items, poking, touching, grabbing, pushing, blocking someone's way, or intimidating physically. Physical bullying can escalate into assault. If these behaviors have a sexual component, the behavior is considered sexual harassment or sexual assault.
  — *Cyber bullying*: in recent years people have used the internet to harass and intimidate others, often through instant messaging, MySpace, Facebook, or simply email.

- A bully often *excuses his behavior in a passive-aggressive way* by claiming, "I was just joking." The problem, of course, is that the behavior was not funny. This is a very common way bullies deflect responsibility for their destructive behavior.

- *The issue is intent.* Does one person want to intimidate or harm another? If he does, it's bullying.

> Never be bullied into silence. Never allow yourself to be made a victim. Accept no one's definition of your life, but define yourself.
>
> *Harvey S. Firestone*

ASSESSMENT INTERVIEW 3

For the Victim of Bullying

1. Tell me what happens when the person (or people) try to intimidate you.
2. When does it tend to occur most often? Do you see a definite pattern in the time and place when this occurs?
3. What precipitated the bullying? Was there a misunderstanding or something else that caused it at first?
4. How have you handled the problem? How effective has your solution been?
5. Who are the people who support you and encourage you to be strong?
6. If you've tried to stand up to the bully, what happened? Does anyone stand up to that person?

7. Have you talked to anyone in authority about the problem? If so, what has this person done to help you?

For the Parents of the Victim

1. How has the experience of being bullied hurt your teen?
2. When did you first become aware of the problem? Is it a new problem, or has your teen always had trouble standing up for himself?
3. In what kinds of situations has he exhibited inner strength and resolve?
4. Have you talked to school officials (or other appropriate authorities) about the problem?
5. What is your plan to help him stand up to the bully?
6. What insights and skills does your child need?
7. What insights and skills do you need?

4 : WISE COUNSEL

Bullies are part of every school, and any child can become a victim. Long before acts of violence actually occur, *threats and harassment* are common, and often children don't tell anyone because of *fear of what may happen.* It is essential that *parents talk to their children on a regular basis* about not only their schoolwork and friends but also their safety. Parents should take a genuine interest in their child's school experiences—both the good and the bad.

Parents should ask their children *direct questions* about what's going on at school and how they feel about it. Frustrations and fears may be evident, even if they seem insignificant. If parents have *ongoing communication* with their children, when big issues come up, their teen will feel safe talking to them about what's going on. *Creating a safe, loving environment* in which kids can talk is one of the surest safeguards to preventing their getting hurt.

Parents play a critical role in helping their teen deal with a bully. Unless there is a threat of physical harm, it may not be wise to jump in to protect the child. Instead, the parent's role is to *listen and provide comfort,* but also to *impart insight and skills* so that the teen knows how to stand up for himself. Rushing in to "fix" the problem leaves the teen feeling powerless and even more vulnerable to bullies. In situations like these, *love means equipping and supporting, not rescuing.*

Parents can play an active role in defining a school environment and should get involved in parent-teacher meetings, becoming activists for their child's safety and education. At after-school activities, such as drama, sports, or music, parents may have the opportunity to connect with other parents, while at the same time showing genuine care and concern to their teens.

It is estimated that nearly 30% of teens in the United States are involved in school bullying—as either a bully or as a target of bullying. In a recent nationwide survey of students in grades 6–10, 13% reported bullying others, 11% reported being the target of school bullies, and another 6% said they both bullied others and were bullied themselves.

www.familyfirstaid.org /bullying.html

ACTION STEPS : 5

1. Talk about It

- (For the teen) Bullying is a serious problem. If you are being bullied, talk with your parents or someone else in authority about it.
- (For the parents) Face the fact that bullying is undoubtedly happening at your child's school in some way, shape, or form. Open up the conversation with your children about bullying. In talking with him, be aware that he may be on either end of the spectrum—either bullying or being bullied. Tactfully share with him your own experiences as an adolescent and ask him about bullying at school. Work to create an atmosphere of openness—don't tell him to "get over it" or "be tough."

2. Deescalate

- (For the teen) Learn how to properly respond to bullying. Though it is natural to lash out at the perpetrator, this will only further escalate the situation. Rather than bullying back, avoid adding to the tension and respond sensibly, rather than in anger, and get out of the situation.
- (For the teen) While counterviolence is never appropriate, assertiveness always is. Any bullying should be reported immediately to the appropriate school authorities.

3. Build Confidence in Setting Boundaries

- (For the parents) Though every school is required to have an emergency response plan in case of bomb threats or fire, few schools have any established plan for handling bullying. By educating your teen in how to handle threats, you build your teenager's confidence and lessen the likelihood that bullying will actually occur.
- (For the teen) Boundaries discourage bullying behavior. By setting up a specific action plan—including what to say, what to do, whom to talk to, and how to get help—you empower yourself to respond to bullying, rather than becoming a silent victim.

4. Choose Friends

- (For the teen) Understand this principle: You are who you spend time with. The apostle Paul was very open about this concept: "Bad company corrupts good character" (1 Cor. 15:33). Find a peer group in which you help to build self-confidence and good character in one another.
- (For the parents) Help the process by encouraging your teen to be involved in extracurricular activities, such as sports, dance, choir, band, church youth groups, or other after-school programs.

6 BIBLICAL INSIGHTS

I can do everything through him who gives me strength.

Philippians 4:13

Victims of any kind of abuse feel hopeless and powerless. They need reassurance that they aren't alone. God is with them and will give them wisdom and direction, and supportive adults can help them take steps to protect themselves.

Alexander the metalworker did me a great deal of harm. The Lord will repay him for what he has done. You too should be on your guard against him, because he strongly opposed our message.

2 Timothy 4:14–15

Self-protection isn't a luxury; it's a God-given right and responsibility. Alexander the metalworker threatened Paul and Timothy, and in his letter to his protégé, Paul instructed Timothy to be on his guard with Alexander. He also assured Timothy that God's justice would eventually prevail in Alexander's life.

We need to help teens to do all they can to avoid direct confrontation and to be smart in how they handle bullies.

God is our refuge and strength, an ever-present help in trouble.

Psalm 46:1

Even when we feel alone, and even when we feel that no one cares, we can be sure that God sees, cares deeply, and will give us wisdom to deal with any problem. Usually He doesn't rescue us out of those problems but He helps us work through them so that we grow strong in the process.

Do not repay anyone evil for evil. Be careful to do what is right in the eyes of everybody. If it is possible, as far as it depends on you, live at peace with everyone. Do not take revenge, my friends, but leave room for God's wrath, for it is written: "It is mine to avenge; I will repay," says the Lord. On the contrary: "If your enemy is hungry, feed him; if he is thirsty, give him something to drink. In doing this, you will heap burning coals on his head." Do not be overcome by evil, but overcome evil with good.

Romans 12:17–21

Our natural instinct is to seek revenge and hurt those who have hurt us, but God leads us in a different path. We can be sure that His justice will eventually reign, but we aren't the instruments of His wrath. We can leave the bully in God's wise and strong hands.

With this assurance, we can be strong, refuse to remain a victim, and overcome evil by forgiving the offender, setting good boundaries, and when necessary learning to stand up strong for what is good and right in a way that deescalates a volatile situation or relationship.

PRAYER STARTER :7

Father, this young person feels hurt and hopeless. Help him be assured that You know exactly what's been going on, how much it hurts, and that You are strong to support him. Give him wisdom to stand up for himself, to say no to those who hurt him, and win their respect by his strength and resolve. Thank You, Lord, for Your grace, truth, and power . . .

RECOMMENDED RESOURCES :8

McGraw, Jay. *Jay McGraw's Life Strategies for Dealing with Bullies.* Aladdin Hardcovers, 2008.

Peretti, Frank. *No More Bullies: For Those Who Wound and Are Wounded.* Thomas Nelson, 2003.

Romain, Trevor. *Bullies Are a Pain in the Brain.* Free Spirit, 1997.

Websites

U.S. Department of Education: http://www.ed.gov/about/offices/list/osdfs/resources. html#safeschool

National School Safety and Security Services: http://www.schoolsecurity.org/resources/links.html

Center for the Prevention of School Violence: http://www.ncdjjdp.org/cpsv

SafeYouth Violence Prevention Resource Center: http://www.safeyouth.org/scripts/topics/school.asp

National Crime Prevention Council: http://www.ncpc.org/

Career Decisions

1 PORTRAITS

- "It's your second year, Dianne," said the woman behind the desk at the registrar's office. "You need to declare a major. Have you given any thought to what you want to do?" Dianne bit her lower lip. She has been trying to decide on a career path but really had no idea what she wanted to do.
- "Bryan is going to be an architect like his father," his mother proudly reports to a friend. Bryan looks down at his shoes. He wants to make his parents happy, but architecture has never felt right to him.

2 DEFINITIONS AND KEY THOUGHTS

- As they finish high school and begin college, teens begin to think seriously about their future career. *Choosing a career can be a daunting task*, and often teens are *pressured* to make career choices before they are ready to do so.
- It is normal for teens not to know the career path they want to take. It is also *normal for college-aged adolescents to change their career path (and their majors) several times*.
- Often a teen's *career choice depends on gender*. For example, a sports career is a timeless favorite for young men but has never made the top twenty for young women. Similarly, early education is more popular with females than males.

3 ASSESSMENT INTERVIEW

Based on the circumstances, you may want to give these career counseling questions to the teen beforehand or talk through them together to determine what type of career she may want to pursue. Your discussion should help to identify areas of interest and passion. Ask follow-up questions if needed to further explore how the teen's interests can be honed as marketable skills.

1. What are your passions? What interests do you have that get you out of bed in the morning?
2. What accomplishments and achievements have you made thus far? (Even small victories/accomplishments should be listed.)

3. Describe your personality and temperament. What do you love to do?
4. What sort of work attracts you?
5. Do you like to work with your hands?
6. Do you think you would prefer social, relational, or political work?
7. Do you think you would like work that is thought intensive?
8. How much education are you willing to complete?
9. Are you interested in working for yourself or for someone else?
10. Do you want to work alone or as part of a team?
11. Do you want to work in an office?
12. Do you want to work in front of a computer or on the telephone?
13. What about other types of jobs, such as working with your hands—jobs that don't require a college education?
14. How do your interests fit into today's job market needs?
15. How much do you really know about the career possibilities you are considering?
16. What are some ways you think you might be able to test out the career choices you are considering?

WISE COUNSEL : 4

In the past, adolescents were often employed in the town's factory or their father's fields before they reached their teens. Today, however, things have drastically changed. For many teens, career choices *aren't at the top of the list* of pressing issues. As society has become more complex and fewer parents are actively present to help their children grow into adulthood, *many teens are more interested in building a social network* than they are in preparing for the future. At some point, obviously, young people need to be actively thinking about their future and *exploring their gifts and vocational calling.*

Many young people who want to please God seem paralyzed by the *fear of "missing God's will."* While many teens expect God to reveal to them the college they should attend, the major they should choose, and the job they should take, *God is more concerned with their character, faith, and love* (Gal. 5:6). It is unrealistic to expect divine "handwriting on the wall," but God's Word clearly states His will for us: to obey Him and to bring glory to Him by *whatever* we do (1 Cor. 10:31).

When it comes to making life decisions, generally God guides us through the use of our natural gifts and abilities and through the counsel of Christian parents and others who are close to us. Any career can glorify God, as long as it does not lead an individual into sin. Encourage the teen to *find what she loves to do, what makes her feel alive, and what is most fulfilling to her.* While it may not be the most desirable career in the eyes of the world, choosing a job she feels "called to" will be the best for her. For more insight into the common adolescent struggle of life direction, refer to the section God's Will.

If you are helping a teen explore career possibilities, make sure to keep a perspective that *the timeline in making a career choice is years long.* Don't become too consumed with the process, and help the teen not to become overly concerned with choosing a career at this point.

Some young people will naturally and willingly *follow their parents in a career*. Perhaps genetics predisposes them to pursue a similar line of work, or familiarity with a parent's career points them down the same path. Parents, however, make a big mistake if they assume a child will necessarily want to follow their path, and they make an even bigger mistake if they try to force the young person into a career.

If the teen is ready to begin applying for jobs, give some counsel on the *interview process*. This should be a time for both the employer and the prospective employee to gather information. The company human resources director has a set of questions for people interviewing for a position. Those interviewing can also ask some important questions. *These questions should help the teen learn more about the company and the career field she is interested in pursuing.* The teen can bring up these questions during a job interview, and reviewing the questions beforehand will help eliminate nervousness.

Apart from formal job interviews, encourage the teen to use this list to initiate interviews with professionals already working in her field of interest. For example, she may want to talk with a doctor, an engineer, a teacher, or a journalist. If an adolescent presents herself in a mature manner, most professionals are more than willing to share about their experiences and their job. There is no substitute for hearing about a career from those who live and work in it!

1. Can you describe a typical day on the job? (When does your day start? What is the first thing you do when you get to work?)
2. How did you get involved in this career?
3. Would you get into this line of work again, right now?
4. How has the field changed recently or how might it change in the future?
5. What is your favorite part of this job?
6. What is your least favorite part of this job?
7. What surprised you the most when you started working in this field?
8. What is the typical salary range for someone in this line of work? (People are typically uncomfortable stating their salaries, but if the question is asked in this more general way, an idea of the range in salary can be given.)
9. What advice would you give me, or anyone, if I planned to make a career in this field?
10. What are employers typically looking for when interviewing or hiring applicants in this line of work?
11. Is there much room for new people wanting to begin this career?
12. May I talk to you in the future if I have additional questions?

Note: Remind the teen that it's a good idea to send a thank-you note after an interview. This will help to leave a good impression on the person who met with her and create the possibility of future networking.

ACTION STEPS 5

For many teens today, career possibilities can seem endless. There are many ways to explore occupations, with parents, teachers, and friends being key components in the process. Here are some suggestions to help teens explore career options.

1. Explore

- In some cases, parents, teachers, or others discourage a young person's pursuit of a particular career, and they may push hard toward the one they prefer. In families that are very active in the church, some young people are pressured into working in the ministry. Also, some valid career choices, such as becoming a chef or an artist, may be seen as frivolous. Explore any career path you find interesting, even if others tell you it's the "wrong" career path for you. The process itself is enlightening, and through it you will probably discover a path that is right for you. It may mean a few false starts, but if you are prepared for that possibility, making the decision to change to another career will not be overwhelming.

2. Shadow Someone at Work

- One way to explore a career choice is to shadow someone working in the field of interest. Some high schools offer these opportunities in their career center. Check with your counselor or ask your parents to arrange a shadowing experience for you. Spending a day with a cook, a police officer, a doctor, an accountant, or a worker in any field will be enlightening, either piquing your interest or letting you know it's not the career for you.

3. Keep Things in Perspective

- Remember that you are only exploring career options and not making a choice now for what you will do for the rest of your life. Keep things in perspective. It's likely that your interests will change over the next few years, so don't feel pressured to make a decision now.
- If your parents seem alarmed by the career you want to explore, help them understand that you are simply checking out a possibility, not committing yourself to a lifelong job.

The 2005 Gallup Survey found the top ten career choices of female students were:
1. teacher
2. lawyer
3. doctor
4. nurse
5. fashion designer
6. scientist/biologist
7. author/writer
8. veterinarian
9. artist
10. medical field (e.g., lab technician)

The top ten career choices for male students were:
1. sports
2. doctor
3. architect
4. engineer
5. teacher
6. businessman
7. lawyer
8. military
9. scientist/biologist
10. computer-related career

6 BIBLICAL INSIGHTS

"For I know the plans I have for you," declares the LORD, "plans to prosper you and not to harm you, plans to give you hope and a future. Then you will call upon me and come and pray to me, and I will listen to you. You will seek me and find me when you seek me with all your heart."

Jeremiah 29:11–13

Choosing a career is sometimes difficult and confusing, but we can be sure that God wants us to find a path that is fulfilling and rewarding. And God's path always involves knowing Him, loving Him, serving Him, and seeing our primary calling, as Philip Yancey says, as being His "instruments of grace" to the world He loves.

I will instruct you and teach you in the way you should go; I will counsel you and watch over you. Do not be like the horse or the mule, which have no understanding but must be controlled by bit and bridle or they will not come to you.

Psalm 32:8–9

As we pursue God and seek to trust Him as our Lord, He promises to lead us. He has not created us to be controlled like an animal, forced to go in a certain direction. Instead, God calls us to listen to His voice for direction in the Scriptures, in Christian community, and as the Spirit prompts.

The sleep of a laboring man is sweet, whether he eats little or much; but the abundance of the rich will not permit him to sleep.

Ecclesiastes 5:12 NKJV

The purpose of work isn't to become wealthy but to honor God and to be His representatives to those He loves. Your work glorifies God when you do it with joy and excellence—when you "work at it with all your heart" (Col. 3:23–34)—and when you rely on God's strength, not your own. Many people desire to be rich, thinking they will have no more worries. Indeed, money and power give the illusion of freedom, but when there is a reliance on money and power, they are destructive.

And whatever you do, whether in word or deed, do it all in the name of the Lord Jesus, giving thanks to God the Father through him.

Colossians 3:17

Some people think there are "spiritual" jobs and "secular" jobs, but that's not the case. All honorable careers can be pursued for the glory of God and the delight of knowing that we are in God's will if we are obeying what He has put before us. When we see our job as an opportunity to partner with the Holy

Spirit, we will share His truth and love with the people we work and interact with in the workplace.

"You have sown much, and bring in little. . . . And he who earns wages, earns wages to put into a bag with holes." Thus says the LORD of hosts: "Consider your ways!"

Haggai 1:6–7 NKJV

Contrary to popular belief, the reason we work is not only for money. Just as God gave Adam and Eve dominion over the Garden of Eden—to tend and care for it—He gives each one of us "dominion" over our own arena. Our work is a trust from God, and one day we will be called to give an account to Him. Haggai points out the importance of working *for God*, not merely for selfish gain. "[Earning] wages to put into a bag with holes" happens when we work with the purpose of hoarding our wealth. But Scripture exhorts us that no matter how much money we may amass, this approach to work will "bring in little" of eternal significance. This is the reason it is important not to make career decisions solely based on money.

Be anxious for nothing, but in everything by prayer and supplication, with thanksgiving, let your requests be made known to God; and the peace of God, which surpasses all understanding, will guard your hearts and minds through Christ Jesus.

Philippians 4:6–7 NKJV

The counsel in these verses applies to many kinds of worries—including the search for a meaningful career. We can trust that God will lead us, and in that assurance, we can be thankful for every step in the pursuit, knowing that God will lead us where He wants us to go.

PRAYER STARTER 7

Father, thank You for my young friend who wants to find a career that is meaningful and the right fit. Thank You for the abilities, interests, and experiences You've given her. Lead her, Lord, through all the options and opportunities and give her the assurance that You have wonderful plans for her life . . .

RECOMMENDED RESOURCES 8

Friesen, Garry, and J. Robin Maxson. *Decision Making and the Will of God.* Multnomah, 2004.

Guinness, Os. *The Call: Finding and Fulfilling the Central Purpose of Your Life.* Thomas Nelson, 2003.

Hillman, Os. *Making Godly Decisions: How to Know and Do the Will of God.* The Aslan Group, 2002.

Matlock, Mark. *Freshman: The College Student's Guide to Developing Wisdom.* NavPress, 2005.

Phillips, Kelsey. *College Bound on Solid Ground.* WinePress, 2008.

Culture and Media Influence

PORTRAITS : 1

- Fashion, boys, and technology—that's what defines Sarah's life. A cheerleader at her high school and a smart student, Sarah makes friends easily. But with each passing day, she seems to slip farther away than ever from her mom and dad. When she is at home, Sarah is usually plopped on the couch watching TV or on the computer chatting with her friends. "How did it come to this?" Sarah's dad, David, asks. "It seems like just yesterday I was giving her piggyback rides, and now she doesn't even want to talk to me."

- "Mom, you have to buy me one . . . pleeease?" Jake pleaded. Finally, Brittany gave in to her son's pleadings and bought him an iPod Touch for his twelfth birthday, hoping that it would help him be responsible. Now it seems like the earbuds live in Jake's ears. He listens nonstop to music that he downloaded or got from his friends. The other day when Brittany noticed the iPod and picked it up, she was shocked at the vulgar song titles on Jake's playlist.

- "I wish I could come, but Thursday night is our family night," Hannah told her friends. "Dad makes breakfast for dinner, and we pull out all the games— Scattergories, Charades, UNO. It's a blast." Although Hannah's friends couldn't quite understand what could be so fun about hanging out with her family, they kind of wondered if they were missing out on something. Hannah talked about it as though she actually enjoyed spending time with her parents.

DEFINITIONS AND KEY THOUGHTS : 2

- Culture can be defined as *a set of shared attitudes, values, and practices that characterizes a specific group of people.* Across the world, there are many distinct cultures, *influenced by ethnicity, geography, economic level, and religious beliefs.* In the United States, countless subcultures exist.

- An expression of culture, *media is communication designed to reach masses of people.* Whether in the form of newspapers, radio, television, internet, or advertising, *media floods into our lives from every direction.* With new technological discoveries, the sea of communication is growing larger every day.

- Of specific interest to today's teen is *social media*—any media form used to *connect with other people.* Facebook, MySpace, Skype, texting, and online chat rooms are just a few common forms of social media. Social media is especially popular among young people because it provides instant gratification and the illusion of connectedness.

- Consider the many ways our *children are exposed to media* every day, almost constantly hearing, seeing, or experiencing some form, including television, radio, CDs, DVDs, magazines, newspapers, direct mail, email, billboards, movies, MP3 players, hundreds of channels of cable television programming, iPods, cell phones, laptops, wireless internet service, HD television, HD radio, playing any one of thousands of realistic video games on a laptop or phone, video game systems, DVD players mounted in multiple locations in vehicles . . . and the list goes on!

- Media is an *integral part of our culture and lives*, and it's important to realize that, in and of itself, media is not evil. Media is simply *a tool* that has changed how we all live. For many teens, media in the form of iPods, cell phones, internet, and social networking so consumes their lives that *they can lose sight of what life is intended to be*.

- As media infuses every aspect of our daily lives, it sets up two polarities we all tend to bounce between: *watching* and *doing*. When we are watching, we are so interested in a medium that *we spend much of our time watching other people live life*. When we are doing, we are *able to set healthy boundaries to keep media from controlling our lives*, and therefore have more time and energy to be actively involved in *doing* life.

- Teens are especially vulnerable to being swept up in an *overconsumption of media*. After all, various forms of media are readily available and hip. Becoming preoccupied with the images and messages of media *sap the creativity* from young minds as well as *disconnecting* teens from the most important relationships in their lives—family, friends, siblings, youth group. We were created for relationships, and no social media—no matter how advanced—can replace *the need for spending time with others*.

3 ASSESSMENT INTERVIEW

The following questions will help you assess the quality and quantity of time the teen spends with his family.

1. When was the last time you had a meaningful one-on-one conversation with a family member or friend? How often does this happen?
2. Describe your typical family breakfasts and dinners. Where do they take place? Is the television on?
3. What goes on in your home on a typical night? How much are people engaged in watching television, listening to music, or searching the internet? Is there conversation among family members? Is it mostly pleasant or unpleasant?
4. Do you ever play board games or sports with your parents and siblings? If not, do you wish your family played together?
5. Do your parents discuss your use of technology with you? What do they think about it? How does this make you feel?

6. Do you discuss movies, music, or the news with your parents? How do their views influence your choices of media?
7. What are limits you and your parents have set for the use of technology, the amount of time watching television, and the types of movies you will watch? How do your parents enforce these limits?
8. How much time do you spend each day on social networking sites (such as Facebook or MySpace)? How much time do you spend each day in face-to-face conversation?
9. What relationships are most important to you—your family, friends, youth group, co-workers? How do you usually connect with these people?
10. Is God part of your conversations? Do your parents encourage your family to spend time together talking about spiritual things? How do you think you can use media in a way that honors God?

WISE COUNSEL 4

In a world overrun by technology, it's important to establish *healthy boundaries in our use of media*. Though modern technology promises to keep us informed and connected, it can easily become an idol and take over our lives. Like a car or any other human invention, media is not evil in and of itself, but it has *tremendous influence* in our daily lives. While having a healthy appreciation for the technology accessible to us in the twenty-first century, we must *guard against becoming slaves to it*.

"Trash in, trash out," the saying goes, and with regard to media, this is especially true. We know that, while we have access to all manner of media at our fingertips, *not everything printed, recorded, or filmed is beneficial to our growth as Christians*. King David vowed that he would set no evil thing before his eyes (Ps. 101:3), and we should make the same commitment. *Guarding our eyes, ears, and minds from the pollution of the world* is by no means an easy task, and discernment is definitely needed if we are to live in but not be part of this world (John 17:15).

Used in a *God-honoring way*, media can be a tool that helps us connect with and encourage other people, as well as a way to share God's truth with a large audience. *Media is powerful*—it can put us in instant communication with hundreds, and potentially thousands, of people. So we must be careful. When we use media to communicate with others, we need to stop and ask, *What am I communicating?*

While social networking is easy and convenient, *deep, life-changing relationships are not developed in front of a computer screen or through a cell phone*. Encourage teens to schedule hangout time on a regular basis with the people they really care about—friends, youth group members, co-workers, and, yes, family too. Teens who rely solely on connecting through technology will find their *relationships shallow and unsatisfying*.

Counsel teens to look for ways to use media to help them *deepen their walk with God*. They can listen to uplifting music and sermons on their iPod, use online Bible study resources, text their friends and ask how to pray for them, and post encouraging Scriptures and quotes on their Facebook page. The possibilities are endless!

All of us need down time to rest our minds and take a break from the fast pace of life. Our culture puts forth media as *the* way to relax—whether it's TV, movies, or computer games. Media entertainment can be easily enticing. It captures our attention, helps us de-stress, and makes us feel like we're part of something bigger than our own living room. However, passive entertainment can never replace active experience. In the long run, *active experience is critical to a healthy, well-balanced life.*

Passive Entertainment	Active Experience
watching	doing
leisure (no sweating)	energetic (sweating likely)
no discipline required	discipline required
no health benefit	some health benefit
done mostly alone	done with others
no teamwork required	teamwork may be required
tendency to self-focus	tendency to focus on others
connecting with media images	connecting with real people
empty feeling afterward	energized feeling afterward

5 ACTION STEPS

1. Talk with Your Parents about the Media You Use

- Many adults need to learn about technology, and you can help your parents understand why you enjoy being part of a "plugged in" culture. Be willing to show them the websites you access, especially social networking sites, and various types of technology.
- Listen to your parents if they are concerned that media and technology may be interfering with your face-to-face relationships.

2. Become a Student of Entertainment

- One of the biggest problems with many forms of screened entertainment is that viewers become completely passive, not reflecting on the message at all. Be prepared to talk with your family about films and TV programs you see. Discuss the message of the film and its meaning for you.
- Listen to the views of others. Try to understand the reasons they interpret the message differently than you do.

3. Try a Media-Free Experiment

- If you struggle with over-using media, try taking a week off from its use. This won't be easy, but taking a break will help you develop healthier media habits.

- Don't sign on to Facebook, MySpace, or Skype. Use your free time to be with God and to hang out with your friends face-to-face, rather than chatting through a computer screen.
- Choose not to watch TV. Make plans ahead of time to do other things during the times you would normally watch TV. You might use those hours to help and encourage someone else.
- If you try not to use any electronic media at all, challenge yourself to spend time reading books, playing games, or talking with your family.

4. Respect Your Parents' Decisions about Censorship

- While you are living at home, your parents have the responsibility to provide leadership in important decisions. It's entirely appropriate for them to have a list, or perhaps a category rating, of movies, TV shows, and video games that are off-limits in your home.
- If you don't agree with their decision, discuss it with them respectfully and explain the reasons for how you feel. But then accept their decision.

5. Make Pleasing God Your Goal

- The world of media can easily cultivate a selfish mindset. As you make decisions about media use, whether it's movies, TV, music, or internet, ask yourself one simple question: *Does this media please God?* Rather than making your decisions about media based on peer pressure or the goal of having fun, learn to approach media with the desire of glorifying God, not indulging your flesh.

BIBLICAL INSIGHTS 6

Do not love the world or anything in the world. If anyone loves the world, the love of the Father is not in him. For everything in the world—the cravings of sinful man, the lust of his eyes and the boasting of what he has and does— comes not from the Father but from the world. The world and its desires pass away, but the man who does the will of God lives forever.

1 John 2:15–17

We live in an entertainment-drenched culture, and it's very easy for teens (and their parents) to become passive and let this electronic world consume and control them.

Though I am free and belong to no man, I make myself a slave to everyone, to win as many as possible. To the Jews I became like a Jew, to win the Jews. To those under the law I became like one under the law (though I myself am not under the law), so as to win those under the law. To those not having the law I became like one not having the law (though I am not free from God's law but am under Christ's law), so as to win those not having the law. To the weak I became weak, to win the weak. I have become all things to all men so that by all possible means I might save some. I do all this for the sake of the gospel, that I may share in its blessings.

1 Corinthians 9:19–23

God has given us enormous freedom to make choices, but He wants us to use our freedom in positive and constructive ways. When we spend our time, energies, and passions on worthless things, we don't have much left for God.

"Everything is permissible"—but not everything is beneficial. "Everything is permissible"—but not everything is constructive.

1 Corinthians 10:23

Except for pornography and other harmful sites, most of what is available online, on a teen's phone, on TV, or at the movies isn't evil, but it can easily become a distraction from what's most important: God, other people, and God's purposes for us.

7 : PRAYER STARTER

Father, we live hectic, chaotic lives, and sometimes we don't spend enough quality time with the most important of our relationships—You and family. God, help this family set aside ample time to eat meals together, support each other, enjoy fun activities, and have family devotions. May they reflect Your heart, Your character, and Your purposes . . .

8 : RECOMMENDED RESOURCES

Andriacco, Dan. *Taming the Media Monster: A Family Guide to Television, Internet, and All the Rest.* St. Anthony Messenger Press, 2003.

Baeher, Theodore, and Pat Boone. *The Culture-Wise Family: Upholding Christian Values in a Mass-Media World.* Regal, 2007.

Chapman, Gary. *The Family You've Always Wanted: Five Ways You Can Make It Happen.* Northfield, 2008.

Smith, Timothy. *52 Family Time Ideas: Draw Closer to Your Kids as You Draw Your Kids Closer to God.* Bethany House, 2006.

Tomeo, Teresa. *Noise: How Our Media-Saturated Culture Dominates Lives and Dismantles Families.* Ascension Press, 2007.

Cutting

- Emma's mom first noticed the cuts when Emma was doing the dishes one night. Emma told her mom that their cat had scratched her. Her mom was surprised that the cat had been so rough but didn't think much more about it. Emma's friends had noticed something strange as well. Even when the weather was hot, Emma wore long-sleeved shirts. She had become secretive too, as though something was bothering her. But Emma couldn't seem to find the words to tell her mom or her friends that the marks on her arms were from something she had done to herself. She was cutting herself with a razor when she felt sad or upset.

- Suzanne had been depressed for a long time, but suddenly her parents began to notice a difference. She had been sullen and withdrawn, but now she was angry and defiant. Was this progress? She began spending time with a new group of friends who all wore black and had various piercings and tattoos. Her parents tried to connect with Suzanne, but she brushed them off or angrily walked out. And something was very odd; she insisted on washing her own clothes. One morning her mom went into her room after Suzanne had left for school and noticed blood on the sheet. That night Suzanne's parents learned that their daughter had been cutting herself for months.

DEFINITIONS AND KEY THOUGHTS 2

- *Cutting*, seen mostly among teens, is the use of a sharp object for the purpose of *self-injury* or SI, breaking the skin and causing scratches or cuts that bleed. Though primarily an act carried out by girls, cutting is sometimes seen among guys as well and generally begins in the early teen years. Some people continue to cut into adulthood.

- People use a *knife, paper clip, or other sharp object for cutting.*

- Other self-injury methods include biting, burning, and self-beatings.

- The most common parts of the body for self-injury are *wrists, arms, legs, or stomach.*

- Most teenagers who self-injure will *try to hide the burns, cuts, or scars* so nobody will notice. Physical problems with cutting include the possibility of extreme blood loss or infection.

- Often cutting provides *relief from the emotional pain and pressure* the person lives with. The pain could stem from relational loss or rejection. Many teens who cut feel as though they don't fit in with the "in" crowd or they feel that nobody understands them.

- Typically, teens who cut *have not learned how to cope with negative emotions and difficult situations in life*, particularly relationship problems. Their coping skills are not adequate to deal with the overwhelming emotions they are experiencing. Then self-injury becomes *a way for the teenager to deal with bitterness, rage, sorrow, rejection, isolation, desperation, longing, or emptiness*. At the very least, cutting gives the teenager a sense of control over her negative feelings and relief from the emotional pain she has been experiencing, which often makes the act of cutting addictive.

- The leading theory concerning the behavior of self-injury is that *cutting, burning, or hitting oneself externalizes brutal and persistent emotional pain*. A poem published in a newsletter called "The Cutting Edge" sums up the disorder, says Ruta Mazelis, a consultant with the Sidran Institute in Baltimore, an organization that focuses on traumatic stress: "I hurt so much I bleed."

- Ruta Mazelis says, "The self-injury becomes *a coping mechanism* for many of the repercussions in their lives." She strongly believes that most self-injurers suffered a previous emotional trauma. "It tends to be an all-purpose tool for trauma survivors who use it to manage incredibly intense emotions: horror, anger and grief."[1]

- Most therapists agree that *self-injury helps relieve negative emotions, at least temporarily.* "People have so much bad feelings in them—shame, guilt, rage—that they need to let it out," Janis Whitlock, a prominent Cornell University researcher on cutting, says "They punish themselves by injuring or distract themselves by injuring. It helps them blow off steam."[2]

- For some sufferers, the *physical pain of self-injury is outweighed by the emotional relief*, researchers say. For others, *pain is a reminder that they are alive when they feel dead inside.* "It's a way of feeling something in the presence of nothing," Whitlock says.[3] Karen Conterio, chief executive of SAFE Alternatives, a treatment center in Naperville, Illinois, adds, "Blood represents life. There is a warmth to it."[4]

- In 2007 some form of *nonsuicidal self-injury* (*NSSI*) was self-reported by *nearly half of high school students* in the preceding year. NSSI refers to the "deliberate, direct destruction of body tissue without conscious suicidal intent."[5]

3 ASSESSMENT INTERVIEW

1. Tell me what has brought you here today. How can I help?
2. Tell me about your family. How are things going at home?
3. Have you experienced any traumatic events in your past? If you have, please tell me about them.
4. How have you tried to cope with the painful events you've experienced?

5. Tell me about cutting. How do you feel before you cut and when you cut yourself? What does it do for you?

6. How do your friends and family members respond when they find out you're cutting yourself?

7. Who are the people you feel closest to? Tell me about them.

8. If I could share with you some other ways to deal with your pain, would you be interested?

WISE COUNSEL 4

Teenagers who cut, sometimes but not always, have *a corresponding mental health problem* that is associated with the act of self-injury. Depression, bipolar disorder, eating disorders such as anorexia and bulimia, obsessive-compulsive disorder, or compulsive behaviors are common among those who cut. Other *common behaviors or experiences of cutters* include impulsive or risk-taking behavior; use of drugs or alcohol; and/or having lived through something traumatic, such as abuse, violence, or a disaster.

Often cutting is *a way for the teenager traumatized by abuse to "feel" again*. Or it may be a way to relieve the anger and rage she feels toward the abuser or as a means of regaining a sense of control over her life. Once the behavior is started, *the endorphins released by self-injurious behavior can become quite addictive.*

Identifying and reaching self-injurers can be very difficult. What is known about youth self-injury suggests that the *intensely private and shameful feelings* associated with self-injury prevent many sufferers from seeking treatment.

Care providers should *avoid displaying shock, engaging in shaming responses, or showing great pity*. Such reactions may reinforce the self-injurious behavior and its underlying causes.

In "Self-Injury Fact Sheet," Amanda Purington and Janis Whitlock report:

Because cutting is a secret behavior, it is very difficult to get accurate estimates of teenage involvement. However, a recent study found that 17% of young adults hurt themselves regularly.

Cornell University

- Self-injury is most common in youth having trouble coping with anxiety. It is important to focus on skill-building in individual youth, and to identify and remedy the environmental stressors that trigger self-injury.
- Self-injury is most often a silent, hidden practice aimed at either squelching negative feelings or overcoming emotional numbness. Being willing to listen to the self-injurer while reserving shock or judgment encourages them to use their voice rather than their body as a means of self-expression.
- Self-injury serves a function. An important part of treatment is helping youth to find other, more positive ways to accomplish the same psychological and emotional outcome, i.e. explicitly teach coping skills.
- Assessment and treatment should seek to understand why youth self-injure and then build on the strengths youth already possess.[6]

It is important to remember that each adolescent who cuts is different, and not all start or continue for the same reason. In addition, some individuals who cut may not show any of the *warning signs*. Many times cutting is not something a teen can just "get over." It is important to seek the assistance of a professionally trained counselor to *assess the reasons* for the cutting and to begin *appropriate treatment*.

Here are some *risk factors and signs* that have been associated with cutting among adolescents:

Risk Factors

- knowledge that friends or acquaintances are cutting
- difficulty expressing feelings
- extreme emotional reactions to minor occurrences (anger or sorrow)
- stressful family events (divorce, death, conflict)
- loss of a friend, boyfriend or girlfriend, or social status
- negative body image
- lack of coping skills

Signs

- wearing long sleeves during warm weather
- wearing thick wristbands that are never removed
- unexplained marks on body
- secretive or elusive behavior
- spending lengthy periods of time alone
- missing items that could be used for cutting (knives, scissors, safety pins, razors)[7]

5 ACTION STEPS

Help the counselee realize that there are better ways to deal with her problems than cutting—healthier, long-lasting ways that won't leave her with emotional and physical scars.

1. Tell Someone

- People who have stopped cutting often say the first step is the hardest—admitting to or talking about cutting. But they also say that after they open up about it, they often feel a great sense of relief. Choose someone you trust to talk to at first (a parent, school counselor, teacher, coach, doctor, or nurse). If it's too difficult to bring up the topic in person, write a note.

2. Identify the Triggering Problem

- Cutting is a way of reacting to emotional tension or pain. Try to figure out what feelings or situations are causing you to cut. Is it anger, pressure to be perfect, relationship trouble, a painful loss or trauma, mean criticism, or mistreatment?
- Identify the trouble you're having; then tell someone about it.

3. Ask for Help

- Many people have trouble figuring out what is causing them to want to cut. This is where a mental health professional can be helpful.
- Tell someone you can trust that you want help dealing with your troubles and the cutting. If the person you ask doesn't help you get the assistance you need, ask someone else. Be persistent. You need caring people in your life to help you overcome cutting.
- To find a therapist or counselor, ask at your doctor's office, at school, or at a mental health clinic in your community.
- Sometimes adults try to downplay the problems teens have or they think a teen is just going through a phase. If you get the feeling this is happening to you, find another adult (such as a school counselor or nurse) who can verify the legitimacy of your struggle to a parent or therapist.

4. Deal with the Root Issues

- Most teens who cut have deep emotional pain or distress and use cutting as a way to numb the hurt, rather than working through the process of emotional healing.
- Commit to working with a counselor or mental health professional to sort through strong feelings, heal from past hurts, and learn better ways to cope with life's stresses.
- Although cutting can be a difficult pattern to break, it is possible to do so. Getting professional help to overcome the problem doesn't mean you are weak or crazy. Therapists and counselors are trained to help people discover inner strengths that help them heal. Then these inner strengths can be used to cope with life's other problems in a healthy way.[8]

5. Run to God

- No matter how hard you try to stop, cutting is a behavior that is difficult to replace because it is so physically stimulating. To overcome cutting, you need the power and strength of God, which is available to you through Jesus Christ.
- Admit that your will, in and of itself, is not strong enough to resist the urge to cut. Learn to run to God when you experience the confusing emotions that lead you to cut. He is always with you and promises to help you fight temptation.

- Write out and memorize key passages from Scripture that speak to you about your struggle and the presence of God in your weakness. Use these promises to help you fight the urge to cut.
- Remember, you're not alone in this struggle. In Psalm 139 David says of God, "even there [when you feel like cutting], your hand will guide me, your right hand will hold me fast" (v. 10).

6 BIBLICAL INSIGHTS

The LORD is close to the brokenhearted and saves those who are crushed in spirit.

Psalm 34:18

People who cut themselves are engaged in an act of self-loathing and they desperately need God's warmth and support. Assure them that God doesn't condemn them for their behavior. He understands, He cares, and He is present for them.

Come to me, all you who are weary and burdened, and I will give you rest. Take my yoke upon you and learn from me, for I am gentle and humble in heart, and you will find rest for your souls.

Matthew 11:28–29

Jesus promised rest and peace for those who turn to Him and trust Him with their burdens. The first step, though, is to acknowledge that the load we carry is too heavy for us, and we need help.

7 PRAYER STARTER

Lord Jesus, we praise You that You are bigger than our pain. In the midst of brokenness, confusion, and anger, You are right here with us. And with You, there is always hope. Wrap Your child today in Your unconditional love. Give this teen courage to bring her brokenness to You rather than trying to carry the burden alone. I praise You, Jesus, that You are not intimidated by the messiness of our lives and that You delight in healing our hurts . . .

8 RECOMMENDED RESOURCES

Alcorn, Nancy. *Beyond the Cut: Real Stories, Real Freedom.* WinePress, 2008.
_____. *Cut: Mercy for Self-Harm.* WinePress, 2007.
Fresonke, Cherie. *Go in Peace for Teens.* WinePress, 2009.

Parrott, Les. *Helping the Struggling Adolescent: A Guide to Thirty-Six Common Problems for Parents, Counselors, and Youth.* Zondervan, 2000.

Penner, Marv. *Hope and Healing for Kids Who Cut: Learning to Understand and Help Those Who Self-Injure.* Zondervan/Youth Specialties, 2008.

Robson, Abigail. *Secret Scars: One Woman's Story of Overcoming Self-Harm.* Authentic, 2007.

Scott, Sophie. *Crying Scarlet Tears: My Journey through Self-Harm.* Monarch Books, 2008.

Seamands, David. *Healing for Damaged Emotions.* David C. Cook, 1991.

Townsend, John. *Boundaries with Teens: When to Say Yes, How to Say No.* Zondervan, 2007.

Wilson, Jess. *The Cutting Edge: Clinging to God in the Face of Self-Harm.* Authentic, 2008.

Depression

1 : PORTRAITS

- Brent's parents thought he was just going through a phase. He had always been a reasonably happy child, but the stresses of school, relationships with friends, and not making the baseball team in his sophomore year must have taken their toll. He seems to have lost interest in everything. His grades are declining, he doesn't spend much time with friends anymore, and he doesn't even play his guitar. When Brent is at home, he spends most of his time playing video games in his room.

- Peggy's mother died about a year ago, and she's still reeling from the loss. For a few months she felt numb but lately she's exploded in rage at her friends for no apparent reason. As people have backed away, she has turned her rage on God. "How could He have done this to me?" she snarled to one of her few remaining friends.

- Beth has always been moody, but when she entered junior high, her parents and friends noticed that her moods became even more pronounced. Now in high school she has times when she doesn't sleep for days, staying up working on projects and talking incessantly. But at other times she has trouble dragging herself out of bed and getting dressed.

2 : DEFINITIONS AND KEY THOUGHTS

- *Depression* is defined as *feelings of dejection and hopelessness* that last for *more than two weeks.* While everyone has a bad day from time to time, individuals struggling with depression often experience *changes in eating and sleeping habits,* as well as *agitation, irritability, and restlessness.* Depressed people generally lack energy and find little pleasure in activities they once enjoyed, such as playing sports or hanging out with friends.

- Most teens with depression will suffer from *more than one episode.* Between 20 and 40 percent will have more than one episode within two years, and 70 percent will have more than one episode before adulthood. Episodes of teen depression generally *last about eight months.*

- *Dysthymia,* a type of mild, long-lasting depression, *affects about 2 percent of teens,* and about the same percentage of teens develop bipolar disorder in their late teenage years. *Fifteen percent of teens with depression eventually develop bipolar disorder.*

- A small percent of teens also suffer from *seasonal depression*, usually during the winter months in northern latitudes.

- Teen depression can affect a teen regardless of gender, social background, income level, race, or school or other achievements, though *teenage girls report suffering from depression more often than teenage boys.* Teenage boys are *less likely to seek help* or recognize that they suffer from depression, probably due to different social expectations—*girls are encouraged to express their feelings while boys are not.* Teenage girls' somewhat stronger dependence on social ties, however, can increase the chances of teen depression being triggered by social factors, such as loss of friends.

- *Risk factors that increase the chances* of an episode of teen depression include:

  — previous episodes of depression
  — experiencing trauma, abuse, or a long-term illness or disability
  — family history of depression (between 20 and 50 percent of teens who suffer from depression have a family member with depression or other mental disorder)
  — untreated problems (about two-thirds of teens with major depression also suffer from another mental disorder, such as dysthymia, addiction to drugs or alcohol, anxiety, or antisocial behaviors)

- A teen suffering from depression is also *at higher risk* for other problems:

  — Thirty percent of teens with depression also develop a *substance abuse problem.*
  — Teenagers with depression are likely to *struggle with relationships* and have a *smaller social circle.*
  — Depressed teens are more likely to *have trouble at school and in jobs* and take advantage of fewer opportunities for education or careers.
  — Teens with untreated depression are more likely to engage in *risky sexual behaviors*, leading to higher rates of pregnancy and sexually transmitted diseases.
  — Teens with depression seem to *catch physical illnesses* more often than other teens.

- Untreated depression is the *number one cause of suicide*, the third-leading cause of death among teenagers. Ninety percent of suicide victims suffer from a mental illness, and suffering from depression can make a teenager as much as *twelve times more likely to attempt suicide.*

- *Less than 33 percent of teens with depression get help*, yet most teens with depression can be successfully treated if they seek help from a doctor or therapist. Many local health clinics offer *free or discounted treatment* for teens with depression.[1]

- *Bipolar disorder* is a specific form of depression. It is sometimes called "manic depression" because it has *two cycles*: the highs of mania and the lows of depression. *Manic symptoms* include:

  — *severe changes in mood*—either unusually happy or silly or very irritable, angry, agitated, or aggressive
  — *unrealistic highs in self-esteem*, feeling all-powerful or like a superhero with special powers
  — *great increase in energy* and the ability to go with little or no sleep for days without feeling tired
  — *increase in talking* and talking too much, too fast, changing topics too quickly, and not allowing interruption
  — *distractibility*—the teen's attention moves constantly from one thing to the next
  — *repeated high risk-taking behavior*, such as abusing alcohol and drugs, reckless driving, or sexual promiscuity

    Depressive symptoms include:

  — *irritability*, depressed mood, persistent sadness, frequent crying
  — *thoughts of death or suicide*
  — *loss of enjoyment* in favorite activities
  — *frequent complaints of physical illnesses*, such as headaches or stomachaches
  — *low energy level*, fatigue, poor concentration, complaints of boredom
  — *major change in eating or sleeping patterns*, such as oversleeping or overeating

Note: Some of these signs are similar to those that occur in teens who experience drug abuse, delinquency, attention deficit hyperactivity disorder, or even schizophrenia. A physician or psychotherapist can conduct a thorough examination to determine an accurate diagnosis. Treatment includes educating the patient and his family, mood-stabilizing medications, and therapy.[2]

3 ASSESSMENT INTERVIEW

For the Teen

1. On a scale of 0 (deep sadness and hopelessness) to 10 (genuine joy), where would you rate yourself today? Tell me about that.
2. When did you start feeling down? Can you point to any particular event, loss, strained relationship, or other circumstance that might have contributed to the stress you felt at that time?
3. How does your sadness affect you—your motivation, grades, friendships, interests?
4. How do you handle anger?
5. Have you noticed any changes in your eating or sleeping habits?

6. Have you used any chemicals or alcohol to try to numb the pain?

7. Has your circle of friends changed in any way? If so, how?

8. Do you have times when you feel unusually energetic, when you're so focused that you can't sleep because you want to get things done?

9. Have you had any thoughts about hurting yourself?

For Parents

1. When did you first notice that your child had drifted into a prolonged season of sadness and hopelessness?

2. Can you point to any event, strained relationship, family problem, school difficulty, or other circumstance that might have contributed to your child's stress?

3. How has the depression affected your child's motivation, friendships, interaction with family members, sports, and other interests?

4. What emotions does your child identify (hurt, anger, sadness, joy, thankfulness, or other)?

5. Have you noticed any changes in your child's eating or sleeping habits?

6. Do you think your child may be using any kind of chemicals or alcohol to numb the pain?

7. Has your child's circle of friends changed?

8. Have you noticed times when your child feels unusually energetic and so focused that he can't sleep?

9. Is there any indication that your child has any intention of hurting himself?

WISE COUNSEL 4

It's *entirely normal for young people to experience "the blues" occasionally.* Adolescence is full of challenges and changes—physical, social, emotional, and many other changes. These *changes threaten a teen's sense of security* and leave him vulnerable to being hurt easily and often.

These stresses would be difficult for adults, but the *coping skills of teens are less developed and their hormones are more active*—a dangerous combination! Even though their experiences of failure and rejection may be only occasional, they live in fear of these traumas every day.

When a teen's fears, hurt, and anger *disrupt his ability to function* at home and at school, he may have adolescent depression, which needs to be addressed.

In adolescence, *depression can be difficult to diagnose* because many teens are naturally moody, and many of them *can't articulate their perceptions and feelings very well.* To determine if a teen is experiencing depression, look for these *signs lasting more than two weeks*:

- poor performance in school
- withdrawal from friends and activities
- sadness and hopelessness

- lack of enthusiasm, energy, or motivation
- anger and rage
- overreaction to criticism
- feelings of being unable to satisfy ideals
- poor self-esteem or guilt
- indecision, lack of concentration, or forgetfulness
- restlessness and agitation
- changes in eating or sleeping patterns
- substance abuse
- problems with authority
- suicidal thoughts or actions

Risk of Suicide

One of the most significant dangers of adolescent depression is the *risk of suicide*. Each year nearly five thousand young people, ages fifteen to twenty-four, kill themselves. The rate of suicide for this age group has nearly tripled since 1960, making it the *third-leading cause of death in adolescents* and the *second-leading cause of death among college-age youth*. Suicide attempts may be triggered by a specific event in the context of long-term emotional problems. In these cases, the teen believes the new situation is completely *hopeless*. In addition, a pervasive, *oppressive sense of shame* can push a teen over the edge. Four out of five teens who attempt suicide have given clear warnings. Parents and teachers need to look for these *signs*:

- suicide threats, direct and indirect
- obsession with death
- poems, essays, and drawings that refer to death
- dramatic change in personality or appearance
- irrational, bizarre behavior
- overwhelming sense of guilt, shame, or rejection
- changed eating or sleeping patterns
- significant drop in school performance
- giving away belongings

To provide help for teens who are suicidal:

- *Get involved.* Get closer to the teen and encourage him to talk about what's going on, including feelings.
- *Look for the warning signs.* Don't assume they don't mean anything serious—they might!
- *Listen for any talk about suicide.* Ask direct questions and listen carefully.
- *Call for help immediately* if you suspect the teen is contemplating suicide, and especially if he has a plan. Call 911, your doctor, a counseling center, the hospi-

tal, or anyone who can help keep the teen safe.[3] For more resources on helping suicidal teens, please see the section Suicide.

Causes and Treatment

The *causes for depression* can be many; therefore, there must be *many types of treatment*. Understanding each of the possible causes of depression is important for knowing how to treat the depressive symptoms from a holistic viewpoint. Trying any of the following treatment measures can be effective depending on the individual.

- *Biological or neurological imbalance.* For some teenagers, such an imbalance could warrant the use of medication. If you think this may be the case, *a referral to a psychologist or primary care physician* for further evaluation is recommended.
- *Psychological.* Often depression can be dealt with using cognitive-behavioral techniques, such as challenging negative thinking and cognitive distortions. Showing the teen how to *overcome destructive thoughts* can help reduce depressive symptoms without having to resort to medication.
- *Social.* The nature of depression is feelings of loneliness and social isolation. Encourage social interaction even though the teenager is likely to say he doesn't feel like it. Challenge him to join in social activities. *Spending more time with others* may increase the teen's feelings of being wanted and liked, which in turn will *enhance his feelings of self-worth, purpose, meaning, and hope.*
- *Spiritual.* Unfortunately, there are many well-intentioned (and sometimes ill-intentioned) members in the church who will accuse those struggling with depression of being distant from God and not praying enough. Though this may be true, it is not always the most likely cause. If the depression is a result of sin, it should be dealt with through *confession and receiving forgiveness*. Otherwise, counselors and spiritual mentors should encourage teenagers to *turn to God in prayer and Bible reading*, focusing especially on verses that promise that He is near, even if they don't feel that He is near. Help them see how God has *protected them and worked in their lives.* This will help them increase their faith in God. Active devotion to God will always be rewarded in the long run for those who diligently seek Him.

Treatment for teen depression may include *therapy, medication, and altering behavior patterns.* And in many cases, *involving parents in at least some aspects of therapy is profitable for everyone in the family.* A wide range of medications are available to help moderate the mood swings and give the teen a stronger emotional foundation and a clearer mind to make good choices.

5 ACTION STEPS

For the Teen

1. Watch Physical Health

- Research shows that thirty minutes of moderate daily exercise is very helpful in elevating mood. Try to set aside time every day to exercise in some way—bike, run, swim, walk, play a sport. Ask a friend to work out with you—it makes it harder to avoid the activity if someone is waiting to do it with you.

- Have a routine medical checkup and work with a doctor or dietitian to develop a diet program. Better eating habits (for example, less sugar and more vitamins) can be a big help.

- Make sure you are getting adequate sleep (preferably going to sleep before midnight). Poor sleep patterns can sap your energy and fuel a negative mindset.

2. Tackle the Root of Your Depression

- Try to think about what situation(s) might be behind your feelings of depression. Take some time to examine *why* you feel this way. Are you stressed, overwhelmed, discouraged, isolated?

- If you have recently suffered a significant loss, acknowledge the loss and allow yourself to grieve. Give yourself permission to feel upset but also find ways to come back to the light, recognizing both the pain of the loss and the opportunity for future happiness in Christ.

- Carry a "daily mood log" and record times when you feel most depressed, what is happening when you feel this way, and what you are thinking at these times.

3. Get Social Support

- Choose not to isolate yourself. When you feel depression coming on, call a friend. Work on building solid relationships with other people who will help build you up; choose to be with them rather than giving in to the down feeling.

- Get involved in a small group or Bible study at your church. Seek out people with whom you can be honest about your struggles.

- Learn to laugh. Don't take life too seriously! Schedule time with the specific purpose in mind of having fun, and make sure you're not setting unrealistic performance expectations for yourself.

4. Reframe Your Thinking

- Use Scripture to challenge your negative statements and beliefs. For example, if your thought is, *I'm totally worthless; I have nothing to give anyone*, meditate on passages such as Psalm 139. Use biblical truth to reformulate your view of yourself as a precious child of God—bought with the blood of Jesus Christ!

- During the next week, write down ten things you like about yourself, with at least three of them being physical characteristics. Choose to rejoice in the unique way that God has created you, rather than comparing yourself to other people.

5. Pay Attention to Spiritual Issues

- Do you have any unconfessed sin that may be promoting a negative mindset? Are you bound by guilt and shame over your sin? Christ died for your sin and has promised to forgive you if you believe in Him. Confess your sin to God and trust that He will keep His promise (see 1 John 1:9).
- Do you need to forgive someone else for something he did to you? Forgiving, even if the other person doesn't admit his wrong, is a means of moving toward personal health.
- Think about the motivations of your life. Are they grounded in your desire to have a stronger connection with Christ? When we are motivated by something other than our love for God, frustration and depression can ensue.

For Parents

1. Look for the Signs

- Be a student of your child's behavior and moods. Your counselor can give you a list of symptoms of depression and suicidal ideation. Be honest about your child's lifestyle and mood. Some parents overreact and cause friction in the relationship with their child, but many don't notice overt signs at all.
- To get a realistic appraisal of your child's well-being, talk to teachers, coaches, and other adults who have seen your child over an extended period.

2. Get Involved

- Parents can take action in several different ways. Opening up a dialogue with your child is essential. Let him know that you care and that you want to provide love and support.
- Schedule a physical exam for your teen to rule out any physiological problem that might be the cause or a contributor to the depression.
- Notice the events and relationships that cause changes, for better or worse, in your child's life.

3. Provide a Network of Support

- Talk to a few trusted friends, teachers, principals, or coaches to let them know your concerns and ask for help. These people may not be trained therapists, but they can pay more attention and show more love to a child who desperately needs them.
- Depression is a serious problem that can't be overcome by sheer willpower. Your child needs lots of support.
- Shower your child with genuine love, affection, and praise. Don't be critical if he is not performing at his best.

4. Go to a Professional

- Some teens "snap out of it" when their circumstances change or they have a few weeks to process a painful event in their lives, but many stay locked in a downward spiral of hopelessness and helplessness. If your child's problems persist, find a competent professional therapist who is trained to address the obvious symptoms of depression as well as your child's hidden hurts and fears.

5. Ask for God's Guidance

- Trust God to guide you in this journey through your teen's depression. Pray for your teen and also for wisdom in knowing how best to reach out to him.
- Remind yourself daily of the fact that, while you love your child, God created him, and His love is far greater! Encourage your struggling teen to meditate on Scriptures that affirm God's love, provision, and care.

6 BIBLICAL INSIGHTS

So do not fear, for I am with you; do not be dismayed, for I am your God. I will strengthen you and help you; I will uphold you with my righteous right hand.

Isaiah 41:10

The process of overcoming depression may take time, but we can be sure that God is with us each step of the way to support, encourage, and love us—even when we feel alone and hopeless.

But now, this is what the LORD says—he who created you, O Jacob, he who formed you, O Israel: "Fear not, for I have redeemed you; I have summoned you by name; you are mine. When you pass through the waters, I will be with you; and when you pass through the rivers, they will not sweep over you. When you walk through the fire, you will not be burned; the flames will not set you ablaze. For I am the LORD, your God, the Holy One of Israel, your Savior."

Isaiah 43:1–3

The Scriptures contain wonderfully encouraging truths about God's love for us. In this passage, Isaiah quotes God saying that He knows us intimately and He will walk with us through the darkest days of our lives. We can be confident that He will lead us to truth, light, and hope.

Weeping may remain for a night, but rejoicing comes in the morning. . . . You turned my wailing into dancing; you removed my sackcloth and clothed me with joy, that my heart may sing to you and not be silent. O LORD my God, I will give you thanks forever.

Psalm 30:5, 11–12

No one is immune to discouragement and heartache. We may wish that life were carefree, but we won't experience it while we are on earth. All of us experience seasons of loss, but God meets us in our pain and sooner or later restores our joy.

For we do not have a high priest who is unable to sympathize with our weaknesses, but we have one who has been tempted in every way, just as we are—yet was without sin. Let us then approach the throne of grace with confidence, so that we may receive mercy and find grace to help us in our time of need.

Hebrews 4:15–16

Even Jesus, when He was on earth, experienced a tremendous sense of loss and abandonment. There is, in fact, nothing we endure that Jesus didn't suffer too. Because He understands, we know that He never condemns us for hurting, and He's very patient with us as we take steps to deal with our grief, anger, and pain.

PRAYER STARTER 7

Lord Jesus, I thank You that we can run to You, even in the darkest times of depression. We desperately need Your comfort and encouragement today. Overwhelm my young friend [these parents] with Your unfailing love and remove the spirit of fear. Be Lord over their minds and their emotions. We thank You, Jesus, that You are a solid rock and a refuge in the midst of painful emotions and confusion. Teach this young person to trust in Your unchanging promises even when life takes unexpected turns. We thank You, Jesus, that nothing—not even depression—can separate us from You . . .

RECOMMENDED RESOURCES 8

Fitzpatrick, Elyse, and Laura Hendrickson. *Will Medicine Stop the Pain? Finding God's Healing for Depression, Anxiety and Other Troubling Emotions.* Moody, 2006.

Fresonke, Cherie. *Go in Peace for Teens.* WinePress, 2009.

Hart, Archibald D., and Catherine Hart Weber. *Is Your Teen Stressed or Depressed? A Practical and Inspirational Guide for Parents of Hurting Teenagers.* Thomas Nelson, 2008.

Jackson, Nisha. *Helping Teens Survive the Hormone Takeover: A Guide for Moms.* Thomas Nelson, 2006.

Nelson, Gary E. *A Relentless Hope: Surviving the Storm of Teen Depression.* Wipf and Stock, 2007.

Piper, John. *When the Darkness Will Not Lift: Doing What We Can While We Wait for God—and Joy.* Crossway Books, 2007.

Vernick, Leslie. *Defeating Depression: Real Hope for Life-Changing Wholeness*. Harvest House, 2009.

CDs

Hart, Archibald D., and Catherine Hart Weber. *How to Help Your Hurting Teen I-II*. Focus on the Family Radio Broadcast.

Organizations

American Academy of Child and Adolescent Psychiatry

3615 Wisconsin Ave. NW

Washington, DC 20016-3007

202-966-7300

Fax: 202-966-2891

clinical@aacap.org

www.aacap.org

American Association of Suicidology

4201 Connecticut Ave. NW, Suite 310

Washington, DC 20008

202-237-2280

For help finding treatment, support groups, medication information, help paying for your medications, your local Mental Health America affiliate, and other mental health–related services in your community, please visit http://www.nmha.org. *If you or someone you know is in crisis now,* seek help immediately. Call 800-273-TALK (8255) to reach a 24-hour crisis center, or dial 911 for immediate assistance.

Destructive Dating Relationships

PORTRAITS 1

- Mary had always been a sensitive child, so her parents were surprised when she began spending time with William when they were both juniors in high school. William was a tough young man, though he tried to be pleasant when he came to pick Mary up for a date. Over time Mary's demeanor changed. She began to withdraw from the family and she never wanted to talk about William. Soon Mary showed signs of depression and would become angry when her parents tried to talk with her about her boyfriend. Months later one of her friends told her parents that William had been beating Mary in places that didn't show.

- Rich had been a regular in his church's youth group and he played in the youth band on Sunday morning. One Sunday he met Rebecca, a cute girl he had seen at school. They talked for a while, and a friendship began. She had a reputation for being kind of wild, and that made her even more attractive to Rich. One day during lunch, an assistant principal found them in a car in the school parking lot. They were engaged in oral sex. When Rich's parents demanded an explanation, he told them he liked Rebecca. He said, "It's not that big a deal. At least we didn't have sex!"

DEFINITIONS AND KEY THOUGHTS 2

- Destructive dating relationships involve everything from *emotional enmeshment, abuse, violence, to sexual intimacy.*

- *Emotional enmeshment* happens when an individual loses her identity in the *overwhelming desire to be accepted by another.* In a dating relationship, enmeshed couples try to be together all the time, are possessive of their partner, and often appear as "carbon copies" of each other.

- Rather than celebrating the unique way God created them, emotionally enmeshed couples *rarely discuss their differences or conflicts* for fear it will cause them to break up. Individuals in this sort of relationship feel obligated to "rescue" their partner, and are *quite likely to stay in a relationship even when abuse is present.*

- Dating violence has become more common today. Statistics now show that one in five teens in a serious relationship reports having been hit, slapped, or pushed by a partner.[1] In addition, about 25 percent of young women in college reported experiencing an *attempted or completed rape* while in school.[2]

- Many teens go on *group dates* instead of going out as couples, and the experience is rarely referred to as a "date." On the positive side, these groups offer some protection and are a way teens relate to one another. But sometimes these groups engage in "group think" and apply peer pressure for everyone to participate in the group behaviors. *Sex and drinking can become the norm.* "Ask your teen to think about what she would do if she weren't in a group," says Sabrina Weill, author of *The Real Truth about Teens and Sex.* "Say to her, 'If nobody was drinking a beer, would you? If nobody your age was having sex, would you?'"[3]

- Regardless of what culture tells us, *supervision of teens is essential.* Teens have sex whenever parents aren't around. Sex isn't just for the backseat of cars anymore. With more mothers in the workforce, often there's no one at home from the time school is out until parents get home from the office, and those hours are invitations to teen sex. It's not surprising that researchers at the RAND Corporation have found that *teens are more likely to have sex when there is little after-school supervision.*

- Cell phones provide instant communication without parents being aware of it. *Cell phones and text messaging* are the tools of the trade when a teen is looking for the best parties, sharing photos, and gossiping about others. "*Sexting*," generally defined as sending sexually explicit photos and videos via text message, has become very common among teens.[4] Parents should not allow pictures or video texting capability on their kids' cell phones, and they need to be sure to monitor their kids' activities very closely.

- *Teens meet people online.* Internet sites, like MySpace, Facebook, and Xanga, where teens can post pictures and trade messages, allow teens to meet lots of new people. The ease of connecting with new people is amazing, but so are the *dangers.* "Parents need to understand that this is a very real risk," says Parry Aftab, executive director of wiredsafety.org. Therefore, especially for young teens and children, parents should monitor *all* internet activity.

- *Girls now initiate.* Today it's common for girls to take the initiative in relationships. Sometimes *girls can become aggressive in pursuing sexual activity.* They may be trying to prove themselves to their friends or they may want to exercise the right to initiate they believe they have.

- Often teens see nothing wrong with *oral sex.* Studies have found that some 50 percent of teenagers, ages fifteen to nineteen, have engaged in oral sex. "I have an eleven-year-old middle schooler who came home saying that a boy wanted her to have oral sex with him in the parking lot," says Tonja Krautter, a psychologist in Los Gatos, California, who works with adolescents. "A lot of kids have this idea that it's no big deal."[5] In fact, oral sex is now considered the new "good night kiss." Yet, according to the Centers for Disease Control, it is resulting in *serious consequences*—one in four U.S. teenagers has contracted at least one STD.

- In spite of our sex-saturated culture, *many teens remain ignorant about sex.* Parents still are the most important source of information for children to learn about sex, and most authorities suggest they need to *talk to their children about sex by the time they are ten years old.* This conversation should not consist of a one-time sit-down "talk" but should really be *appropriate ongoing discussions* as the children are growing up. Many teens are misinformed through their peers and the internet.

ASSESSMENT INTERVIEW 3

For the Teen

1. Tell me about your relationship with your boyfriend.
2. What attracted you to each other?
3. Has there been violence or threats of violence?
4. When did things start to turn rough? How did it occur?
5. In what other ways does he make you feel unsafe, used, hurt, or afraid?
6. What happens when you resist or hesitate to go along with his demands?
7. Have you tried to get help before? If you have, what happened? Why didn't it work?
8. What do your friends say about him?
9. What do your parents think about the relationship and its effects on you?
10. Are you afraid for your physical safety today?
11. If I can help you develop a plan to protect yourself, are you interested?

For the Parents

1. Describe the nature of your teen's dating relationship and why you're concerned about her.
2. Has your child's behavior changed in any way since the relationship began? If so, how?
3. Do you suspect violence, threats of violence, or coercion of any kind? What are the signs these are happening?
4. Have you tried to talk with your teen about your concerns? How has she responded?
5. Who are some good role models (peers, relatives, friends) your child respects? Have any of them tried to talk with your child about this problem? If so, what was the result?
6. Do you have a plan to help your child set healthy boundaries and reclaim her life?

1 in 3 teens reports knowing a friend or peer who has been hit, punched, kicked, slapped, choked, or otherwise physically hurt by his or her partner. Nearly 80% of girls who have been physically abused in their dating relationships continue to date their abuser.

Teenage Research Unlimited, www. loveisnotabuse. com/statistics_ abuseandteens.htm

WISE COUNSEL 4

Times have changed. Only a few years ago, girls waited for the phone to ring and expected their boyfriend to ask them for a date. Today, however, "even the concept of dating is outdated," says Beth-Marie Jelsma, a psychotherapist in Rochester, New York. And *kids in junior high are often very interested in sex and relationships, and many of them are ready to experiment.* Parents need to understand the *new youth culture* so they can help guide their kids through it more effectively.

With the plethora of date rape drugs and incidents among junior high, high school, and college students, *teens need to protect themselves* by adhering to the following:

- Go out only with friends you trust.
- Let someone know where you are at all times.
- Create a "buddy system" when out with friends to keep one another accountable.
- Do not accept drinks or food from people you do not know.

Positive, healthy dating relationships have these characteristics:

- *Trust*: People tell each other the truth, they don't gossip, and they don't get jealous when their girlfriend talks to someone else.
- *Respect*: People value each other as they are; they don't demand that they be someone they're not. They know "yes" means yes and "no" means no. They don't demand compliance and they don't try to manipulate by using intimidation, self-pity, or other kinds of demands.
- *Mutual support*: All of us are selfish to some degree, but we can have healthy relationships only to the extent that we can look beyond ourselves and care for others. Love isn't the same as enmeshment, which is losing our identity in our desire to be accepted by another.
- *Clear communication*: Every other factor in a relationship depends on clear communication—the ability of people to connect and relate their thoughts, feelings, and desires to each other. Communication comes naturally for some but much harder for others. All of us, though, can learn the basic skills of speaking truth and active listening.

Dating relationships almost always start out with high hopes, but some *deteriorate into abuse and demands.* If the boyfriend does any of the following, it is a warning sign:

- He is *resentful* if his girlfriend does not comply with his requests.
- He forces her to have sex in any way at any time.
- He criticizes her for the way she looks, talks, or behaves and tells her that she'll never find anyone else to love her.
- He wants to filter whom she talks to, where she goes, and what she does.
- He demands to know where she is at all times.
- He hits her or threatens to hit her.[6]

ACTION STEPS 5

When their teen children are threatened with violence or coercion of any kind, the parents' responsibility is to protect and equip their child. The first priority is to protect the child from harm, but quite often teens are deeply enmeshed in these destructive relationships, and they don't want to pull away. They experience a powerful pairing of hope and fear: hope that this person will truly love them and fear that they'll be hurt or abandoned. These emotions are strong in any person, but teens are especially vulnerable to manipulation when they are insecure about their identity.

For the Teen

1. Date Someone of Like Faith

- Second Corinthians 6:14—"Do not be yoked together with unbelievers"—can apply to dating relationships, because dating relationships are the precursor to marriage.
- Dating someone who is serious about his faith is a clear biblical command for the Christian. Even if the individual claims to be a Christian, it is important to evaluate his level of spiritual maturity as an important factor in determining compatibility. To have a godly relationship, it is critical for both partners to be able to encourage and build up one another in faith.

2. Set Your Boundaries ahead of Time

- In moments of passion, saying no to sexual temptation can be very difficult. Before going out with your boyfriend, decide on healthy boundaries and specific standards that will guide your interactions with him. Some guidelines might include:

  — Go only on group dates.
  — Plan dates in advance, rather than just "seeing what happens."
  — Do not spend time alone together at each other's home.
  — Do not lie down together.
  — Do not hang out in a bedroom.
  — Avoid dark or lonely places in town.
  — Do not touch or caress each other's body.
  — Stay away from parties or gatherings where alcohol, drugs, and sexual acts will be present.
  — Treat your boyfriend as a treasure belonging to God.

3. Practice Holiness

- Often we try to get "as close to the line" as we can, but God commands us to stop flirting with sin and pursue pleasing Him. Sexual temptation is not something that can be fought by mere good intentions. Even the best standards can be cast aside in the heat of the moment for sexual gratification.

- God calls us to holiness, which means running away from sexual temptation. Sexual sin is a trap and a consuming monster, but it does not satisfy. In your own strength, you cannot fight sexual temptation and win. That's why Scripture says, "flee" (see 1 Corinthians 6:18).

4. Get Input from Family and Friends

- As a young person, you need the input of older, wiser couples who have healthy marriages. They can help you determine if you are dating a person who is good for you. Enlist the support of a couple in your church or community who is willing to hold you accountable to high standards for dating and who can offer you sound biblical advice.

- Get to know your boyfriend's parents. While this may sound old-fashioned, remember that if you do decide to get married, you will be interacting with his parents on a regular basis. Specifically, a guy should look at the way his girlfriend treats her father and a girl should observe how her boyfriend treats his mother. These attitudes are clues into the behavioral tendencies your partner will show in dating and marriage.

5. Place God at the Center of Your Relationship

- Just because two Christian people are dating does not guarantee that the relationship will honor God or that it will work out. Pray about dating someone, rather than just jumping in based on how you feel.

- Read God's Word with the person you are dating and pray together. It will work wonders in strengthening your relationship and will put your focus in the right place.

- As you evaluate your relationship, ask yourself, *Is this person helping me draw closer to Jesus or is he drawing me away from Him?* Any relationship that is dulling your spiritual senses cannot be God's will for you and needs to be broken off.

For the Parents

1. Open Lines of Communication

- Quite often the last person teens in destructive relationships want to talk to is their parent. In some cases, they believe they've tried to talk before, but their parents refused to listen. And in virtually all cases, the teens feel deeply ashamed and confused about what's going on in their lives. They don't want to expose their shame to anyone who might condemn them.

- Begin with assurances of your love, not with your demand for compliance. Statements such as, "I love you and, no matter what, I'm here for you," do wonders to break down barriers, but these statements must be sincere.

- Become a kind and strong advocate. In many cases, teens will be slow to trust their parents' assurances, so be prepared to prove your sincerity before you expect your child to be open with you.

2. Encourage Spiritual Growth and Accountability

- Godly dating relationships are not just about not having sex. The beauty of two Christians dating is that their relationship should challenge and encourage each other to know God better. Help your teen build her dating relationship on a spiritual foundation by looking to encourage and support her boyfriend in his faith. Fun should not be the sole goal of their relationship.

- Challenge your teen to seek out accountability with a youth pastor or leader who can help her fight temptation by growing spiritually.

3. Study God's Design for Relationships

- God cares intimately about our human relationships, including dating relationships. Rather than scolding or shaming your teen, open up Scripture together and begin to find out what God has to say about dating.

- God has created sex, but He warns of the potential danger of its being used for manipulation and exploitation. God's Word clearly states that we should avoid sexual immorality (1 Thess. 4:3) and that intimate physical activity is a gift and expression of the marriage vow (1 Cor. 7:4–5). Ultimately, it is not a matter of just "obeying the rules."

BIBLICAL INSIGHTS 6

Love must be sincere. Hate what is evil; cling to what is good. Be devoted to one another in brotherly love. Honor one another above yourselves.

Romans 12:9–10

Often people in abusive relationships are very confused about the nature of love. They confuse manipulation for affection and coercion for belonging. Healthy relationships are always based on two crucial factors: trust and respect. When these are present, communication is honest, love is sincere, and inevitable conflicts can be resolved.

Love is patient, love is kind. It does not envy, it does not boast, it is not proud. It is not rude, it is not self-seeking, it is not easily angered, it keeps no record of wrongs. Love does not delight in evil but rejoices with the truth. It always protects, always trusts, always hopes, always perseveres. Love never fails.

1 Corinthians 13:4–8

This classic passage of Scripture describes the nature of loving relationships. Abusive people act in the opposite way, though they may claim that what they are doing is loving. It's important for people in abusive relationships to have a better definition of love—and to settle for nothing less in their dating relationships.

7 PRAYER STARTER

Heavenly Father, we thank You for the beautiful gift of love. I pray for my friend today as she seeks out your guidance in dating. Give Your child strength and grace to resist temptation and wisdom to discern Your will. Surround this teen with godly friends and mentors to guide her in the journey toward a God-honoring marriage. Grant patience to wait for Your timing, and keep changing and molding this teen into the godly woman You created her to be. We rest, Lord, in knowing that Your timing is always best, even in dating . . .

8 RECOMMENDED RESOURCES

Beair, Kimberly. *First Comes Love, Then What? Challenging Your Assumptions on Dating, Love and Commitment.* Tyndale House, 2007.

Clark, Chap. *Next Time I Fall in Love: How to Handle Sex, Intimacy, and Feelings in Dating Relationships.* Wipf and Stock, 2004.

Clark, Jeramy, and Jerusha Clark. *Define the Relationship: A Candid Look at Breaking Up, Making Up, and Dating Well.* Random House, 2004.

Cloud, Henry, and John Townsend. *Boundaries in Dating.* Zondervan, 2000.

Discipline

- Gretchen's parents are divorced, and she lives with her mother. Out of her pain and lack of understanding as to why her family is not together, she plays her mom and dad like they are violins, skillfully using guilt on her mother to get what she wants and lying to her father. At this point, her parents have just about given up. Gretchen tries to rule both houses and expects to do whatever she wants to do. Her dad cannot stand her any longer, but her mom is willing to try once more to create an environment of love and boundaries for her daughter.
- Brandon is changing. In fact, now that he just turned seventeen and is nearly finished with high school, he has been challenging his parents' rules. He has been going out with young adults who are older than he and living on their own. His parents have told him they disapproved of his behavior and expressed their disappointment with the crowd he is hanging out with, knowing they smoke marijuana and party frequently. Brandon has threatened to move in with his friends if his parents don't ease up on their rules. In his parents' eyes, he is still only a teenager and needs parental supervision. The tension is mounting as Brandon's actions and his parents' expectations are ever widening.

DEFINITIONS AND KEY THOUGHTS | **2**

- *Discipline* is one of the most misunderstood of all parental responsibilities. It has come to mean punishment, whether physical or the withholding of privileges. The intent of discipline, however, is to *help guide and instruct a growing child*.
- Parents need to understand the nature of the period of adolescence so they aren't surprised by the *conflicting emotions and needs* of their teens. With some insight into the conflict going on in their teen's life, they can *provide support and guidance* instead of being threatened by the teen's struggles.
- Adolescence is a time of *increased stress and experimentation* when teens are attempting to carve out their own sense of uniqueness that is separate from their parents.
- Some teens are compliant and pleasant during this transition time in their lives, but many resist their parents in their attempts to be separate. While this period is

challenging for parents, it is important to remember that this season is *especially challenging for teens.*

- Parents need to find the right blend and *balance between their child's growing independence and their need for direction.* The type of discipline they use and how they administer it are very important.

- In 1990 Dr. Foster Cline and Jim Fay, in their practical and encouraging book *Parenting with Love and Logic*, identified the following parenting styles: drill sergeant (authoritarian), the helicopter (permissive), and the counselor/consultant (authoritative). Sometime later, a fourth parenting style began to appear in literature. This fourth style was called the neglectful parent.

  — *Drill sergeant/authoritarian* parents are inflexible, lecturing, and controlling. They use harsh words and humiliation, display anger, punish, and may be cruel. They are domineering, critical, pushy, intrusive, shaming, and demanding. This parent sends the message: "You can't think for yourself. I have to think for you. You are stupid, and if left up to you, you will make bad choices and mess things up."

  — *Helicopter/permissive* parents are overprotective and doting, and they do not hold their teens to a specific standard. They use emotional control and guilt, are intrusive, and demand compliance "for your own good." They insist on making decisions for their teens, take over when a child neglects his responsibilities, and make excuses for him when he fails. This parent communicates: "You are fragile and weak. You need me to think for you and take care of you. You will not be able to survive the pressures of life without my protection and help."

  — *Counselor/consultant/authoritative* parents are supportive and empowering. They believe in their children and welcome mistakes as opportunities for their children to learn valuable lessons. They treat their teens with respect and build a relationship of trust. They share personal stories of success and failure, offer insights, guide them in exploring alternatives, and allow natural consequences. These insightful, effective parents communicate: "You are a pretty neat kid. I believe you can figure out how to handle life; and even if you mess up, you are just the kind of person who will learn from your mistakes and handle things differently next time."

  — *Neglectful* parents are absent, physically and/or emotionally, and unavailable. They are indifferent, distant, self-absorbed, unstructured, detached, and uncaring. These parents impart the message: "You are not important to me. You are not worth caring about. You have your life to live, and I have mine. Try not to cause me any problems, because I really don't care to be involved."[1]

ASSESSMENT INTERVIEW 3

For the Teen

1. How would you describe the environment of your home and family—comfortable, loving, strict, legalistic?
2. How do you relate to your parents? Do you trust them?
3. What boundaries have your parents set for you (dating, curfew, driving, and so on)?
4. How do your parents discipline you?
5. How do you respond to your parents' discipline? How does it make you feel?
6. What specific things do you think are unreasonable in your parents' discipline? Have you expressed this to them?
7. What are some reasonable compromises in the family rules that you could suggest to your parents?

For Parents

1. How did you relate to your parents when you were a teen?
2. How did they discipline you? How did you respond?
3. (*Explain the four parenting styles outlined in the section Definitions and Key Thoughts.*) Which of these best describes your parenting style? What has the impact of your style been on your child and on your relationship with your child?
4. Describe the level of trust between you and your child. When do you enjoy being around each other? When is there tension?
5. Describe the most pleasant, positive period in your relationship with your child, even if it was years ago. What contributed to that experience? What is different today?
6. How do you and your spouse view discipline of your child? Where are there points of common ground? Where are there disagreements? How do your disagreements affect you, your relationship with your spouse, and your relationship with your child?
7. (*Explain the nature of adolescence and the child's task of creating a separate identity.*) As your child creates his own identity, do you celebrate or are you threatened by the difference and the distance it causes? Explain your answer.
8. What is your hope for your relationship with your child? What would a respectful adult-adult relationship look like a few years from now?
9. What can you do to be sure you have that kind of relationship? What are the barriers to achieving it?
10. What is your next step in determining how to be the parent God wants you to be for your teen?

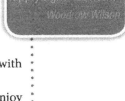

When correcting a child, the goal is to apply light, not heat.

Woodrow Wilson

My dad is the boss . . . until Grandma comes over. Then he's just one of us.

A child in Kids Say the Greatest Things about God

4 WISE COUNSEL

For the Teen

The adolescent years can be a rocky time for parent-teen relationships. A teen may be simply trying to *express his independence* and figure out who he is, but *his parents may interpret his behavior as rebellion and enforce unreasonable discipline*. If teens are to survive—and enjoy—their teenage years, *the key is honest communication* with their parents, rather than manipulating, lying, or overreacting. While simple conversation may not seem like the "cool" thing to do, much of the conflict that parents and teens experience could be eliminated if they would talk to each other.

Rather than giving their parents the silent treatment and refusing to talk to them, teens need to learn to express intelligibly what they are feeling. Encourage teens to sit down with their parents and *express their frustration with the restrictions they are placing on them*. Rather than lashing out at their parents, they should suggest plausible compromises to rules they feel are unreasonable.

Teens must be careful to approach their parents in a *respectful manner*, remembering that they are called to honor them, whether or not they agree with their rules. They should *listen to their parents* and really *try to understand* where they are coming from. If their parents seem unpredictable, constantly changing the rules about curfew, borrowing the car, having friends over, and other issues, teens should suggest that together they write out what is expected and what is not allowed, so there is no confusion.

Remind teens to *thank God for their parents*. Whether or not they feel love for them right now, God has given their parents to them as a gift. They should look for the positives and learn from them, while expressing their appreciation for all their parents do.

For the Parents

Authors Scott Turansky and Joanne Miller observe that often the parent, in an effort at correction, focuses on controlling the teen's behavior at the expense of their relationship. They insist that discipline isn't complete until the *relationship between parent and child is restored and strengthened*.

Punishment focuses on past misdeeds, but *genuine discipline focuses on the child's growth, future, and increased wisdom*. Too often parents take action to control their child's bad behavior out of anger. Discipline, however, has an opposite motivation—lovingly wanting to point the child in a positive direction.

Parents need to *avoid extremes* in their reactions, which might include yelling and violence, smothering attention, or neglecting the child and walking away.

If the parents need time and space from a heated conversation to think and come up with a plan of how to respond to a child's defiance, they can *take a time-out to regroup*. In most cases parents need at least twenty minutes to calm down and think clearly (and maybe call a trusted, wise friend for advice).

Parents should give the teen a chance to explain. Sometimes parents *misunderstand* their child's behavior or words. It's never a bad idea to ask a child to explain his perspective. *Listening often clarifies things* for both parents and their children.

Children can be asked to *come up with appropriate consequences*. Too many parents dictate consequences to their adolescent children, but the kids don't feel respected. Instead, after talking about the situation, a parent can ask, "What do you think are the proper consequences for this?" Often teens will come up with consequences that are more severe than those of their parents. When this happens, the parents can scale them back as they help their children grow in their belief in themselves.

Some parents are so controlling that they debate every decision their teens make. This is a big mistake. It's much healthier (for everybody) to *let smaller choices pass without comment*, and engage in meaningful conversation about those that really matter.

When parents threaten but fail to back up their threats, kids become confused and tend to see their parents as not really believing what they say. *Parents should not set requirements on their kids that they aren't willing and able to back up.*

At the same time, since parents are prone to be as reactive and overly emotional as their teens, they must be willing to *apologize quickly for mistakes and sins*. Teens long for relationships with their parents (and everyone else in their lives) that are genuine, and that means that people "own" their faults. When parents are willing to admit their mistakes, it goes a long way toward *building trust*.

ACTION STEPS 5

For the Teen

1. Discipline Yourself

- Realize that, while you may dislike your parents' rules, there will always be rules in life. Don't just hold your breath until you can get out of the house; learn to discipline yourself.

- Begin to develop personal standards. Don't make decisions just because "Mom and Dad said so." A vital part of growing up is learning to make wise choices and take responsibility for the consequences.

- Own up to your mistakes. Don't lie or hide what you have done. Honesty is always the best option.

2. Talk about Your Frustration

- Immature people overreact to or ignore what bothers them. Mature people listen and respond. Rather than yelling and stomping off to your room, learn to put your feelings into words. Many times needless conflict stems from miscommunication.

- Talk about the issue at hand, rather than attacking your parents. Just because they won't lend you the car does not make them "horrible parents."

- Avoid sweeping generalizations in talking about an issue. When emotions flare up, it's easy to blow things out of proportion.

- When you are angry or hurt, take a step back and try to understand why your parents have set the guideline they have. For example, if you haven't completed your homework, it is reasonable for your parents not to lend you the car.

3. Choose to Respect Your Parents

- Respect for parents is not an option in Scripture—it's a command. As long as you are living at home, you are under your parents' authority.
- Remember that your parents are people too—people who have sacrificed a whole lot for you since the day you were born. Your attitude should be one of gratefulness for all they have done, not making demands and bossing them around.
- Learn to serve your parents. For a change, ask what you can do to help them. It will do wonders for your relationship.

4. Work toward a Compromise

- Rather than insisting on your own way, look for common ground as you talk with your parents.
- Controlling your frustration can be extremely difficult, but remember, if you can't control yourself, your parents are very unlikely to grant you more freedom.
- Listen to your parents' reasoning and try to respect their decisions even if you don't agree. Remember, you're not the "boss" of your own life.

For Parents

1. Listen

- Few adults have the patience to listen to and really hear their adolescent. Let go of your agenda, at least at first, and do all you can to try to get inside the head and heart of your teen. Start by asking questions.
- Our belief is that most kids will lie when they believe they are in trouble. The skill of listening creates a climate of trust and understanding that will allow the truth to come out. An important goal of a parent is to be a good listener.

2. Guide

- It's time to shift your approach to your teen, or child as young as twelve, from being his authority to being his guide. To be a fair and responsible guide, you need solid information. This is where listening is important.
- As a guide, your task is not to tell your teen how he violated a rule and let you down. The best way to be a guide is to lead your child to discover for himself what happened and why, and what needs to be done in the future. Your role is to continue the conversation until your teen sees the issue as it is, even if you need a few time-outs along the way to ease emotional tensions and calm yourselves down.

3. Negotiate

- Once you have convinced your teen that you care and understand, you have proven your commitment and compassion. When you have helped him comprehend and own his transgression or poor decision making, you are ready to help him face the consequences of his action.

- Most parents simply impose sanctions that are usually punitive and rarely make much of a dent correcting the cause of the poor behavior. It does not work to try to shame a teen into changing his behavior.

- First, listen to your teen and help guide him into admitting and acknowledging the infraction.

- Next, work with him to bring to light the contributing circumstances and thinking that caused the problem and the reason they caused it.

- Lastly, require your teen to help determine the discipline for his behavior. Keep in mind that it is important to establish a monitoring process to ensure that what you decided together actually happens. If it doesn't work or doesn't happen, then you come back together, discuss it, and decide on an alternate course of action.[2]

4. Stay Consistent

- At this time in his life your teen will need you to stay as consistent and available as possible.

5. Be a Student of Your Teen's World

- To be a student of your teen's world means you get to know well the people who influence him. This includes teachers, coaches, youth group leaders, and other parents, especially the parents of the kids in your teen's cluster.

- It's most important to become a supportive and engaged friend of your kid's friends. Many parents think that their teen wants them to disengage and back off from his world, but the opposite is true, as long as the parent does not invade the child's world.[3]

- While invading your teen's world would include possessiveness and a desire to micromanage, engaging in your teen's life can powerfully reinforce your love and support, while giving your teen freedom to make his own decisions.

- Engaging in your teen's world requires time and effort, but the results are definitely worth it. Engaged parents learn to value what their teenager cares about (i.e., sports, dance, music, theater) and find ways to encourage his natural talents.

6. Maintain a Commitment to Dialogue

- It is the parent's responsibility to make sure the lines of healthy and warm communication remain open between the parent and child.

- Dialogue is two-way—respectful discussions that contribute to the trust and depth of the relationship in a way that ultimately builds up both the child and the parent.[4]

7. Hold on to Your Role as the Adult

- You are a parent, but you are also a caring and committed friend. Sometimes friends say difficult things, and sometimes friends intervene in the best interest of their friend. By virtue of the role we have as parents, we have the responsibility, even mandate, to make sure our friends are well served, well cared for, and well developed.

- It is fine and good to be your child's friend, provided you never lose sight of the fact that your role is one of authority, leadership, and careful setting of boundaries.[5]

6 BIBLICAL INSIGHTS

"The Lord disciplines those he loves, and he punishes everyone he accepts as a son." Endure hardship as discipline; God is treating you as sons. For what son is not disciplined by his father? If you are not disciplined (and everyone undergoes discipline), then you are illegitimate children and not true sons. Moreover, we have all had human fathers who disciplined us and we respected them for it. How much more should we submit to the Father of our spirits and live! Our fathers disciplined us for a little while as they thought best; but God disciplines us for our good, that we may share in his holiness. No discipline seems pleasant at the time, but painful. Later on, however, it produces a harvest of righteousness and peace for those who have been trained by it. Therefore, strengthen your feeble arms and weak knees. "Make level paths for your feet," so that the lame may not be disabled, but rather healed.

Hebrews 12:6–12

Discipline is an important aspect of raising children. But parents must always remember to administer discipline within the boundaries of and toward the goal of providing training and instruction for children that will lead toward a maturity that is focused on serving others.

Train a child in the way he should go, and when he is old he will not turn from it.

Proverbs 22:6

As parents, our task changes as our kids mature. All along the way, however, our job is to equip, guide, and train them. By the time they are adolescents, our job isn't to control them any longer but to help them discover their "bent" and become healthy, confident young adults.

My son, do not despise the LORD's discipline and do not resent his rebuke, because the LORD disciplines those he loves, as a father the son he delights in.

Proverbs 3:11–12

Discipline is not usually fun when it's happening, but God's Word affirms that discipline is for our good, not merely to punish us. God wants to shape and change us to be more like Jesus, and one of the main ways He shapes a teen is through the influence of his parents. God disciplines us out of love. He is always working for our good, even when it hurts.

Whoever loves discipline loves knowledge, but he who hates correction is stupid.

Proverbs 12:1

Midcourse corrections are part of life. God's wisdom constantly challenges our assumptions and guides us along the right path—and sometimes, He uses parents to do that!

PRAYER STARTER 7

Lord Jesus, help us learn what You have in mind when it comes to discipline in the family. Give these parents honesty, mercy, wisdom, and gentleness in consistently and lovingly disciplining their teen. Give them an extra measure of Your grace so they can respond to conflict constructively, rather than lashing out in anger or neglecting to deal with the problem at all. We pray for the teenager as he is growing into an adult. Make his heart teachable and willing to accept instruction. We pray for good communication and that You, Jesus, would continue to build a healthy relationship between these parents and their child . . .

RECOMMENDED RESOURCES 8

Assor, Avi, Guy Roth, and Edward L. Deci. "The Emotional Costs of Parents' Conditional Regard: A Self-Determination Theory Analysis." *Journal of Personality* 72 (February 2004): 47–88.

Caldwell, John. *Raising G-Rated Kids in an R-Rated World*. Pleasant Word, 2007.

Christie, Les. *When Church Kids Go Bad: How to Love and Work with Rude, Obnoxious, and Apathetic Students*. Youth Specialties, 2008.

Clark, Chap, and Dee Clark. *Disconnected: Parenting Teens in a MySpace World*. Baker Books, 2007.

Cline, Foster, and Jim Fay. *Parenting with Love and Logic*. NavPress, 2006.

Clinton, Tim, and Gary Sibcy. *Loving Your Child Too Much: Raising Your Kids without Overindulging, Overprotecting or Overcontrolling*. Thomas Nelson, 2006.

Nelsen, Jane, and Lynn Lott. *Positive Discipline for Teenagers: Empowering Your Teens and Yourself through Kind and Firm Parenting*. Random House, 2000.

Roth, Guy et al. "The Emotional and Academic Consequences of Parental Conditional Regard: Comparing Conditional Positive Regard, Conditional Negative Regard, and Autonomy Support as Parenting Practices." *Developmental Psychology* 45 (July 2009): 1119–42.

Drugs and Alcohol

1 PORTRAITS

- Stephen's parents noticed that the levels in the bottles in their stock of vodka seemed to be going down each weekend. At first, they assumed each other was having a private drink. As the weeks went on, they talked and realized there had to be another explanation. They talked to Stephen, but he denied knowing anything about it. Months later he missed his curfew. When they called him, he slurred his words. There was no doubt about it. He was drunk.

- Dawn's grades began to deteriorate, and she became involved with a new group of friends at school. Her mother noticed that her eyes were bloodshot many days when she came home from school. She thought Dawn just wasn't sleeping enough. Finally, she talked to Dawn, who told her mother that she'd been smoking weed every day for the past four months.

- James's parents noticed that he had been acting very strangely. He had been a pretty happy boy but had become sullen and angry. One day his mother realized a lot of money was missing from her purse. It had happened before, but she had assumed she had just lost it. Now she suspected something else. She confronted James, and he denied he had taken the money. Weeks later he was caught stealing from a store in town. When the police arrested him, they found a bottle of Ecstasy on him.

2 DEFINITIONS AND KEY THOUGHTS

- Factors such as *wealth, the community environment, and the presence of mental health problems* affect substance abuse by teens.

- *Affluent youth reported significantly higher substance use* than inner-city students, consistently indicating more frequent use of cigarettes, alcohol, marijuana, and other illicit drugs.

- According to the White House Office of National Drug Control Policy, *more teenage girls than boys* now smoke and abuse prescription drugs. Girls also are starting to use marijuana and alcohol at a higher rate than boys.

- *The most commonly used illicit drug in the nation is marijuana*, and this is the drug of choice of most teens who use drugs. Some also use prescription drugs, inhalants, hallucinogens, and cocaine.

- More teens are in treatment with a *primary diagnosis of marijuana dependence* than for all other illicit drugs combined. Smoking marijuana leads to changes in the brain that are similar to those caused by cocaine, heroin, or alcohol.[1]

- According to the National Institute on Drug Abuse, marijuana today is *more dangerous* than it was in the sixties and seventies. Some reports estimate that today's marijuana is five times *stronger* than it was in the seventies, while other reports estimate it is as high as twenty-five times stronger than that of earlier decades.

- The *stages of addiction* for a particular substance or behavior are *experimentation, misuse, abuse, and addiction.*

Experimentation:
— In the first steps of using alcohol or drugs, teens often respond to the invitation of peers to try it.
— They are excited about doing something forbidden.
— Often they begin at the bottom rung of substances, such as wine coolers.
— They experience the thrill without serious consequences.

Misuse:
— Teens like the feeling of getting high.
— Lying becomes a lifestyle.
— They develop a new peer group and want to fit in socially by continuing to use.
— They may set limits on their use, but occasionally they go over their limit.
— They begin to experience problems at home and at school.

Abuse:
— Throughout the day, teens think about getting high.
— They regularly break their self-imposed limits.
— They experience significant difficulties at home and at school.
— They regularly lie, steal, and hide their use from those who love them.

Addiction:
— Teens are consumed by the substance and become willing to sacrifice their dreams and dignity to gain access to it.
— They blame others for the consequences and difficulties caused by their use.
— Every aspect of life deteriorates: social, mental, emotional, and spiritual.
— They have to use to feel "normal."

- Christian kids, especially those from sheltered environments, may be particularly *prone to drug and alcohol use* because of the novelty when they are first exposed to it.

- During the teenage years, *friends have major influence*, so preventing drug and alcohol use starts with building healthy, godly friendships. Involvement in a youth group or Bible study, such as Young Life, is a great way to have clean, positive fun. Many times teens start using because of peer pressure. *Positive peer pressure* can be just as powerful, however.

3 ASSESSMENT INTERVIEW

For the Teen

1. When did you start using or drinking?
2. Has your drug use increased recently? If so, can you explain why?
3. Has anyone ever suggested that your drug use or drinking created a problem for you or for her? What did she tell you?
4. Have you experienced anxiety, panic attacks, shakes, or hallucinations when you didn't use or drink?
5. What is your level of drug use now? Do you want to stop? Why or why not?
6. Have you tried to quit? If you have, what happened?
7. How would quitting affect your life for the better? How would it make your life harder in the short term?
8. How do you pay for the drugs, pills, or alcohol?
9. Does anyone in your family drink to excess or use drugs? If so, how do you think you've been affected by that person's behavior?

For the Parents

1. When did you notice that drinking or using drugs was a problem for your child?
2. What are the signs you noticed? How severe do you think the problem is?
3. What has happened when you have tried to talk to your child about this problem?
4. Are there others in the family who have a substance abuse problem?
5. What is your plan to help your child quit?
6. What is your responsibility?
7. What is your child's responsibility?

4 WISE COUNSEL

In dealing with drug and alcohol abuse, there is *no substitute for early awareness.* The more the teen uses, the more addicted she will become. If there is any suspicion of the teen's involvement with drugs and/or alcohol (based on the warning signs below), ask the teen straightforwardly.

Warning signs in teens of drug and alcohol use, include:

- changes in friendships
- unwillingness to bring new friends home
- unexplained absences from home
- secretiveness
- mood swings
- changes in sleeping and eating habits

- problems with money
- impulsive behavior
- lack of motivation
- red eyes, vomiting, or other physical problems
- poor memory, glazed expression

The issue of drug or alcohol use cannot be ignored. *It's not just a phase* the teen is going through. *Drugs and alcohol kill,* and the most loving thing you can do for the teen is confront her about her use. Enlist the help of a professional counselor in dealing with a using teen. Due to the highly addictive nature of these substances, *quitting isn't an easy matter.*

ACTION STEPS 5

For the Teen

1. Examine the Consequences

- In the moment it's easy to give in to peer pressure and use alcohol or drugs just because it's the cool thing to do. But take a step back and look at the cold, hard facts about these substances. Do some research.
- Drugs and alcohol are addictive and highly destructive to both you and the people around you. When you feel the urge to use, remember that these substances have the potential to destroy both your life and the lives of the people you love.

2. Remove Negative Influences

- Just "trying" to resist drugs and alcohol will not work. Don't put yourself in situations—parties, bars, raves—where you know these substances will be present. Even the strongest person can easily give in to "just one time," which can lead to addiction.
- Choose friends wisely. Don't hang out with people who use alcohol and drugs. Sure, you may think it won't bother you, but the continual influence of peer pressure can easily wear you down.
- Take up a new hobby. Join a sports team. Do something you find fulfilling. Choose to invest yourself in things besides just getting high.

1 in 4 high school students drank alcohol before the age of 13. High school students are drinking earlier with each passing year.

CDC Youth Risk Behavior Surveillance, 2005

3. Get Help

- Visit a professional counselor. Join a support group. Study the cycle of addiction for yourself. Be proactive in fighting alcohol and drug use, but don't try to fight on your own.
- Surround yourself with supportive, encouraging people who will hold you accountable and help you get a fresh start.

4. Run to God

- Alcohol and drugs never satisfy. No matter how much you use or how drunk you get, you will always end up feeling empty.
- Only an intimate, personal relationship with Jesus can truly satisfy you forever. Jesus, the creator of all good things, including pleasure, wants you to experience the pure pleasure of His presence.

For the Parents

1. Set up Accountability

- Your teen needs support and accountability to fight any addiction. As a parent, you can help your teen navigate the difficult waters of addiction by creating an atmosphere of honesty. Sit down with your child and set up clear guidelines that will help keep her away from drug and/or alcohol environments.
- A professional counselor can provide valuable assistance, and 12-step groups can offer a safe, positive environment. Your counselor or pastor can provide referrals.

2. Work to Fill the Emptiness in Your Child's Life

- Some parents think it's their role to monitor their wayward child every waking moment to assure that she doesn't drink or use again. The bigger goal, however, isn't stopping the immediate use, but building a new sense of hope and purpose in the child's heart.
- Short-term goals are important, but we can't forget the long-term goal of equipping the child for a lifetime of responsible behavior.
- Help your teenager get involved with athletics and hobbies to discover things she loves. Whether it's basketball, gymnastics, ballet, or hiking, help your teen learn to enjoy life without using drugs or alcohol.

3. Increase Relational Time

- Positive relationships are very powerful in the life of an individual struggling with alcohol and drugs. Often, using alcohol and drugs provides a context for making friends and feeling loved and accepted.
- While it may be the natural tendency to shame and judge the teen for her negative decisions, it is essential that parents make their unconditional love clear. Go out of your way to let your kid know that you love her and invite her to spend time with you, playing sports, shopping, going to see a movie, or some other enjoyable activity.

4. Write a Contract

- With the help of a lay or pastoral counselor, write a contract with your teen, stating that she will stop using and agree to get immediate help for the problem.

- The contract needs to be clear and unequivocal, including steps to take, benefits for compliance, and consequences for failure. You, as the parent, must agree to enforce these consequences. Be prepared to follow through.

5. Enlist Support

- Dealing with an addicted teen can be very trying, and there is no way that you can handle it on your own. Ask God for guidance and wisdom. He knows your teen's heart far better than you and He will never stop loving her.
- Get involved with a support group for parents of teens who are using drugs and/ or alcohol and learn more about the nature of addiction.
- Ask friends and church members to pray for your teen. Don't give up. God never stops pursuing His children, even in the midst of their sin.

BIBLICAL INSIGHTS : 6

Be very careful, then, how you live—not as unwise but as wise, making the most of every opportunity, because the days are evil. Therefore do not be foolish, but understand what the Lord's will is. Do not get drunk on wine, which leads to debauchery. Instead, be filled with the Spirit.

Ephesians 5:15–18

The issues surrounding drug and alcohol abuse aren't about substances; they are about the meaning and purpose of life. We need God's wisdom to know what's important and how to communicate with grace and truth to a teen who is struggling with a substance. Our teen (and we) may have made some very foolish choices, but now is the time to follow the leading of God and carve out a hopeful future.

Do you not know that your body is a temple of the Holy Spirit, who is in you, whom you have received from God? You are not your own; you were bought at a price. Therefore honor God with your body.

1 Corinthians 6:19–20

The measure of God's love for us is that He paid the ultimate price to rescue us. He gives us freedom from the slavery of sin, but with that freedom comes the responsibility to live for Him and make something of our lives—to honor Him in all we do.

Who has woe? Who has sorrow? Who has strife? Who has complaints? Who has needless bruises? Who has bloodshot eyes? Those who linger over wine, who go to sample bowls of mixed wine. Do not gaze at wine when it is red, when it sparkles in the cup, when it goes down smoothly! In the end it bites like a snake and poisons like a viper.

Proverbs 23:29–32

Counselors tell us that the number one reason addicts decide to change is desperation. When they realize they've ruined their lives and poisoned relationships with those they love, they find the courage to get help. That is a pivotal moment for them—and for the family.

7 PRAYER STARTER

Lord Jesus, we thank You that when we are tempted, You promise to always provide a way of escape. I pray for my friend as she struggles to be controlled no longer by drugs or alcohol. We believe, Jesus, that You are stronger than any addiction. By the power of Your Spirit, give Your child grace and strength to say no to the pleasures of this substance. Surround her with godly friends who will encourage her in this journey . . .

8 RECOMMENDED RESOURCES

Brotherton, Marcus. *Buzz: A Graphic Reality Check for Teens Dealing with Drugs and Alcohol.* Multnomah, 2006.

Fresonke, Cherie. *Go in Peace for Teens.* WinePress, 2009.

Lookadoo, Justin. *The Dirt on Drugs.* Revell, 2008.

May, Gerald G. *Addiction and Grace: Love and Spirituality in the Healing of Addictions.* HarperOne, 2006.

Shellenberger, Susie, and Kathy Gowler. *What Your Daughter Isn't Telling You.* Bethany House, 2007.

Townsend, John. *Boundaries with Teens: When to Say Yes, How to Say No.* Zondervan, 2007.

CDs

Dobson, James C. *Preparing for Adolescence: How to Survive the Coming Years of Change.* Gospel Light, 2000.

Eating Disorders

PORTRAITS : 1

- Janet was a star student and athlete in her sophomore year at school, but in the past few months, her coach has been concerned because Janet is losing weight. "It's no big deal," Janet insisted, but on trips with the team, the coach noticed that Janet hardly ate at all. "I'm not hungry. I'm fine," she protested. A few weeks later, she weighed only eighty-three pounds, even though she was five foot eight.

- Rachel and her friends would love to be models. They spend their money on the latest clothes and use up hours looking at fashion magazines. One of them noticed that at the end of lunch each day, Rachel almost always excuses herself and goes to the bathroom. One day her friend followed her without being noticed and heard Rachel vomiting. When her friend confronted her, Rachel began to cry. "Please don't tell my parents," she pleaded.

DEFINITIONS AND KEY THOUGHTS : 2

- *Body image and eating disorders* often go hand in hand. For most young women, the pressure to be thin and pretty drives them to look constantly in the mirror and jump on and off the scales to measure their weight. The problem, however, is the distorted view most of these young women have of their body. *Malnourished and often underweight, they still view themselves as fat.*

- The *media* plays a big role in today's society when it comes to body image. The *primary message* the media gives through actresses and models is that *skinny is pretty.* When a young woman feels fat, ugly, and out of control, she uses her eating habits as a way to have power over her life. Not eating puts her in control of her body and *makes her believe she can become the image the media portrays as acceptable.*

- It's important for teenagers to remember that *their body is a temple of God.* Psalm 139:13–14 says, "For you created my inmost being; you knit me together in my mother's womb. I praise you because I am fearfully and wonderfully made." *In God's eyes, we are perfect just the way He created us!*

- Eating disorders are characterized by an *obsession with food and compulsive behaviors related to eating.* Quite often, these behaviors are attempts to gain control of the person's life due to excessive anxiety and stress.

- According to Dr. Ken Weiner, medical director of the Eating Recovery Center and national expert in the treatment of eating disorders: "Eating disorders are complex conditions that can arise from a variety of potential causes and affect a wide demographic of American women—including children and teens."[1]
- *Ninety percent* of people with eating disorders are women. *Twenty-seven percent of girls twelve to eighteen years old* have significant eating disorder symptoms. *Thirty-one percent of female college students* have an eating disorder.
- The *long-term effects* of eating disorders can be frightening. Anorexia and bulimia have a *high rate of relapse*, as much as 30 to 50 percent. Because anorexia and bulimia are *complicated, multifaceted diseases*, individuals with eating disorders may require *ongoing treatment* to achieve a lasting recovery.
- The two primary types of eating disorders are *anorexia nervosa* and *bulimia nervosa*.

Anorexia

- Anorexia nervosa is a disorder that causes individuals to *severely restrict their caloric intake*.
- Anorexics are *obsessed with body image* and long to be thin. They believe that being thin is attractive, and they are afraid of gaining weight.
- They *obsess about their food* and engage in *self-starvation*.
- They may take *diet pills, laxatives, or water pills* to lose weight and may *exercise too much*.
- No matter how much weight they've lost, when anorexics look in the mirror, *they think they're too fat*. People with anorexia may become so malnourished that their lives are in danger.
- If it isn't treated, anorexia can cause *significant health problems*, such as:

  — stomach problems
  — heart problems
  — irregular periods or no periods (amenorrhea)
  — fine hair all over the body, including the face
  — dry, scaly skin

Bulimia

- Bulimia involves *two primary behaviors*: eating a lot of food at once (called bingeing) and then throwing up or using laxatives to remove the food from the body (called *purging*).
- After a binge, some bulimics *fast or overexercise* to keep from gaining weight.
- People with bulimia may also use *water pills or diet pills* to control their weight.
- They are very *secretive* about their bingeing and purging behavior.

- Bulimics are usually *close to normal weight*, but their weight may fluctuate. If it isn't treated, bulimia can cause *significant health problems*, such as:

  — stomach problems
  — heart problems
  — kidney problems
  — dental problems (from throwing up stomach acid)
  — dehydration (not enough water in the body)

Warning Signs of Anorexia and Bulimia

- unnatural concern about body weight (even if the person is not overweight)
- obsession with calories, fat grams, and food
- use of any medicines to keep from gaining weight (diet pills, laxatives, water pills)
- throwing up after meals
- refusing to eat or lying about how much was eaten
- fainting
- over-exercising
- not having periods
- increased anxiety about weight
- calluses or scars on the knuckle (from forced throwing up)
- denying that there is anything wrong
- A study by the National Association of Anorexia Nervosa and Associated Disorders reported that 5–10 percent of anorexics die within ten years after contracting the disease, 18–20 percent of anorexics will be dead after twenty years, and only 30–40 percent ever fully recover. The mortality rate associated with anorexia nervosa is twelve times higher than the death rate of all causes of death for females fifteen to twenty-four years old. Twenty percent of people suffering from anorexia will prematurely die from complications related to their eating disorder, including suicide and heart problems. Only one in ten people with eating disorders receive treatment.

ASSESSMENT INTERVIEW 3

For the Teen

1. How do you normally handle painful emotions such as hurt, fear, and anger?
2. Describe your most important relationships. Who are the people who make you feel valuable and secure? Who are the ones who neglect you or demand too much of you? How do you respond to those people?
3. When do you feel most safe and happy? What makes you feel that way?
4. What do you think about food? How much do you think about it?

129

5. What do you think of your body? What would it take for you to feel beautiful?
6. What do your friends, teachers, and parents say about your weight loss [your bingeing and purging]?

For the Parents

1. When did you suspect that your child had a problem with food and body image?
2. What are the signs and symptoms you've noticed? Who else has noticed them?
3. Have you tried to talk to your child about this? If you have, what happened?
4. Describe your family. What might cause your child to feel out of control and the need to control something (like food) to feel more secure?
5. How do you handle stress and disappointment?
6. What do you know about the nature of eating disorders? (*Explain as necessary.*)
7. Has your child recently seen a physician for a physical?
8. What kind of treatment have you considered for your child?

4 WISE COUNSEL

Some parents overreact when their child misses a meal because she's preoccupied with something at school or distraught about an argument with a friend. On the other hand, *some parents ignore obvious warning signs* that their child is in grave physical and emotional danger from an eating disorder. Look for *definable patterns* of behavior that suggest or demonstrate a problem.

Determine the severity of the problem, and if appropriate, *seek professional help.* (*Note*: In almost all cases, professional help will be necessary.) Treatment of an eating disorder must involve a *multidisciplinary team* composed of a medical doctor, nutritionist, and therapist, working with the client and her family. Every person designated to be a part of the support team should be in constant and *open communication* with one another.

It is essential that the teen get a *thorough physical*. A *physician* will be able to tell if weight loss or vomiting is from some other problem besides anorexia or bulimia, and the doctor can also determine any physical complication that has already occurred because of the disorder.

A *nutritionist* will be able to provide *up-to-date nutritional education, monitor food intake* and patterns of eating, and *construct a meal plan* that will be healthy for the teen.

A *professional therapist* who specializes in eating disorder treatment will be able to employ counseling theory and techniques proven to help *alleviate dysfunctional thoughts, beliefs, and coping mechanisms* that are currently prompting the eating disorder.

If the teen is anorexic, *individual therapy* is most appropriate. If the teen is bulimic, *group counseling* and support has been found to be highly effective.

Quite often in the family of a child with an eating disorder, *everyone feels out of control* but is *trying to cope in different ways*. One may try to find security by controlling weight and body shape, another may drink or use drugs to numb the pain, and another may shop or work to fill up the emptiness. Even in relatively healthy families, when one member develops an eating disorder, every family member experiences *confusion, doubt, and hurt*. Everyone needs to *process* the *pain, anger, and fear*.

Eating disorders are very serious signs of a deep emotional wound. Sometimes people who are that desperate give up on trying to control their lives and find meaning. Instead, they think of ending their lives. Be alert for statements of *hopelessness* and, especially, to any *plans the person may have to commit suicide. Talk openly and honestly* about this issue. For more information, see the section Suicide.

ACTION STEPS 5

For the Teen

1. Seek Professional Counseling

- Eating disorders are very serious and, if left untreated, can become a life-and-death issue. Some individuals may need to find an inpatient clinic to get the help they need.

- There is no substitute for professional psychiatric care in working through the roots of addiction (these include self-image, past abuse, control issues, and low self-esteem) and learning to fight the temptation of food manipulation.

2. Identify Your Ideal Weight and Stick to a Healthy Diet

- It is important for you to identify your healthy weight based on your height and body type. This can be easily done using a health manual or the internet.

- One practical way to fight an eating disorder is by planning out your meals to ensure that you have a healthy, balanced diet. This ensures that you are getting the vitamins and nutrients your body needs to stay healthy.

3. Look for Triggers

- The environment you put yourself in—people you're with and images that you admire—may trigger the urge to starve yourself and/or binge and purge. Additionally, stress and anxiety in your life (parents, boyfriend, school, work, sports performance, and so on) can often precipitate an eating disorder as a means of anxiety control.

- Every eating disorder starts in the mind—with how you see yourself and how you see food. Fighting the urge to binge and purge or starve yourself starts with identifying and changing your faulty thought patterns. If the primary motivation behind the eating disorder is that you think you're fat, begin getting others around you to help you understand the truth. If you are overweight, set up an exercise plan to get rid of extra pounds in a nondestructive way.

- Many times, eating disorders are more about control, achievement, and people-pleasing than food. Many young women struggling with eating disorders feel as though they cannot live up to the expectations of others and therefore feel that they have no control of their lives. Dealing with an eating disorder involves tracing these attitudes to their source and reshaping personal beliefs.

4. Keep a Journal

- A journal is a good way to relieve stress and also identify patterns that may be influencing your eating disorder. Write down your feelings, frustrations, and stresses.
- Use the journal to record your specific food intake each day, your bingeing/purging, and the thoughts that go through your mind that day about food. Be honest! This process may be difficult but is extremely helpful in objectively identifying the root causes of your eating disorder.

For the Parents

1. Consult a Physician

- One of the first steps is to get the teen to a doctor who can determine her health and detect any other causes for the problem or corollary damage from the disorder. With this information, the situation becomes much clearer.

2. Open Up Conversation

- The real issue isn't the food; it's relationships and all of the tension, anger, fear, hopes, and dreams in the teen's heart. Don't focus only on nutrition, calories, and vomiting. Those are important, but they aren't causes.
- It may be painful to hear that your child doesn't feel loved and safe, but voicing these perceptions is essential to healing and growth. If you feel threatened by your child's honesty, get help for your own insecurities. Your child needs you to be there and to listen without correcting or defending.

3. Watch for Triggers

- Most people with eating disorders have predictable patterns of thought and behavior that have become routine. Certain triggers propel the behavior. Fashion magazines, mirrors, talk about body image, and tension in the family can cause people with eating disorders to use food to control themselves and their environment. Help the teen identify the triggers.
- Consider asking the teen to write about her activities and feelings in a diary or a journal. This may help you identify a pattern and the triggers.

4. Consider Inpatient Treatment

- If the teen is experiencing significant health problems, hospitalization may be necessary to save the teen's life. After stabilization, the teen may then be transferred to a treatment center designed to treat people with eating disorders.

- Don't underestimate the physical and emotional damage this problem can cause.

5. Build a Relationship of Trust and Affirmation

- In the course of treatment, many buried but powerful emotions will come to the surface. Throughout this process, be your teen's biggest cheerleader and choose to affirm her all along the way. Acknowledge any wrongdoing you've committed, and take strong steps to communicate love and forgiveness.

BIBLICAL INSIGHTS 6

We demolish arguments and every pretension that sets itself up against the knowledge of God, and we take captive every thought to make it obedient to Christ.

2 Corinthians 10:5

People with eating disorders have distorted thinking. They need an environment of emotional support and clarity of thought—grace and truth. During the process of healing deep emotional wounds and learning new life skills, teens (and their parents) will need to search the Scriptures to find the truth about their identity in Christ, the Spirit's power to change lives, how to speak truth in love, and many other valuable lessons.

Jesus looked at them and said, "With man this is impossible, but with God all things are possible."

Matthew 19:26

Eating disorders affect every aspect of the teen's life: physical, emotional, spiritual, and relational. The tangled web of distorted thinking, misguided perceptions, and strained relationships can seem impenetrable and hopeless, but nothing is impossible with God. Countless men and women have depended on Him and have found true peace and strength.

The LORD your God is with you, he is mighty to save. He will take great delight in you, he will quiet you with his love, he will rejoice over you with singing.

Zephaniah 3:17

The amazing love of God dissolves our fears and shatters our shame. It takes time for His grace to work its way deep into the heart of someone who struggles with an eating disorder, but sooner or later the fear and compulsive controlling behavior are replaced with genuine joy.

7 PRAYER STARTER

Heavenly Father, we praise You today for the gift of food. I lift up my friend to You as she tries to experience Your love, grace, and peace. Jesus, nothing is impossible with You. Fill my friend with the knowledge of Your love and Your wisdom. Give Your child grace and strength to chart a new way of thinking and new ways of relating to You and to others. Reassure my friend of Your never-failing love and care as she begins this journey toward healing . . .

8 RECOMMENDED RESOURCES

Alcorn, Nancy. *Starved: Mercy for Eating Disorders.* WinePress, 2007.

Cruise, Sheryle. *Thin Enough: My Spiritual Journey through the Living Death of an Eating Disorder.* New Hope, 2006.

Hersh, Sharon A. *Mom, I Feel Fat: Becoming Your Daughter's Ally in Developing a Healthy Body Image.* Random House, 2001.

Jackson, Nisha. *Helping Teens Survive the Hormone Takeover: A Guide for Moms.* Thomas Nelson, 2006.

Jantz, Gregory. *Hope, Help, and Healing for Eating Disorders.* Random House, 1995.

Larimore, Walt, and Mike Yorkey. *God's Design for the Highly Healthy Teen.* Zondervan, 2004.

McClure, Cynthia. *The Monster Within: Facing an Eating Disorder.* Baker, 2002.

Mintle, Linda. *Breaking Free from Anorexia and Bulimia.* Strang Communications, 2002.

Fatherlessness

PORTRAITS 1

- Nine years ago, when Dustin was only six, his father died in a car accident. His mother was already working, and with only one income, their grief was compounded by financial problems. His mother had to sell the house and they moved across town to an apartment. They didn't know anyone there, but it was all she could afford. Under the strain, his mother became sullen and withdrawn. Dustin desperately needed adults to guide him during his high school years but, instead, he relied on a peer group, the only ones who accepted him.

- Jan's parents went through an acrimonious divorce when she was twelve. In his desire to get as far away as possible, her father moved across the country and rarely calls. Now, four years later, Jan feels as though there is a huge hole in her heart. Not seeing the connection, she has begun making herself available to boys who are willing to make her feel loved, if only for a short while.

- Bill's father is consumed with his work. Throughout his childhood, Bill watched as his mother pleaded with his dad to spend more time with the family, but his father worked eighty to ninety hours each week and rarely took vacations. When he came home at night, he was so tired he regularly ate dinner in front of the television. He felt he needed to keep the grueling work hours to provide for his family, but they just thought he didn't care about them. Eventually this resentment drove the family apart.

DEFINITIONS AND KEY THOUGHTS 2

- Not having a father in the home as a result of death, divorce, or merely an uncaring parent can have long-term effects on young adults. *Emotional instability, relational problems, and difficulty trusting others* can be just a few of the consequences of fatherlessness.

- Of all the parental relationships, adolescents report being *least close to nonresident fathers*.

- Children whose fathers assumed 40 percent or more of the family's care tasks had *greater cognitive achievement* and performed better on tests than children whose fathers were uninvolved.

- Fathers tend to *disengage from children they no longer live with*—making less frequent calls and visits with each passing year.

135

- The *income of male householders is 51 percent* greater than that of female householders, creating a difficult financial situation for single mothers.
- Children who live with one parent are significantly more likely to have a *poverty-level household income* and are more likely to display depression, antisocial behavior, and school problems. Teenage girls from single-parent homes are at greater risk of bearing a child out of wedlock.[1]
- Even among homes where both parents are present, many dads are *emotionally and physically absent* from their teens. During their adolescent years, teenagers *need the acceptance and support of their father* more than ever. Henry Biller and Robert Trotter, authors of *The Father Factor*,[2] found that most fathers who live in the home spend *less than thirty minutes per day* with their children.
- Fatherlessness is not an automatic sentence to a life of failure and heartache. In the case of a deceased father, *the legacy that is left behind communicates to the children that they are loved and blessed.*
- Regardless of an individual's relationship with his father, *our heavenly Father promises to always protect and provide for His children.* God's love is *unconditional and never failing.* To the teenager struggling with the lack of a father, this love can be hard to accept or understand. But God promises to be a *"father to the fatherless"* (Ps. 68:5), and this promise is important for all of us.

3 ASSESSMENT INTERVIEW

For the Teen

1. When and how did your father leave your life?
2. Describe your relationship with him before he died, left, or became emotionally distant.
3. How did your mom cope with the loss of her husband?
4. How did you cope initially?
5. What are some things you've missed by not having a loving, supportive father?
6. Are there any men who have helped to fill that hole in your life? If so, who are they and how have they related to you?
7. Is there any man you really admire and would like to have a stronger relationship with?
8. Through this experience, what are some painful but important lessons you're learning about God being your father?

For the Parent

1. Under what circumstances did your teen's father die, leave, or become emotionally unavailable?
2. What was your child's relationship with him like before he died, left, or became distant?
3. How has your teen coped with the sense of loss?

4. How have you coped with your sense of loss?

5. When you try to talk to your teen about the pain of not having a loving, supportive father, how does he respond?

6. Is there a man in your child's life (a coach, grandparent, uncle, or family friend) who fills in the gap in some way? If so, what impact does this person have on your child?

7. How can you help your child process the loss more effectively?

8. Are there men your child respects (or might respect) who could build a relationship with him?

WISE COUNSEL : 4

God has created the family and each person in the family to play crucial roles so that *children develop into healthy adults*. Teens are going through perhaps the most difficult developmental time of their lives, and they rely on the nurturing touch of both their mother and father to give them the *love and guidance* they need. When a father isn't physically and/or emotionally present, the teen may feel *a genuine sense of loss*, usually coupled with confusion, because the losses experienced by absence are harder to identify than the losses suffered from abuse. When a teen doesn't have the presence of a committed father, he will likely experience *a deep, gnawing pain*.

Quite often the children aren't the only ones who are devastated by the loss of their father. Their *mother can suffer deep emotional wounds* no matter how the loss began: from divorce, death, or emotional absence. Grandparents are also affected. Different people *cope in very different ways*. Some get busy, some become absorbed in fixing others' problems, some become depressed and withdrawn, and some become defiant. Even if it is better that a father is out of the home, there is a *painful loss* in a family when a father is not a part of daily life.

The most common ways people cope with deep emotional wounds are to *minimize* ("Oh, it's no big deal. It doesn't really bother me.") or *excuse* ("He couldn't help it. He had to leave us for his own good."). But the loss can be devastating. A mom needs to be *honest about her own struggles*, being careful *not to burden her children* with the need to take sides, be a "best friend," or worse, be a personal therapist.

No one can take the place of a dad in a teen's heart, but a wise, loving coach, uncle, grandparent, or friend of the family can fill in some of the holes and *help the teen take steps forward*. Such a relationship *should not be forced*, but when there seems to be a natural affinity between an adult and a child, the mother should look for ways to *encourage the relationship*.

Fatherlessness is a tragedy, but *God can use anything to teach us life's most valuable lessons*. With insight and courage, the remaining members of the family can learn more about God as *the most gracious, wise, and supportive Father* anyone can imagine. And they can trust Him to bring other men into their lives to provide good models for teens who are searching for direction.

Fatherlessness is a rarely discussed but tragic reality in today's world. In 2007 almost 1 out of every 4 children (22.6%) were living in a household without their father. Nearly half of all children in disrupted families haven't seen their father at all in the last year.

Childstats.gov

5 ACTION STEPS

For the Teen

1. Don't Blame Yourself

- Do not allow an absent parent to destroy your self-esteem and make you feel worthless. It is never a kid's fault if a parent chooses to leave. Parents are responsible for their children's welfare and well-being, not vice versa. Taking the blame for your parents' failures may be a natural impulse, but it is not an appropriate one.

- Use Scripture to fight your feelings of guilt and reaffirm in your mind your unique worth to God. He does not see you through the eyes of your parents' failures. He sees you as a unique individual whom He loves.

- The same God who created you and knit you together in the womb will take care of you, even if your parents are neglectful or not present. He is your heavenly Father, who loves you perfectly and will never let you down. If you can't rest in the arms of your earthly father, rest in God.

2. Learn to Forgive

- No matter how your father has treated you, the command to forgive remains. If he has abused or abandoned you, forgiveness is extremely difficult. You will need to rely on God's grace to enable you to forgive.

- Forgiveness is a choice, but letting go of the hurt takes time. Consider seeing a professional counselor to work through the bitterness and anger you may have toward your father.

- If possible, talk to your father in person, with the mediation of a counselor, if necessary. Express to him the pain and brokenness you feel—your anger, hurt, frustration, and grudges. Tell him of your desire to forgive him. This will not make the pain magically go away, but it will free you from the bondage of bitterness and begin the healing process.

3. Look for Godly Role Models

- Every teen needs the input of older, wiser adults who care about him. If your father is not actively involved in your life, ask a teacher, coach, or youth group leader to mentor you. Spend time with this person, ask him questions, listen to his advice, and learn from him.

- With access to the internet and printed media, you have huge amounts of wisdom in the form of books, sermons, articles, and other formats. Seek out wise and godly authors who know God's Word and learn from their writings.

4. Invest in Others

- Rather than having a pity party because your life is so bad, choose to invest your time and energy in helping other people. Get involved with after-school programs, Big Brother Big Sister, or local outreaches through your church. Often God uses our brokenness to help other people in similar situations.

- Focusing on yourself and your past will only lead to anger and depression. While these issues need to be worked through in a counseling setting, reaching out to help hurting people around you may change your perspective in amazing ways.

For the Parent

1. Be Honest about the Loss

- Denial may seem like a good short-term solution, but it leaves deep, un-healed wounds. Be honest about the pain of losing your spouse. As you learn to grieve and take steps to rebuild your life, you can offer insight and encouragement to your children.

2. Provide Love and Support

- Some mothers try to fill the hole in their children's heart caused by the absent father by pouring themselves into the vacuum. They try to protect their children from being hurt again, micromanaging their lives and robbing them of self-reliance. Don't withdraw into your pain, but don't smother your kids either.
- Seek help to know how to be a single mother to a teen who is trying desperately to carve out his sense of identity.

3. Point Your Teen toward Men Who Can Fill the Gap

- Be observant. What men does your teen trust and respect? These people may be able to step into your child's life and fill the gap. Sometimes the most obvious choices don't work out for some reason. Be patient and persistent.
- Don't force a relationship, but notice and nudge your teen toward relationships with men who can play a significant role in shaping his life in a positive direction during these important years.

4. Uncover God's Lessons

- Nothing is a surprise to God, and He will use every painful event in our lives to teach us the most important lessons we can learn. The absence of a father in the home is one of the biggest tests any family can face, but even then, God is there to comfort, teach, and guide. Help your child look to God for the help He longs to give.

> 90% of all homeless and runaway children are from fatherless homes. 85% of all children that exhibit behavioral disorders come from fatherless homes.
>
> *Centers for Disease Control and Prevention*

6 : BIBLICAL INSIGHTS

But you, O God, do see trouble and grief; you consider it to take it in hand. The victim commits himself to you; you are the helper of the fatherless.

Psalm 10:14

In times of trouble, the psalmist didn't despair. God sees the evil in the world, and the fatherless can trust in God's promise to help them in their time of need.

Not only so, but we also rejoice in our sufferings, because we know that suffering produces perseverance; perseverance, character; and character, hope. And hope does not disappoint us, because God has poured out his love into our hearts by the Holy Spirit, whom he has given us.

Romans 5:3–5

Even in our darkest hours, God has a wonderful plan to meet us there, teach us important lessons, and shape our character. We may not know why we experience the suffering of being fatherless, but we can be sure that God will produce something good if we trust Him.

Sing to God, sing praise to his name, extol him who rides on the clouds—his name is the LORD—and rejoice before him. A father to the fatherless, a defender of widows, is God in his holy dwelling. God sets the lonely in families.

Psalm 68:4–6

In the Scriptures and in the life of Christ, we find that God has a special place in His heart for the lost, the hurting, and "the least of these." God longs to be a "father to the fatherless."

7 : PRAYER STARTER

Our Father, we thank You that You are our Abba, our dad to whom we can always run without fear. Even if we are abandoned or hurt by our earthly father, You never stop loving us with Your incomprehensible love. Wrap Your arms around this precious son of Yours. Reassure my friend of Your goodness and the truth of who You really are. Heal brokenness with Your perfect love, and take away the power of fear. Teach us to trust You, Jesus, as a Father who always works for our good . . .

RECOMMENDED RESOURCES 8

Blankenhorn, David. *Fatherless America: Confronting Our Most Urgent Social Problem.* Harper, 1996.

Clark, Chap, and Dee Clark. *Daughters and Dads: Building a Lasting Relationship.* NavPress, 1998.

Robinson, Monique. *Longing for Daddy: Healing from the Pain of an Absent or Emotionally Distant Father.* Waterbrook Press, 2004.

Stringer, Doug. *Who's Your Daddy Now? The Heart Cry of God to a Fatherless Generation.* GateKeeper, 2007.

Stroop, David. *Making Peace with Your Father.* Regal Books, 2004.

Thomas, Pamela. *Fatherless Daughters: Turning the Pain of Loss into the Power of Forgiveness.* Simon and Schuster, 2009.

Wright, H. Norman. *A Dad-Shaped Hole in My Heart.* Bethany House, 2005.

Forgiveness

1 PORTRAITS

- When Michael went to high school, his demeanor changed. He had been fairly happy in middle school, but after taking abuse from seniors for most of his freshman year, he became increasingly sullen, angry, and defiant. Clearly he was taking everything they said and did very personally. His bitterness affected every relationship.

- Beth's parents divorced when she was eleven, but she found comfort in her relationships with her friends. Now as a junior in high school, a misunderstanding with her best friend has fractured her web of friendships. It was over a boy, and now Beth hears ugly gossip about her from all over the school. Furious and feeling betrayed, Beth can't sleep at night and she's lost weight because her stomach is upset most of the time.

- Felicia was angry—at her parents, the army, and God. Her dad was transferred again, just at the time she had finally developed some good friendships and found a home at the high school. She knew a transfer was possible, but she hoped her dad would have a longer stint this time. Now she faces more upheaval, more uncertainty, and more strain in finding a new set of friends. "Why does God do this to me?" she moans.

2 DEFINITIONS AND KEY THOUGHTS

- The Bible describes *forgiveness* in two ways: as the *release from a debt* (Matt. 18:21–35) and the *refusal to take revenge* for an offense (Rom. 12:17–21).

- *Unforgiveness* is the refusal to absolve the debt and the insistence that the person pay in some way for the offense. Choosing not to forgive can ultimately result *in bitterness, resentment, anger, relational tension, unrealistic demands on God and others, defensiveness, and even physiological problems.*

- Forgiveness is both *a choice and a process.* Author Philip Yancey calls it "the unnatural act" because everything in us cries out for revenge. Quite often, when we face our refusal to forgive, we also come to grips with the damage we've experienced from the offense. When we forgive, the process usually involves *the process of grieving our losses.*

- A 2001 study revealed a correlation between reviewing hurtful memories and measures of the stress response (EMG, heart rate, blood pressure). When subjects were encouraged to think forgiving thoughts, *the stress response was diminished.* Similar findings were seen in an October 2003 study of 108 college students. The health benefits of forgiveness may include:

— decreased anger and negative thoughts
— decreased anxiety
— decreased depression and grief
— decreased vulnerability to substance use[1]

According to Everett Worthington Jr., one of the world's leading researchers on forgiveness:

People who won't forgive the wrongs committed against them tend to have negative indicators of health and well-being: more stress-related disorders, lower immune-system function, and worse rates of cardiovascular disease than the population as a whole. In effect, by failing to forgive they punish themselves. Unforgiving people are also thought to experience higher rates of divorce, which also reduces well-being, given that married men and women consistently do better on most health barometers, including longevity. In contrast, people who forgive may have better health, fewer episodes of clinical depression, longer marriages and better "social support," another indicator of well-being. This latter means forgiving people get along better with others, who in turn come to their aid in social-support situations.[2]

> For if you forgive men when they sin against you, your heavenly Father will also forgive you. But if you do not forgive men their sins, your Father will not forgive your sins.
> *Matthew 6:14–15*

ASSESSMENT INTERVIEW 3

For the Teen

1. Tell me about the disappointments and hurts you've experienced.
2. How did you respond (your feelings and actions) to those people and events?
3. How do you currently relate to the people who hurt you? Describe how you think about them, feel about them, and act toward them.
4. What does forgiveness mean to you? How can a person know if she's forgiven someone?
5. Whom do you know who is good at forgiving others? Is this trait admirable and attractive to you? Why or why not?
6. How are anger and hurt addressed in your home? Is forgiveness modeled?
7. How do you think bitterness affects the offender? How does it affect the person who is bitter?
8. What would happen if you forgave those who hurt you?

For the Parents

1. How has resentment affected your teen's life (relationally, emotionally, spiritually, physically)?
2. How have conflict resolution and forgiveness been modeled in your home?

3. What are the events and who are the people who have hurt you? What are the events and who are the people who have hurt your teen?
4. Who has modeled forgiveness to you? to your teen?
5. How can you be a good example of forgiveness for your teen?
6. How would choosing to forgive affect your teen's life?

4 WISE COUNSEL

In his letter to the Ephesians, Paul instructs his readers and us: "Get rid of all bitterness, rage and anger, brawling and slander, along with every form of malice. Be kind and compassionate to one another, forgiving each other, just as in Christ God forgave you" (4:31–32). We can't forgive by sheer will. As Paul indicates, our ability to express forgiveness to others is directly related to *the depth of our experience of God's forgiveness* of us for our own sins. When we have trouble forgiving, we need to first look at our own hearts and dig more deeply into God's grace and love for us. Then *out of the deep well of God's grace for us, we can choose to forgive* those who have hurt us.

Many people, however, *misunderstand* the nature of forgiveness.

- It doesn't mean that wrongs done to us are acceptable.
- It doesn't imply that the wounds don't hurt or will stop hurting as soon as we choose to forgive.
- It doesn't mean that we have to now trust the person who betrayed us.
- It doesn't absolve the offender from some or all of the consequences of the offense.
- It isn't the same thing as reconciliation. Forgiveness is unilateral; reconciliation requires both people to take steps toward each other.
- It doesn't demand that the other person change or express sorrow.
- It doesn't require that we become passive victims again.
- It is a sign not of weakness but of great strength of character.

Forgiveness:

- *releases us* from the self-imposed bondage of bitterness and recriminations
- *frees our minds and hearts* to enjoy life and build positive relationships
- *is a choice*, often a difficult choice, to refuse to take revenge in any way or to be happy when the other person suffers
- *draws us closer* to God because we often have to go deeper into God's grace toward us if we are to forgive others
- *produces empathy* for the offender, *humility* because we realize we are sinners who need God's forgiveness, and *gratitude* for God's grace

Almost always people *feel justified* in their resentment and bitterness. They cling to the hope that justice will be done, sometimes feeling they should be the instru-

> If your brother sins, rebuke him, and if he repents, forgive him. If he sins against you seven times in a day, and seven times comes back to you and says, "I repent," forgive him.
>
> *Luke 7:3–4*

ment of that justice. When this process takes root in a person, she can see herself as a victim, and in that role, she makes *three demands*: that the person pay for what she did, that God or someone fill the hole created by the offense, and that a guarantee be given that no one will ever hurt her again. These demands set up the bitter person to be hurt again and again, and the *bitterness multiplies*.

ACTION STEPS 5

1. Learn about Forgiveness

- Many people, including many who are Christians and regularly attend church, don't understand the nature of forgiveness. Your counselor will give you Scripture passages and principles that will give you a foundation for a discussion of this crucial topic. Allow your counselor to clarify particular points so that you will have no misconceptions.

2. Be Honest about Your Feelings

- We don't forgive those we excuse, and our forgiveness is shallow when we minimize the damage inflicted by another's offense. Many people have buried their true feelings of hurt for a long time, and bitterness has become a lifestyle of anger and demands.
- Write a life history of unpleasant experiences and hurts to uncover events that have never been resolved. Be honest about your feelings concerning these people and events. Honesty is the foundation for genuine forgiveness, resolution, and healing, and it might even lead to restored relationships.

3. Set Good Boundaries

- If you are in an ongoing, destructive relationship, wounds are repeatedly inflicted, and they won't stop because you choose to forgive. Your counselor will help you find ways to set boundaries, to say no to the offender, and to protect yourself from more abuse.
- In some cases, such as in friendships, you can withdraw from unsafe people and find new friends.
- If the unsafe person is a family member, you will need to look to an adult to help you. If you have a supportive parent, ask that parent to find a way to bring a stop to the abusive treatment, provide protection for you and other family members, and shape a new family culture. Your counselor will refer you to people who can help.

4. Be Encouraged by God's Love

- Facing the reality of how we've been hurt by others is a watershed in our lives. We can become bitter or we can pursue God's love and wisdom like never before. God is never surprised by the events in our lives, and He wants to use even the most painful things to teach us important lessons about His love, mercy, grace, and forgiveness.

6 : BIBLICAL INSIGHTS

Therefore, as God's chosen people, holy and dearly loved, clothe yourselves with compassion, kindness, humility, gentleness and patience. Bear with each other and forgive whatever grievances you may have against one another. Forgive as the Lord forgave you.

Colossians 3:12–13

We can forgive others only to the extent that we've experienced God's forgiveness in our lives. The more deeply we sense God's amazing grace, the more we'll be willing and able to forgive those against whom we have grievances. Jesus chose to forgive His enemies when they were in the process of crucifying Him, and He has forgiven every one of the sins we will ever commit. Only when we begin to grasp this incomprehensible love can we extend unconditional forgiveness to others.

But Joseph said to them, "Don't be afraid. Am I in the place of God? You intended to harm me, but God intended it for good to accomplish what is now being done, the saving of many lives."

Genesis 50:19–20

Joseph was betrayed by his brothers and sold into slavery in Egypt. Years later God orchestrated events and used Joseph to save the lives of his family. His brothers were understandably afraid that Joseph would take revenge and kill them, but Joseph had a different perspective. He realized that God had used their anger and betrayal, and all the pain he had suffered because of their sins, for the good purpose of rescuing the entire family from famine. We may not be able to see the cause and effect of God's plan to use others' sins for good purposes in our lives, but we can trust that He is doing just that.

Make every effort to live in peace with all men and to be holy; without holiness no one will see the Lord. See to it that no one misses the grace of God and that no bitter root grows up to cause trouble and defile many.

Hebrews 12:14–15

Without a genuine experience of the grace of God, people naturally become bitter toward those who hurt them. When this happens, everything in their lives becomes "defiled"—poisoned by anger, resentment, defensiveness, and demands.

PRAYER STARTER : 7

Jesus, You know every act of injustice, every incident of abuse, every harsh word, and every hurt that has been inflicted on my young friend. And I know that it breaks Your heart. Fill her heart with the deep knowledge of Your love, grace, and forgiveness. Then free my friend to forgive the people in her life who have caused hurt. By the power of Your Spirit, break down any walls of bitterness and resentment and open up her heart to the reality of the unconditional forgiveness You showed on the cross . . .

RECOMMENDED RESOURCES : 8

Brauns, Chris. *Unpacking Forgiveness: Biblical Answers for Complex Questions and Deep Wounds.* Crossway Books, 2008.

Demoss, Nancy Leigh. *Choosing Forgiveness: Your Journey to Freedom.* Moody, 2006.

Kendall, R. T. *Total Forgiveness.* Charisma House, 2007.

MacArthur, John. *The Freedom and Power of Forgiveness.* Crossway Books, 2009.

Sanford, John Loren, and Paula Sanford. *Choosing Forgiveness: Turning from Guilt, Bitterness, and Resentment towards a Life of Wholeness and Peace.* Charisma House, 2007.

Smedes, Lewis B. *The Art of Forgiving.* Random House, 1997.

Stanley, Charles F. *The Gift of Forgiveness.* Thomas Nelson, 2002.

Gangs and Violence

1 PORTRAITS

- Tim had given up on school. Never a good student, he drifted away from the friends he had enjoyed as a child and began hanging out with a new group. As Tim spent more time with them, his demeanor changed. He became tough, angry, and defiant. When his mom tried to talk to him about what she saw, he exploded.

- Juan always wanted to belong, and in middle school he found a group that gladly accepted him. His parents suspected this new group was up to no good, but they had no idea that their son had joined one of the most notorious gangs in the city. A few months after he joined the gang, he was one of four arrested for stealing from a gas station. When the police searched the young men, they found crack cocaine and Ecstasy on them.

2 DEFINITIONS AND KEY THOUGHTS

- The Bureau of Justice Assistance defines a gang as "an organization of tightly bonded youth who are joined together and controlled by a criminal leader. A gang is often conceived and nurtured by an individual who uses it as a vehicle to raise himself or herself to a position of power among his or her peers."[1]

- *Leading risk factors for gang involvement* include:

  — low income
  — learning disabilities (children with learning disabilities are three times more likely to join a gang)
  — low achievement in school and little involvement in school activities
  — no involvement in positive activities outside of school
  — friends and peers who are delinquent
  — low exposure or attachment to conventional rules, expectations, and role models
  — feelings of fear in school (28 percent of those joining gangs reported fear in school, while only 2 percent of those who did not join gangs reported fear in school)
  — early involvement in petty theft
  — behavioral disorders in the primary grades[2]

- In 2005 the National Alliance of Gang Investigators Associations reported:

  Once found principally in large cities, violent street gangs now affect public safety, community image, and quality of life in communities of all sizes in urban, suburban, and rural areas. No region of the United States is untouched by gangs. Gangs affect society at all levels, causing heightened fears for safety, violence, and economic costs.[3]

- While gangs may look appealing initially to *teens who are desiring acceptance*, the gang life is rife with *violence, drugs, immorality, and running from authorities. Gang fights*, whether within or between gangs, are often fatal, and once an individual joins a gang, it is very difficult to get out.

- Gangs are not something to play around with. It is far easier to *say no initially* then to be caught in a web of violence and death threats. The *longing for community* is innate to being human, but joining a gang is not the solution. A *strong support network* grounded in family, friends, school activities, and youth group will help a teen avoid the gang scene.

ASSESSMENT INTERVIEW 3

For the Teen

1. Tell me about your friends. What are they like? What attracted you to them?
2. What kind of impact has your time with them had on you—positive and negative?
3. Do you feel that you need them for protection? Explain your answer.
4. What's your home life like? Describe your relationship with your family members.
5. Do you want to get out of the gang and stop the violence? Why or why not?
6. What risks do you face if you choose to leave the gang?
7. How can I help?

For the Parents

1. When did you first suspect your child might be involved in a gang or in violent behavior?
2. Have you noticed any gang-related clothes, handshakes, or signs?
3. What do you think attracted your child to these people?
4. Describe the impact this involvement has had on your child and on the family.
5. How has your child responded when you've tried to talk about it?
6. Who have been the most positive influences in your child's life? How does your child relate to these people now?
7. What is your hope for your child?
8. How can you support and guide the changes that need to be made?

4 WISE COUNSEL

It's not surprising that studies show a large number of violent criminals and gang members in the country grow up in *single-parent homes* led by a mother. The *absence of a father's love and guidance* is a primary cause of kids joining gangs. In addition, teens who haven't found a secure and *meaningful place* in their family, school, sports, and community are at risk to join gangs to find relationships. Those who join gangs want a place to belong and a sense that their life matters to someone. They are:

- desperate to belong and be cared about
- needing recognition, higher status, and acceptance
- longing for excitement
- wanting structure and protection
- needing cash (that they get from stealing, drug sales, and so on)

To *keep teens out of gangs* and away from violence and drug use, parents can:

- *enroll children in school activities* from the time they are in grade school so involvement in sports, music, clubs, and other activities becomes part of their normal routine and they meet other kids who have some ambition and relational skills
- *stay involved in their child's life* by asking questions, encouraging the child to invite other kids to the house, and showing interest in all activities
- *teach and model the ability to handle difficulties*
- take time to *know their child's friends, teachers, coaches, and activity sponsors*
- limit home *exposure to movies and music* that glorifies violence, premarital sex, and other destructive behavior
- reinforce and model *ambition and a commitment to excellence*
- talk often about the *consequences* of choices, and help the child learn from the examples (both good and bad) of others[4]

5 ACTION STEPS

For the Teen

1. Find a More Positive Environment

- To take steps away from gang involvement and toward healthy relationships and a positive future, the following are essential:

  — You must want to make the change. Listen to your counselor talk realistically about the consequences of the path you are on.
  — Realize that you have a lot to live for. Focus on the love and support of adults in your life.

— Realize that leaving the gang will be one of the most difficult and the most important choices of your life.

— Don't just stop gang activity; replace it with more positive involvement in sports, music, or work.

— Get rid of gang-related clothes and other paraphernalia. Change your language and stop using gang-related signs and handshakes.

— Take small steps away from the gang instead of stopping all at once. A gradual approach will minimize the risk of violence toward you from the gang.

2. Get the Support of Others

- If you are involved with a gang, you need to get the support of people who can help you. Getting out of a gang is not something you can do on your own. Support groups are a good way to work through issues alongside of people who are struggling with the same thing.

3. Find a New Group of Friends

- When you decide to stop hanging out with your gang friends, you must realize the weightiness of this decision. You will likely become an enemy of your former "friends," but true friends are people who really care about you and have your best interest in mind.

- Seek out new friends in your school or youth group who are not involved with the gang life. Join a sports team, take up a new hobby, volunteer at your church, get an after-school job. In short, do something to involve yourself in a non-gang community.

4. Turn to God

- Breaking away from gang life is a difficult journey, one of loneliness and rejection. Know that, in the darkest and most difficult times, when you feel like no one cares, God is there, and His love for you will never change.

- Even when you feel like giving up and giving in, God is committed to changing you. By the power and grace of God, you can live your life as a free man.

- Without God, walking away from a gang is next to impossible, but in a thriving, intimate relationship with Him, God can work beyond your imagining. He can heal your heart, surround you with a new community, and give you a fresh start in life.

For the Parents

1. Look at the Home Environment

- Often teens join gangs to find the acceptance and purpose in life they haven't found at home or with other adults. The first step, then, is to take a hard look at your lives, the home environment, and the kind of adult community you are involved with.

- Unless the home and community atmosphere become affirming and positive, any efforts to remove your child from a gang may prove futile. Take steps to improve your child's environment.

  —Give your teen consistent love, comfort, and acceptance in the home so he is not trying to seek it elsewhere.
  —Rather than always pointing out the negatives, affirm your teen for what he does well—i.e., sports, school, helping around the house.
  —Use parental control on the TV and internet to keep your teen from watching violent movies and websites. Pay attention to the video games your child is playing.

2. Seek Sound Advice

- All teens struggle with security and significance, but those who have joined gangs or gotten involved in criminal activity of any kind have chosen to try to get their basic emotional and relational needs met by people who will lead them astray. For them, the road back is hard. You need expert advice to know how to guide your child. The issues involved are explosive and dangerous. Find a skilled counselor to help you navigate these turbulent waters.

3. Enlist Support

- If you suspect your child is involved in a gang, habitual violence, or criminal activity of any kind, ask for help from family members, school counselors and teachers, and your church. Ask them for advice, enlist their involvement, and ask those who believe in God to pray for your child's direction in life.

6 BIBLICAL INSIGHTS

The cords of the grave coiled around me; the snares of death confronted me. In my distress I called to the LORD; I cried to my God for help. From his temple he heard my voice; my cry came before him, into his ears. The earth trembled and quaked, and the foundations of the mountains shook; they trembled because he was angry. Smoke rose from his nostrils; consuming fire came from his mouth, burning coals blazed out of it.

Psalm 18:5–8

When teenagers feel so desperate that they commit to a gang, they need the assurance that the Lord has the power to rescue them.

For nothing is impossible with God.

Luke 1:37

The story of the gospel is one of hope. People who seemed to be lost forever have experienced God's grace as they repented and found meaning and purpose through Christ. Even if a teen is deeply involved in gangs, violence, sex, and drugs, there's still hope. Nothing is impossible with God.

He has showed you, O man, what is good. And what does the LORD require of you? To act justly and to love mercy and to walk humbly with your God.

Micah 6:8

Parents of teens in gangs need to understand what God wants for them. They can't change the past, but they can make decisions today that are good, right, and noble. No matter how bleak the situation may look, they can cling to God, walk humbly with Him, and love their children by showing grace to them and speaking truth.

PRAYER STARTER 7

God of peace, we desperately need Your wisdom in dealing with gangs and violence in this teen's life. I know, Lord, that You hate violence and the destruction it brings to the people You have created. Give these parents grace to help and give this teen wisdom and strength to respond to threats and temptation with grace not anger. By the power of Your Spirit, protect him from anyone who tries to inflict harm. Because of Your love, Jesus, bring godly friends into this teen's life to encourage and build him up . . .

RECOMMENDED RESOURCES 8

Garbarino, James. *And Words Can Hurt Forever: How to Protect Adolescents from Bullying, Harassment, and Emotional Violence.* Free Press, 2003.

Huber, Wolfgang. *Violence: The Unrelenting Assault on Human Dignity.* Augsburg Fortress, 1996.

Merrill, Cirven, and Sandra Merrill. *The Gang Gun Violence Prevention Handbook.* AuthorHouse, 2008.

Miles, Al. *Violence in Families: What Every Christian Needs to Know.* Augsburg Fortress, 2002.

Morris, Wilda K. *Stop the Violence! Educating Ourselves to Protect Our Youth.* Judson Press, 2001.

Obsatz, Michael. *Raising Nonviolent Children in a Violent World.* Augsburg Fortress, 1998.

Quarles, Chester L. *Staying Safe at School.* B & H Publishing Group, 2000.

God's Will

1 PORTRAITS

- Jennifer is a bundle of conflicting desires. She has good grades and a very good score on her SAT, and she's been accepted to an excellent school of engineering. But Jennifer also has a tender heart for children, especially poor children. She's been involved for the past couple of years in caring for kids in a homeless shelter in her city. She knows that an engineering degree will open a lot of doors for her future, but her heart is really with the kids. She has asked different people for advice, and their input is as conflicted as her desires.

- Bob loves music. He has played in a band for a couple of years, but he's really interested in being a producer. He has big plans to move from his home in the Midwest to Nashville or Austin, where he believes he'll have the best opportunity. His father, however, insists that he go to college and get a degree. He doesn't want Bob to "throw his life away" on the "empty dream" of a career in music.

- Susan won a scholarship to a fine university out of state, but her close friends are going to in-state schools. Her parents aren't rich, but they said they're willing to pay the tuition if she wants to stay closer to home. She knows that would put an added financial burden on her parents, and she's having a hard time weighing the options.

- Jim has been looking forward to joining the Marines since he was in junior high, but his father's landscaping business isn't doing well, and he could use Jim's help. His dad isn't putting pressure on him to join the business, but his girlfriend is begging him to stay so they can get married.

2 DEFINITIONS AND KEY THOUGHTS

- *Discovering the will of God* for a career path, marriage, place to live, and other major choices is *one of the biggest challenges* of adolescence. Virtually all teens struggle with these decisions and need some *guidelines and insights* to make wise choices.

- Some of the choices teens face are *moral issues*, questions of right and wrong, such as involvement in premarital sex, stealing, or lying. Many decisions, however, have *no moral implications*. They deal with questions of desire, opportunity, and the best fit for a person. Pastor John Piper observes:

The Bible does not tell you which person to marry, or which car to drive, or whether to own a home, where you take your vacation, what cell-phone plan to buy, or which brand of orange juice to drink. Or a thousand other choices you must make. What is necessary is that we have a renewed mind, that is so shaped and so governed by the revealed will of God in the Bible, that we see and assess all relevant factors with the mind of Christ, and discern what God is calling us to do.[1]

- In discerning the path our lives should take, *the answers to the following questions should align*:

    1. What does our heart tell us?
    2. What do the people closest to us say?
    3. What does our community of faith affirm?

- Since many of the decisions we have to make are between two good options, the choice is often not clear. In these times we must *depend on past experience, the advice of people we trust, and our own sense of God's direction. If we are seeking to live a life that is pleasing to God, we can be sure He will guide our choices.*

ASSESSMENT INTERVIEW 3

1. Tell me the choice you're concerned about today.
2. What are the options you have considered?
3. If you picture a future in each career path [pursuit or relationship], what do you envision for each one? Which one seems most attractive to you? Why is that?
4. What would your teachers, coaches, parents, and friends say are your talents and skills? Do you agree with them? Why or why not?
5. Are there any biblical principles or directives that are guiding you? If so, what are they?
6. What input have you gotten from people who know you best? Do you value their insights into your life?
7. As you pray, do you have a sense that God's Spirit is leading you in a direction? Explain it to me.
8. What are the doors that are open to you at this point?
9. Are you willing to do God's will if He shows it to you clearly?
10. On a scale of 0 (not at all) to 10 (completely), how well would you say you are obeying God and pursuing Him now?
11. How will you be convinced that you know what God wants you to do?

WISE COUNSEL 4

Teens (and their parents) can become quite *stressed about important choices*. Decisions about college, career, and marriage are *crucial* ones for anyone, but *fear of making the wrong choice* can cloud the real issues and confuse even those who ardently pursue God's best. We can trust that *God wants us to know and follow His will* far more than we want to. He is a loving Father who delights in guiding His children. We can rest in His love and be confident He will lead us.

Some parents insist that their perceptions and desires are undoubtedly the best for their children and they aren't open to any conversation about their child's desires and opportunities. Parents need to realize that their "child" is *becoming an adult* and increasingly needs to be treated with respect. *Open dialogue* is far more effective—for the immediate choice and the long-term relationship—than demands for compliance.

Not all questions about God's will have a clear-cut answer. Moral issues are spelled out in the Bible, but sometimes, even those have *nuances and different applications* that must be considered.

There is *no guaranteed formula* or certain matrix a teen can use to determine the best path for the decisions without moral implications, but the following should be considered:

- *Desires.* What does the person really want to do? How long has she wanted to do it? Is it just a sudden impulse or a deep, long-simmering desire?
- *Gifts and abilities.* Does the teen show aptitude for this path? In relationship decisions, what effect do the two people have on each other?
- *The Scriptures.* Does the Bible speak directly to the choice? If not, are there biblical principles that apply?
- *Wise input.* What is the considered opinion of mature people who know the teen and have experience in guiding young people toward God's will?
- *Opportunity.* Is a door open, or does the teen long to do something that simply isn't possible? For instance, a teen may want to be a PhD-level scientist, but if she scored very low on her SAT and can't get into college, that dream may have to be relinquished. Or she may think being a professional musician would be exciting, but if she lacks talent, she will need to find another career choice.
- *The Spirit's nudge.* When the teen prays and seeks God's wisdom, what is the sense she has about God's leading? We must be careful here. Some of us mistake our desire for God's Spirit, or in relationships we may confuse aroused endorphins for God's stamp of approval.

Quite often God unfolds His will as we walk with Him *one step at a time.* Trusting Him as we move through life is the key to a faithful journey.

5 ACTION STEPS

1. Have Confidence in God

- *Usually teens don't come for help about major decisions unless they are confused and discouraged about their inability to figure out what path to choose. One of the tasks of the counselor, then, is to demonstrate confidence that God will reveal His will and that the teen will discover and follow it.*
- You can be sure that God will direct you, but His answer may not come quickly. It may unfold gradually. Put your confidence in Him and be patient.

Rejoice always; pray without ceasing; in everything give thanks; for this is God's will for you in Christ Jesus.

I Thessalonians 5:16–18 NASB

2. Grow in Your Commitment to God

- You may feel like a tangled mass of conflicting desires, but if you have a heart for the Lord and are willing to obey Him no matter where He leads, you will know His direction.

- To help you become increasingly obedient to the Lord, it is very helpful to have somebody in your life to disciple you in God's Word and help you be accountable to making wise decisions. Find a godly mentor, youth pastor, or mature adult to walk with you as you make difficult life decisions and learn to obey God's commands.

- The commitment to obey is a prerequisite to knowing God's will. For instance, in 1 Thessalonians 5:16–22 Paul writes: "Always be joyful. Never stop praying. Be thankful in all circumstances, for this is God's will for you who belong to Christ Jesus. Do not stifle the Holy Spirit. Do not scoff at prophecies, but test everything that is said. Hold on to what is good. Stay away from every kind of evil" (NLT). In Matthew 6:33 Jesus says, "But seek first his kingdom *and his righteousness*, and all these things will be given to you as well."

> We're not necessarily doubting that God will do the best for us; we are wondering how painful the best will turn out to be.
>
> *C. S. Lewis*

3. Become Familiar with the Ways God Guides

- Some teens think that God will speak to them in a vision or that His plan will magically appear to them in some super-spiritual way. You must understand that God has already been guiding you and shaping your life. He will continue to lead you if you trust Him.

- The elements God uses to guide us include the Scriptures, our desires, open doors of opportunity, the counsel of people who know and love us, and the Spirit's nudging. These don't create a formula, and God works in different ways in people's lives, but throughout history, people have found God's path through these means.

> I know God will not give me anything I can't handle. I just wish He didn't trust me so much.
>
> *Mother Teresa*

4. Consider the Implications of the Options

- You may be focused on how you feel and what you want right now, but you need to consider the long-term implications of your options.

- For a career choice, try to "shadow" someone for a few days in your field of interest. For a college choice, visit the schools you are considering. In a relationship, project how current patterns of relating will play out years in the future. Your counselor can help you do this.

6 BIBLICAL INSIGHTS

If any of you lacks wisdom, he should ask God, who gives generously to all without finding fault, and it will be given to him. But when he asks, he must believe and not doubt, because he who doubts is like a wave of the sea, blown and tossed by the wind.

James 1:5–6

God delights in revealing His will to His children, but He wants us to trust that He will, indeed, lead us. When we ignore His leading, we can effectively miss what He has for us.

Therefore, I urge you, brothers, in view of God's mercy, to offer your bodies as living sacrifices, holy and pleasing to God—this is your spiritual act of worship. Do not conform any longer to the pattern of this world, but be transformed by the renewing of your mind. Then you will be able to test and approve what God's will is—his good, pleasing and perfect will.

Romans 12:1–2

To discern God's path we don't have to be super spiritual, and there's no magic involved. We do need to spend time with Him and be willing to obey as He leads us. As our minds are renewed by the work of the Spirit and as we grow in trusting God, we find that our lives are increasingly in tune with God's heart. We learn to want what He wants, to care about the things He cares about, and to let our heart break about the things that break His heart.

Be joyful always; pray continually; give thanks in all circumstances, for this is God's will for you in Christ Jesus.

1 Thessalonians 5:16–18

God's will isn't always something "out there" in the distant future; it's responding to God in faith right now, thanking Him, trusting Him, following Him in caring for others and being involved in His work this minute.

Call to me and I will answer you and tell you great and unsearchable things you do not know.

Jeremiah 33:3

So I say to you: Ask and it will be given to you; seek and you will find; knock and the door will be opened to you. For everyone who asks receives; he who seeks finds; and to him who knocks, the door will be opened.

Luke 11:9–10

Jesus promises to give us everything we need for making decisions that please Him as we move through our lives. He can be fully trusted to lead us.

PRAYER STARTER 7

Father, my young friend needs wisdom in making decisions. Make her heart receptive to the leading of Your Spirit, and free my friend from fear of making the "wrong" choice. Give her confidence in the truth You have revealed in Scripture. Bring godly counselors into her life to help her sort through confusing choices. Guide my friend with Your peace that passes understanding . . .

RECOMMENDED RESOURCES 8

Cloud, Henry, and John Townsend. *God Will Make a Way: What to Do When You Don't Know What to Do.* Thomas Nelson, 2002.

Friesen, Garry, and J. Robin Maxson. *Decision Making and the Will of God.* Multnomah, 2004.

Hillman, Os. *Making Godly Decisions: How to Know and Do the Will of God.* The Aslan Group, 2002.

Omartian, Stormie. *Praying God's Will for Your Life: A Prayerful Walk to Spiritual Well-Being.* Thomas Nelson, 2001.

Runcorn, David. *Choice, Desire and the Will of God: What More Do You Want?* Hendrickson, 2003.

Sittser, Jerry. *The Will of God as a Way of Life: How to Make Every Decision with Peace and Confidence.* Zondervan, 2004.

Swindoll, Charles R. *The Mystery of God's Will.* Thomas Nelson, 1999.

Grief

1 PORTRAITS

- Tom hasn't been the same since his brother died while skiiing at the lake last summer. Tom had been driving the boat, and his brother tried to spray some friends on a dock. He hit one of the piers and died instantly. Since then, Tom has lost interest in everything he had enjoyed and has withdrawn from his friends.
- Kim's dad is in the air force, and their family has moved every couple of years since she was born. When she was young, it didn't seem to bother her, but the last time was when she was a sophomore in high school. She had grown really close to a group of friends at school and at church, but then they moved and she was having to start all over again. She felt angry and depressed.
- John's parents fought like cats and dogs his whole life, so he thought their divorce would bring welcome relief. It didn't. Instead, he feels as though he has lost any stability he had. He misses his dad and blames his mom for kicking him out. He knows better, but that's how he feels.
- Sarah had a charmed life: she had good grades, was a cheerleader, and had a handsome boyfriend. But her life crashed around her when she became pregnant. She wrestled with the decision of what to do and chose to get an abortion. Since that day, her demeanor has changed. She is no longer the happy, optimistic young woman she had been. She's angry, ashamed, and withdrawn.

2 DEFINITIONS AND KEY THOUGHTS

- Grief is *emotional suffering caused by a sense of loss.*
- Many people think of grief only in relation to death, but *any kind of significant loss* requires the process of grieving to resolve the pain and find hope for the future. For teens these losses might include their parents' divorce, changing their network of friends, moving to another city, abuse, abandonment, a family member's poor health, loss of bodily function from an accident, or any other kind of misfortune.
- In our culture of instant gratification, people aren't very good at grieving, and young people often haven't had *good adult models of grieving* to watch and follow.
- The Family Caregiver Alliance reports:

Grief is a natural process, an intense fundamental emotion, a universal experience which makes us human. It is a process that entails extremely hard work over a period of many painful months or years. People grieve because they are deprived of a loved one; the sense of loss is profound. The loss of a spouse, child or parent affects our very identities—the way we define ourselves as a husband, wife, parent or offspring. Moreover, grief can arise from the survivor's sudden change in circumstances after a death and the fear of not knowing what lies ahead.[1]

- Grief often involves a *wide range of emotions*, including sadness, anger, and guilt. The person feels a *deep sense of loss and hurt*, but this may be coupled with *anger at God* for allowing the loss or at people who failed to stop it. In addition, the person may experience intense *guilt* for not being able to prevent the problem, not responding with the same level of feeling he thinks he should, or being overwhelmed instead of being able to "put it behind" and keep going as if nothing happened.

- It's been found that 15 percent of people who've lost a loved one may be likely to experience "*complicated grief.*" This form of grief is more severe than the normal grief experienced because of loss. It is different than depression and anxiety and can be recognized by the *extreme, often negative changes in all close relationships.* Complicated grief is marked by "a sense of meaninglessness, a prolonged yearning or searching for the deceased and a sense of rupture in personal beliefs."[2]

- Many years ago, Elisabeth Kübler-Ross, a nurse working with cancer patients, noticed that people go through *five distinct stages of grief: denial, bargaining, anger, grief, and acceptance.*[3] Later this pattern was observed in other types of loss. Understanding the grief process takes away much of the confusion and uncertainty for people as they try to face the reality of what has happened to them.

  1. *Denial.* At first, we may be in shock at the news of a person's death or other tragic loss. Our attempts to numb the pain feel "normal" because we want to avoid painful, present realities. Instead of facing the painful facts of our life, we say things like, "Oh, it wasn't so bad," or "I guess I must have caused it somehow."

  2. *Bargaining.* When we come face-to-face with the reality of our pain, the most common response is to try to swap something to fix the problem as quickly as possible. We might try going to church to buy relief, we might try to be nicer to somebody we've hurt, or we might try even harder to put a lid on our anger around other people. Bargaining is certainly a step forward beyond denial, but it looks for a quick fix, not genuine resolution. Sadly, many people never get past this stage and they stay stuck trying to make deals with God and people for the rest of their lives.

  3. *Anger.* Sooner or later some of us will give up on making deals and we realize the full force of our loss. At that moment, we become furious at those who hurt us, at those who failed to protect us, at ourselves for taking so long to come to grips with it, and with God for allowing it all to happen. Hurt people

are angry at every stage of the process, but in the third stage, their anger is intense and focused.

4. *Grief.* After weeks or months, the wave of anger subsides. Now we face the gnawing hurt that has been under the surface of our anger all along. We feel deep sadness, often bordering on depression, when we realize how much we've lost and can never regain. Staying busy distracted us and numbed us for a while, but in this stage, we aren't using any anesthetics any longer. In one of the most poignant moments recorded in the Gospels, John tells us that Jesus wept at the tomb of His friend Lazarus (John 11:25). The Son of God, who knew He was going to raise His friend from the dead, was still overcome with grief over the loss.

Jesus understands our sense of loss too. In this stage, we grieve the wounds we can easily identify. A more difficult task, but one that is just as necessary, is identifying the losses that often remain hidden—the pain that comes from the absence of someone we love, for example.

Many psychologists say it takes at least two years to go through the stages of grief and resolve a significant loss. This insight gives us patience and persistence to keep going through the painful memories and emotions until we arrive at the last stage.

5. *Acceptance.* God made us with the capacity to grieve losses so that we can learn valuable lessons and move on with our lives. This process can be excruciating, and there are no shortcuts. If we keep taking steps down this path, eventually we realize that the wounds heal, the brokenness mends, and tremendous lessons are learned—lessons about God, others, ourselves, and what really matters in life. No longer are we haunted by the pain of the past. We still bear the scars of those wounds, but scars are signs of healing. We no longer have gaping wounds that demand our attention and make us feel threatened by any and every bump in life's road.

3 ASSESSMENT INTERVIEW

1. Tell me about how you're feeling today.
2. Describe what happened that makes you feel sad.
3. How did you feel when it happened?
4. Have you experienced other emotions, such as anger or guilt? Tell me about that.
5. How has your sense of loss affected you physically?
6. How has it affected your relationships and your functioning each day?
7. When are your best times? When do you feel particularly sad?
8. Do you ever feel hopeless, as if the pain will never go away?

WISE COUNSEL 4

The *stages of grief*, as outlined under Definitions and Key Thoughts, aren't clean and simple. Those who grieve lurch forward at one point with a fresh insight but stay stuck for a while as they process new information. They *drift back and forth* from bargaining—trying to resolve the pain as quickly as possible—to fury over a fresh reminder of their pain.

Through it all, teens who are grieving will have times of feeling that God is very close, but at other times it will seem as though He has forgotten them entirely. Throughout this journey of resolving past hurts so they don't control the present, the teen who is grieving can be confident that *God knows, God cares, and God is with him.*

The role of the caregiver is to *normalize the process of grieving* so the teen isn't confused or surprised by the powerful emotions involved. Without this insight, people usually stay stuck in denial or bargaining instead of taking steps forward.

ACTION STEPS 5

1. Accept Support and Comfort

- People who are hurting from loss may want the pain to go away immediately, but that doesn't happen with genuine loss. Talk about your loss with others who care about you and accept their support.

- *A study of the emotional life of Christ shows that the feeling most often ascribed to Him in the Gospels is compassion. As you grieve your loss, you need the genuine empathy and support of others. Admit your need and allow yourself to feel Christ's compassion and the compassion of others. Welcome the time they want to spend with you, receive their help, and depend on their understanding.*

2. Understand the Stages of Grief

- Powerful feelings of sadness, anger, and guilt may surprise you, and you may assume these feelings need to be denied or suppressed. Go over the stages in the grieving process with your counselor so that you will know what to expect in each stage.

3. Realize Grief Is Normal

- Grief encompasses a number of changes. It appears different at various times, and it comes and goes in people's lives.
- Grief is a normal, predictable, expected, and healthy reaction to a loss.
- The way you grieve is your own personal journey, and no one should tell you how to deal with your loss. Even if people don't understand the way you are grieving, they should respect it. However, if your grieving is prolonged in a manner that is detrimental to you and your relationships, you should expect your counselor

and those who care about you to gently challenge you so that you can move on through the grieving process.

4. Expect Complicated and Powerful Emotions

- You will need help processing the emotions that come with your loss. Find someone who can guide you as you deal with these feelings. Your counselor, pastor, or youth pastor will probably be able to assist you or refer you to someone who can.
- If you have other feelings, such as anger, guilt, and fear, they add to your emotional confusion and threaten your stability. Be willing to talk about these feelings and accept them as steps along the healing process.

5. Stay Connected and Maintain Friendships

- Powerful, unwanted feelings may cause you to look for acceptance through sexual activity or to withdraw, even from people who love you. Identify a few people who care, who don't offer pat answers and quick solutions, and who will be true friends during the grieving process.
- Don't become isolated from people, but seek meaningful connections with others.
- Make a list of friends to call.
- Locate a grief support group.

6. Get Help if You Feel Hopeless, Depressed, or Suicidal

- *If the teen expresses signs of depression, consider referring him to a physician or counselor who can help. And if the teen talks about ending his life, talk openly and honestly about these ideas. If he has a plan, get help immediately.*

6 BIBLICAL INSIGHTS

The Lord is close to the brokenhearted and saves those who are crushed in spirit.

Psalm 34:18

When we feel sad and alone, we can be sure that God weeps with us and cares deeply about us.

Be merciful to me, O Lord, for I am in distress; my eyes grow weak with sorrow, my soul and my body with grief. My life is consumed by anguish and my years by groaning; my strength fails because of my affliction, and my bones grow weak.

Psalm 31:9–10

Grieving affects every aspect of our lives. In Psalm 31 David describes the physical impact of loss in his life, as well as his emotional pain expressed in weeping. Many have suffered deep loss and, with God's help, have survived.

For men are not cast off by the Lord forever. Though he brings grief, he will show compassion, so great is his unfailing love. For he does not willingly bring affliction or grief to the children of men.

Lamentations 3:31–33

Grief is a season we all have to endure from time to time, but it doesn't last forever. If we take courageous steps into and through the process, we'll grow stronger and wiser.

My soul is weary with sorrow; strengthen me according to your word.

Psalm 119:28

Though we may be angry with God because He didn't prevent the loss, we can find wisdom and strength if we go to the Scriptures. There we find men and women who struggled with their losses too, and they trusted God to help them through their pain.

PRAYER STARTER 7

Father, You weep with us when we weep. We can run to You in our pain and brokenness, and You promise to welcome us with open arms. I pray for my friend as he is grieving this loss. Our hope is in You, Jesus—the One who will right every wrong in the end. Reassure my young friend of Your infinite love and care. Strengthen him even in the midst of grief and fill the void with Your kindness, grace, and peace . . .

RECOMMENDED RESOURCES 8

Dunn, Bill, and Kathy Leonard. *Through a Season of Grief: Devotions for Your Journey from Mourning to Joy.* Thomas Nelson, 2004.

Exley, Richard. *When You Lose Someone You Love.* David C. Cook, 2009.

Kubler-Ross, Elisabeth, and David Kessler. *On Grief and Grieving: Finding the Meaning of Grief through the Five Stages of Loss.* Scribner, 2007.

Lewis, C. S. *A Grief Observed.* HarperOne, 2001.

Rogers, Matt. *When Answers Aren't Enough: Experiencing God as Good When Life Isn't.* Zondervan, 2008.

Wright, H. Norman. *Experiencing Grief.* B & H Publishing, 2004.

———. *Recovering from the Losses in Life.* Baker Books, 2006.

Yancey, Philip. *Where Is God When It Hurts?* Zondervan, 2002.

Guilt

1 PORTRAITS

- Life in Bill's family has been chaotic since he was a little boy. Bill has internalized family stress and now as a teen believes he was somehow responsible for his parents' problems. He has chronic stomachaches and apologizes profusely for the smallest infraction, even when he has done nothing wrong.

- Rita despises herself. When she was in junior high, her parents left her to take care of her three-year-old brother for an afternoon. While she was talking on the phone with a friend, her brother fell in the pool. She called paramedics, and they revived him, but the stigma of failure has haunted her since that day. She tells herself that she's a terrible person and can never be trusted.

- Phil is a pastor's son and he has always felt that people in the church have very high expectations for him. His dad never demanded that Phil read his Bible or pray and he didn't get upset when he didn't obey, but his mother did. Under her close supervision and threats of punishment for any infraction, Phil became very rigid and legalistic. His dad has tried to help him enjoy life, but he just can't. Failure of any kind, Phil presumes, isn't an option.

2 DEFINITIONS AND KEY THOUGHTS

- Guilt is *a feeling of regret or remorse caused by real or perceived failure* to live up to a standard of behavior. Unless these feelings are resolved, the person may develop a pervasive and devastating sense of shame—the perception of being a hopeless failure.

- *Guilt and shame are related*, but they are quite different. Guilt says, "I *did* something bad." Shame says, "I *am* bad."

- *True guilt* occurs when a *moral law has been violated; false guilt is a burden of responsibility* for failing to live up to our own or someone's expectations. Many adolescents are actively and assertively trying to earn acceptance by pleasing people, so they become susceptible to false guilt.

- Psychologist and author Les Parrott observes:

  Everyone who works with adolescents works with guilt. Talk with young people who struggle with depression, loneliness, inferiority, alcoholism, drugs, critical attitudes, premarital sex, eating disorders, anxiety, spiritual doubt, God's will, masturbation, grief, or almost any other problem and you will find adolescents who struggle with guilt as well.[1]

- Neurological research confirms that feelings of guilt create an overactivity in the same brain regions that are involved in depression.[2]

ASSESSMENT INTERVIEW 3

1. How long have you struggled with guilt or shame? Tell me how it affects you.
2. When did these feelings begin? What were the events that caused you to first feel this way?
3. How have you tried to resolve these feelings?
4. Do you think the feelings come from genuine sin or from feeling that you haven't measured up to someone's (perhaps your own) unrealistic expectations? Tell me more about that.
5. If the feelings are the result of sin, have you confessed the sin to God and experienced His forgiveness? If so, how do you explain your continued feelings of guilt and shame?
6. If the feelings are a failure to meet unrealistic expectations, tell me about your home life. How stable and secure has it been? What has been expected of you?
7. What words would you use to describe yourself?
8. How would it change your life if you knew you were forgiven by God and accepted by those you trust?

WISE COUNSEL 4

Prolonged feelings of guilt and shame *destroy a teen's self-concept.* Teens are emotionally fragile, and feelings of guilt and shame can take root very easily. In talking with teens, look at more than just actions and behaviors. Quite often, by the time they reach out for help, teens are experiencing *pervasive and powerful feelings of self-hatred and hopelessness.* They may *mask their shame* by staying busy or having lots of friends but they seldom let anyone know what they're really thinking and feeling. Begin to reconstruct their sense of identity during this crucial time in their development.

Relationships with parents are the most determinative in shaping a teen's self-concept and the ability to resolve true and false guilt. Look for patterns in the messages (verbal and nonverbal) the teen's parents communicate and help the teen understand how the family's struggles can be internalized with such thoughts as: *I can't do anything right. If my parents aren't happy, it's my fault. Nobody could love someone as awful as me.*

If one or both parents are willing to come for help, assist the whole family in *resolving past pain* and dealing with present stresses in relationships.

Many people, even those who have been Christians for years, don't really believe that *God loves them unconditionally and forgives all their sins*. They believe they have to somehow pay for their sins by feeling bad enough long enough. Stress with the teen the reality of God's forgiveness and acceptance of her.

Many people believe in *a form of penance* and they get on a *guilt-penance treadmill* that promises to give relief but actually deepens their sense of guilt and shame. Here's how it works: They feel guilt for a sin or shame for failing to please someone, so they pull out their spiritual whips to lash themselves with accusations and self-punishment. After a while, they hope they've done it enough but they are now more convinced that they are worthless and hopeless. Discouraged, they are susceptible to temptation or try even more desperately to please and they fail again, which triggers another round of self-flagellation. Many teens and adults live on this treadmill all day every day, and they believe it's their best hope for happiness.

Feelings of hopelessness and shame quickly produce *self-defeating thinking and self-blame* called *morbid introspection*. The teen may spend hours each day examining her motives, feelings, and behaviors, beating herself up for being so "stupid," "awful," or "worthless." This daily exercise only leads to more of the same the next day and the next and the next.

5 ACTION STEPS

1. Determine the Source

- Determine if you feel guilty because of sin or because of some issues that were out of your control.
- Seek God patiently. Just because you feel guilty doesn't mean you have sinned, yet be willing to let God remind you of a sin long forgotten that needs to be resolved.
- If you feel guilty for something out of your control, you still need to find a way to resolve your feelings.

2. Distinguish between True and False Guilt

- True guilt is the feeling of regret for genuine sins. Ask for forgiveness.
- False guilt is unnecessary self-blame. Continuing to punish yourself for being human is useless. Do what you can and move on.

3. Understand the Gospel of Grace

- Study the Scriptures to understand God's unconditional love, forgiveness, and acceptance. Confession of sins is crucial. When we confess, we agree with God that our sins are wrong, but we also acknowledge that He has completely forgiven us through Christ's payment for our sin on the cross.

- *Share passages of Scripture that teach God's love and forgiveness, explain their meaning, and tell how you've experienced God's forgiveness for sin in your life.*

4. Begin to Rebuild Your Self-Concept

- *If the teen is experiencing false guilt and shame, share messages of affirmation and acceptance to replace the thoughts of self-condemnation. You might use passages of Scripture that speak of our identity in Christ, but your warmth and regard will communicate powerfully too.*
- When rebuilding your self-concept, you are trying to return to a state of equilibrium, where you can balance feelings of guilt and acceptance. Often when we're overwhelmed with guilt, we can fall into a pattern of self-punishment or feelings of worthlessness.
- Rebuilding your self-confidence may need to start with forgiving yourself. Part of forgiving and moving on is grieving over whatever it is that was lost, like a relationship, personal freedom, or your reputation. As you grieve, it's important to realize that forgiveness and moving on can only happen because of the forgiveness first offered by Jesus Christ. It is only because of His love, forgiveness, and grace that our self-concept can be secure.

5. Watch for Triggers

- Often those who struggle with false guilt and shame are prompted by certain people, particular times, and specific situations to feel those self-defeating emotions. Identify the people or events that trigger feelings of guilt. Then you can be on guard and learn to deny the guilt feelings that arise.

6. Reinforce Right Thinking

- Change your thinking by focusing on the truth of God's Word and His wonderful love and forgiveness.
- Spend time reading the Bible.
- Ask your youth pastor or some other mature Christian to study God's love and forgiveness with you.
- *Share particular passages of Scripture that are meaningful to you, and let the teen know how God has used these truths to free you from true guilt, false guilt, and shame.*

7. Stay Active

- Do things for other people.
- Practice being forgiving in your relationships.
- By providing encouragement to someone else, you will receive encouragement back and this will increase your feelings of self-worth.

6 BIBLICAL INSIGHTS

Therefore, there is now no condemnation for those who are in Christ Jesus, because through Christ Jesus the law of the Spirit of life set me free from the law of sin and death.

Romans 8:1–2

No matter what we've done, no matter how evil our hearts have been, God is willing to forgive us and set us free through His amazing grace.

If we confess our sins, he is faithful and just and will forgive us our sins and purify us from all unrighteousness.

1 John 1:9–10

Confession is agreeing with God about our sins, and it acknowledges that God has already forgiven us completely through Jesus's death on the cross to pay completely for our sins.

Let us draw near to God with a sincere heart in full assurance of faith, having our hearts sprinkled to cleanse us from a guilty conscience and having our bodies washed with pure water.

Hebrews 10:22

God's forgiveness is a judicial act, but it also draws us close to Him. We aren't only set free from our sins; God invites us to delight in Him as our loving Father.

As far as the east is from the west, so far has he removed our transgressions from us.

Psalm 103:12

God doesn't hold our past sins over our heads and remind us of them when He wants to shame us into compliance. His forgiveness frees us from guilt and allows us to love and serve Him.

7 PRAYER STARTER

God, I thank You that You promise to free us from living under the pain of guilt. I pray for my friend who is struggling with feelings of guilt and shame. Because You have taken the penalty for our sins, Jesus, we are not slaves to our feelings or the lies of this world. Thank You for the cross and Your forgiveness. Reassure Your child of the depth and width and height and length of Your forgiveness and love . . .

RECOMMENDED RESOURCES : 8

Beam, Joe. *Getting Past Guilt: Embracing God's Forgiveness.* Howard Books, 2003.

Fehlauer, Mike. *Finding Freedom from the Shame of the Past.* Strang Communications, 1999.

Howe, Leroy. *Guilt: Helping God's People Find Healing and Forgiveness.* Abingdon Press, 2004.

Humbert, Cynthia. *Deceived by Shame, Desired by God.* NavPress, 2001.

Lane, Timothy S. *Freedom from Guilt: Finding Release from Your Burdens.* New Growth Press, 2008.

Seamands, David. *Healing for Damaged Emotions.* David C. Cook, 1991.

Whelchel, Mary. *Why Do I Always Feel Guilty? Breaking Free from What Weighs You Down.* Harvest House, 2007.

Zacharias, Ravi. *Cries of the Heart.* Thomas Nelson, 2002.

Inferiority

1 PORTRAITS

- Beth is a pretty girl, but her older sister is gorgeous, and everybody knows it. Since she was a little girl, Beth can remember hearing people talk about her sister's beauty. When they looked at her, they often said something like, "And Beth is cute too." Beth has tried to compensate by being an honor student and excelling on the high school volleyball team, but she still feels that she can never measure up.

- Rob grew up in an alcoholic home. His father was a binge drinker who would seem fine for a couple of weeks but then be drunk for several days. His mother felt that things in the home were out of control, and she was determined to protect Rob the best way she could—by smothering him with attention, affection, and directions. No decision was too small for his mother to make for him, even when he was in high school. His father's emotional absence and his mother's command of his life stole from Rob the confidence to make his own decisions.

- Often Sarah wonders if someone will find out how dumb she really is. She's pretty and has fun with her friends but, because she struggles with dyslexia, she is consistently behind in her classes. No one identified the problem until she was a sophomore, so she spent years wondering why she couldn't grasp the things in class that her friends understood so easily. Now she feels that she is too far behind to ever catch up.

2 DEFINITIONS AND KEY THOUGHTS

- During teen years *two tough questions* surface: Who am I? and How do I fit in? Virtually all adolescents *wrestle with their sense of self-worth* and consequently struggle with *feelings of inferiority*—even the brightest, prettiest, handsomest, and most gifted athletically. They *compare themselves* to those around them, and there's always someone more gifted or beautiful or intelligent, or they fear that someone more gifted will come along and knock them off their perch.

- *Symptoms of inferiority* can include:

  — *A lack of confidence.* When teens compare themselves with others and come up short, their fragile sense of confidence is shaken. Then they believe they don't have what it takes to effectively complete a project, make adequate grades, compete in sports, or be a good friend. When this self-perception becomes entrenched, the teen feels a gnawing *sense of shame, helplessness, and worthlessness.*

— *Arrogance.* When comparison makes teens feel superior, they may display an *inflated pride* that they are better than their peers. But comparison has a downside—it inevitably produces a *distorted sense of identity*, creating insecurity for all. Even those who are on top in one area know that they fail in others.

— *Perfectionism.* Some teens try to cope with their feelings of incompetence by *rigidly controlling some area of their lives.* Some keep a strict schedule, some write with judicial precision, some keep their rooms immaculate, some make sure their clothes or hair is perfect, and others find another aspect of life they can perfect to make them feel more secure. This behavior, of course, doesn't address the root issues that caused the feelings of inferiority.

— *Being sullen and withdrawn.* Some teens simply *give up* on playing the game of being accepted and competent, so they withdraw in isolation. They may spend their time playing video games or they may create *a fantasy world* where they are the star, beauty, or hero.

— *Defensiveness.* Teens who believe they don't measure up to their own or others' expectations feel hurt, and a typical reaction is to defend themselves. Psychologist Les Parrott notes:

> To protect themselves from further pain they erect barriers. They may exhibit a disproportionate amount of hostility, criticism, bragging, suspiciousness, or denial. It is too risky for these struggling adolescents to be exposed to additional hurt, so they wear psychic armor. Perhaps the most common defense for these young people is apathy. It is as if they have been injected with emotional Novocain that leaves them with a lethargic I-don't-care kind of attitude.[1]

— *Risky behavior.* To numb their feelings of inadequacy, to add excitement to their lives, and to impress people they admire, some teens engage in risky behaviors. They may use alcohol or drugs, drive when they're high, get into fights, engage in premarital sex, join a gang, or participate in extreme sports.

ASSESSMENT INTERVIEW 3

1. Tell me how you're feeling about life today.
2. What makes you feel confident and happy? What makes you feel discouraged?
3. When was the time you felt most confident in yourself? What was going on at that time in your life that gave you confidence?
4. What are some situations or people that make you feel insecure or inadequate (socially, academically, physically, or athletically)?
5. Tell me about your home life. What messages do your parents give you about your appearance, your abilities, and your wisdom to make good decisions on your own? How have these messages affected you?

173

6. To whom do you compare yourself? What person do you wish you were like?

7. How do you respond when you feel that you aren't measuring up?

8. In your mind, what words and names do you use to describe yourself? What do these tell you about how you really think about yourself?

9. What do you think of God's unconditional love for you? Did you know that the Bible says He's crazy about you? Does that make a dent in how you think and feel? Why or why not?

10. How would your life be different if you felt really confident about yourself?

4 WISE COUNSEL

"Who am I?" "How do I fit in?" "How do I measure up?" These are the questions of adolescence. The *feelings of inferiority are widespread*. Don't be surprised that teens (and adults too, for that matter) struggle with feelings of inferiority. Our *performance- and image-driven culture* actively promotes beauty, strength, and skill in every area of life.

People naturally compare themselves to others, and adolescents make comparisons more than any other age group. This results inevitably in *self-destructive perceptions*. Even when a person feels superior to everyone else, he fears that someone will come along who is bigger, better looking, smarter, or a better athlete. When talking with adolescents, the question is not *if* they struggle with comparison and feelings of inferiority, but *how* this affects them.

In the most positive, healthy families, *parents help their kids identify their strengths and give plenty of affirmation*—not false praise, but "what I like about you" praise that focuses on *gifts, talents, and abilities*. As the teen matures, these parents gradually give more responsibility to their child to make his own choices, knowing he'll make some good ones and some bad ones, but trusting that he'll learn and grow from all of them.

Less-healthy families fail in these areas. They don't help the child identify areas of giftedness and talent and they *don't affirm their child's successes.* They tend either to smother the child with directions or withdraw passively from the child's life at this pivotal time.

The *verbal and nonverbal messages* the child has received throughout his life and now in adolescence shape his self-perception to a remarkable degree. Children from healthier families have the skills to interpret correctly all the messages they receive from the culture and from friends, but those who haven't learned these skills are vulnerable and *absorb destructive messages*.

Differing Responses

Not all adolescents respond to feelings of inferiority in the same ways, so *look for patterns of behavior* that indicate the teen's self-perception and coping style. These may include perfectionism, withdrawal, defensiveness, and risky behavior. Ask some direct questions, but also *look for more nuanced indications* from comments, gestures, and body language. Teens use their *coping styles* because they think they will protect them or help them win approval from others, so they aren't likely to give them up easily.

Not all coping mechanisms are healthy. Unhealthy coping behaviors must be replaced with *new healthy coping mechanisms.* For example, if a teenager copes with feelings of inferiority by obsessively doing homework and being perfectionistic to achieve or earn the acceptance of others, he needs to learn to replace that behavior with another activity. Spending time with other healthy teenagers who will accept him no matter how well he does in school is a healthy alternative. *Perfectionism, withdrawal, defensiveness, and risky behavior are all unhealthy ways of coping* with inferiority and can make the feelings of inferiority even worse because self-concept becomes based on what the person does, not on who he is.

Parental Involvement

Parents may or may not be a significant cause of the problem, but they are almost certainly an *important part of the solution.* If possible, talk to the parents about feelings of inferiority being a normal part of adolescence, so they shouldn't be shocked or demand that their child get over those feelings immediately. They can examine their role in *helping build their child's sense of self-worth and confidence.* Perhaps they have been too passive and uninvolved or perhaps they have smothered the child and robbed him of confidence to make his own choices. They need to identify what their child does well, affirm those talents and attempts to use them, and show increasing confidence in their child's growth in responsibility toward being a competent adult.

Ultimately, helping a teenager overcome inferiority happens by getting good things going for him—getting all trains going in the same direction so to speak by setting him up to succeed and helping him find his gifts, abilities, and talents. Parents can *build confidence* in their children's abilities by encouraging them to play sports, join clubs, take classes, act in plays, participate in anything that interests the child. But *parents shouldn't push children to do things they don't want to do.* That's counterproductive, harming the child's sense of adventure and clouding the relationship between parent and child.[2]

ACTION STEPS 5

1. Be Authentic

- *Many insecure teens may appear withdrawn or seem to be preoccupied with perfectionism or pleasing others, but most of them have antennae that are finely tuned to pick up authenticity or phoniness—especially in adults. Be interested but not too absorbed; be affirming but not syrupy. If the teen perceives your attention as less than genuine, he will discount anything you say.*

2. Identify the Main Cause of Inferiority

- Explore your family background and think about when your feelings of inferiority began. The dynamics of your family or your vulnerability to other factors may have contributed to your feelings.
- Identify the specific coping style—such as perfectionism, defensiveness, or risky behavior—you are using to mask or overcome your feelings. These may seem completely normal ways of behaving to you and the only conceivable way to live, but they are still not right.

3. Learn a New Language of Self-Perception

- Self-perception is a closed system and feeds on your thoughts and self-talk to reinforce your self-image. Memorize a statement or Bible verse that you can write on a card and keep in a pocket that will speak words of life into your heart.

4. Look for New Friends if Necessary

- If the group of friends you hang out with has a part in bringing you down, begin finding new friends. Though this is no easy task, it is imperative for your well-being.
- We are who we spend time with. Before long you talk like the people you hang with, act like them, and live like them. First Corinthians 15:33 says, "Bad company corrupts good character." You will build self-confidence by spending time with people who will encourage you, not put you down.

5. Get Involved in Activities You Are Good At

- You can build confidence in your abilities by playing sports, joining clubs, taking classes, acting in plays, or participating in anything you find interesting. Do things you want to do. Ask your parents for their support and find other mature adults who will help you in these endeavors.

6. Talk about the Impact of Comparison

- *Comparison is the air we breathe in our culture, and it's the nature of adolescents to compare themselves to their friends, models and actors in the media, and everyone else in their world. Discuss the nature of comparison: its goal, its process, its impact on our thoughts, and its power to cause us to feel inferior. Also help the teen understand how to replace these thoughts with positive statements from God's Word.*

7. Affirm Liberally but Genuinely

- *Celeste Holm accurately observed, "We live by encouragement and die without it—slowly, sadly, angrily." Adolescents hunger for people they trust to speak words of love and life to them. They need us to notice what they do well.*

- *Describe in detail the positives about the teen so he will know you really believe what you're saying.*

- *Point the teen in directions where he can use and expand his skills.*

- *For encouragement to have the desired effect, it has to be specific and genuine. It simply doesn't work to say something bland and generic like, "You're great!" Take time to observe, ask the teen what he loves to do, and be sure to ask him why he loves it. Listening to him is one of the most important forms of affirmation you can give.*

BIBLICAL INSIGHTS 6

The Spirit of God has made me; the breath of the Almighty gives me life.

Job 33:4

Young people need to understand that God created them. They aren't an accident or a freak of nature. God has given them talents, abilities, and a temperament that is unique in all the world.

I am the vine; you are the branches. If a man remains in me and I in him, he will bear much fruit; apart from me you can do nothing. . . . As the Father has loved me, so have I loved you. Now remain in my love.

John 15:5, 9

We are only truly ourselves when we are rightly related to God. His grace, forgiveness, and love free us from our past and our sins, and as we walk in the joy and power of His Spirit, His love and strength flow through us. Knowing God and experiencing Him are the source of a wonderful self-concept that is strong, humble, loving, and honest.

Finally, be strong in the Lord and in his mighty power. Put on the full armor of God so that you can take your stand against the devil's schemes. For our struggle is not against flesh and blood, but against the rulers, against the authorities, against the powers of this dark world and against the spiritual forces of evil in the heavenly realms.

Ephesians 6:10–12

The battle for a teen's mind and heart isn't just about the media and conversations with parents. The enemies of our souls, both the invisible spirits and the visible spirits of power and control, want all of us to believe lies about ourselves and about God, and teens are the most vulnerable group in our society to this deception. We need God's truth and love to combat those lies.

7 : PRAYER STARTER

Heavenly Father, we praise You that our identity is not based on what we do or what other people think about us. You proved Your love for us, Jesus, by shedding Your blood! Make my young friend confident today in the truth of who he is in You. We praise You that in our weakness, You are strong and You love to use ordinary people to bring glory to Yourself. Give this teen wisdom in sorting through lies that he believes. Teach him to live in the truth of Your Word and not in his changing feelings . . .

8 : RECOMMENDED RESOURCES

Anderson, Neil T., and Dave Park. *Stomping Out the Darkness: Discover Your True Identity in Christ and Stop Putting Up with the World's Garbage.* Regal Books, 2008.

Clinton, Megan, and Tim Clinton. *Totally God's: Every Girl's Guide to Faith, Friends, and Family (BTW, Guys 2!).* Harvest House, 2008.

Dobson, Ryan, and Marcus Brotherton. *2 Live 4: Why Did You Think You Were Here?* Tyndale House, 2007.

McGee, Robert S. *The Search for Significance.* Student ed. Thomas Nelson, 2003.

Priolo, Lou. *Self-Image: How to Overcome Inferiority Judgments.* Resources for Biblical Living Series. P&R Press, 1997.

Thomas, Angela. *Do You Think I'm Beautiful?* Thomas Nelson, 2005.

Loneliness

PORTRAITS 1

- Samantha had been nervous about going on the trip with the youth group. She was a freshman, so she didn't know many of the older kids. And to be honest, she didn't have many friends in her own class. She had a problem with acne and she didn't see herself as even remotely attractive. She was one of the first ones on the bus, but no one sat next to her. She wished she had stayed home.

- Bradon's older brother was the life of every group he was in. He was funny, clever, and smart, and everyone loved him. But his brother often used Bradon as the butt of a lot of his jokes, and it hurt Bradon's feelings terribly. He tried to smile and act like it didn't matter, but it did. He never felt as though anyone wanted to be his friend.

- Whitney's family moved to town when she was a sophomore in high school, and from the first day, she had a hard time fitting in. She's bright and pretty, but it seemed that every group of girls had a "No Vacancy" sign. Her parents told her to keep trying to make friends, but after a while, she gave up. "I hate all of them!" she yelled at her mom.

DEFINITIONS AND KEY THOUGHTS 2

- *Loneliness* is the common condition of fallen humanity. It is the *painful experience of isolation* triggered by one or several factors, including exclusion or the perception of exclusion from groups, abandonment by a person or family, cultural differences, or a feeling of alienation from God.

- Loneliness tells us that we are alone and cut off from any hope of meaningful interaction, resulting in *sadness, hopelessness, and sometimes anger.*

- Feelings of loneliness are common in our culture, and even more *prevalent in adolescence.* Developmentally, young people are trying to establish their identity and they get much of their self-worth from the acceptance of friends and family. *When they don't feel accepted, they feel abandoned, isolated, and alone.*

- A study of adolescence in America found:

  Chronic loneliness in childhood is related to insecure attachment during infancy, low self-esteem and regard for others, and academic problems. It is also linked to negative emotionality. . . . people who are easily upset or angered tend to report more loneliness than other people. Extreme loneliness is consistently linked to actual peer group isolation and victimization. Fortunately, however, the presence of one stable friendship in a child's life greatly reduces feelings of loneliness, even for kids who have been rejected by the larger peer group.[1]

- *Solitude*, however, shouldn't be confused with loneliness. Many studies demonstrate the *positive impact of regular times of solitude* to provide time and space to think clearly, reflect on things of the day, and get away from the hectic pace of life. One study examined the connection between solitude and physical health. A quote from the author states the findings:

  > The long-term, cumulative benefits of healthy solitude are suggested by my repeated finding that American teenagers who spend some amount of time alone are better adjusted than those who are never or rarely alone. This is a finding that I have verified in three studies: adolescents who spend an intermediate amount of time alone—20–35 percent of waking hours—show more favorable adjustment than those who are rarely alone or who are alone more often. These youths report more positive average emotional states and lower alienation and depression. They were also rated as having fewer problem behaviors by their parents and higher GPAs in school.[2]

- Loneliness has been shown to *decrease the ability of the brain to experience pleasure*.

  > Lonely individuals saw the positive events as less uplifting, less strong, less rewarding than did the non-lonely individuals. . . . And those negative events . . . they saw to be more severe hassles. Loneliness compromises your ability to regulate yourself, and it has a direct effect on some of the stress systems. So if you feel lonely, and you feel lonely for an extended period of time . . . your stress physiology starts to ramp up.[3]

3 ASSESSMENT INTERVIEW

1. When do you feel particularly lonely?
2. When do you feel connected to people?
3. When did those feelings begin? What was going on in your life at that time?
4. Tell me about your family. Do you feel close to them (or to some of them)? Tell me about that.
5. Who is your most trusted friend? Tell me what makes this friendship special for you.
6. What do you think is the most significant cause of your loneliness?
7. How have you tried to connect with people? What happened? How did you respond to their rejection?
8. How do you feel about God? Have you ever felt close to Him? Tell me about that.
9. Who are the people—teens or adults—who are genuinely interested in you? How do they make you feel?

WISE COUNSEL 4

The *feelings of emptiness or abandonment* may be overwhelming, and the teen may not understand the cause of the problem. Explore the *possible factors that may contribute to the lonely feelings*, including broken or strained friendships, moving to a new city and not getting into a group, cultural differences (including race, nationality, or financial disparity), failure to meet an important person's expectations, part of the grieving process, or the sense of being far away from God.

Often loneliness begins at home. Without a firm foundation of love and support from parents, adolescents may have *unrealistic expectations of their friends* at school, unwittingly demanding that they be more accepting than they are able. *Parents need to provide plenty of physical and emotional presence* coupled with strong doses of *affirmation* as they gradually grant more autonomy to their adolescent kids. It's not easy but it's essential for their teens' *emotional and relational health.*

Loneliness almost always is part of *a larger emotional package.* Feelings of isolation and rejection *trigger a wide range of powerful emotions*: anger at those who failed to accept the person, fear that it will happen again, and a sense of shame that she isn't worthy of anyone's love.

The counselor's unconditional warm regard is important to the teen struggling with loneliness. The fact that she came to you is an expression of both need and trust. Build on that connection. Enjoy talking and listening to her.

To be emotionally healthy, people don't have to be friends with everybody but they certainly need one or two people who accept them for who they are. Help the teen identify others (maybe just one person) who might be a real friend to her. The first person she chooses may not respond the way she hopes. Encourage her not to despair but to keep looking for friends she likes and trusts.

ACTION STEPS 5

1. Recognize the Feeling

- Put your thoughts and feelings in writing—possibly in a journal—as a way to determine the source of your loneliness.

2. Realize That Loneliness Won't Last Forever

- It may seem as though your feelings of loneliness are the only emotions you'll have for the rest of your life. Understand that everyone has these feelings from time to time. Your situation is not hopeless. You will not always feel lonely.
- Remember that no one is truly alone if she has God in her life.

3. Examine Your Coping Styles

- Every person tries to compensate for painful feelings in one way or another. For example, some become busy to fill the time, some engage in risky behavior to win acceptance and find excitement, and some passively withdraw into an emotional shell. Talk with your counselor about nonproductive coping styles you may be using that ultimately lead to more isolation.

- Boredom is often a problem when it comes to loneliness. If you are bored, find a new hobby or activity that keeps you busy. If your activity involves being outdoors or in a public place, it will also increase your chance of meeting new people who could become your friends.

4. Build on Positive Relationships

- Take steps to build healthy relationships of trust and respect.

- Identify any healthy, positive relationship in your life—even if it's with an aunt who lives across the country. Think about what makes that relationship positive and pleasant and pursue deepening the relationship even more.

- Allow this good relationship to boost your confidence in your ability to have meaningful friendships. This can encourage you to take steps to find and develop new friends.

5. Get Involved

- Join your church youth group, a Bible study, a service organization or club in your school, or a sports team.

- Volunteer. Volunteering for a community agency is a great way to help others and at the same time engage in meaningful relationships.

- When in a group with other kids, identify the person who looks loneliest and make an effort to befriend that person.

6. Remember How Much God Loves You

- Lonely times can draw you closer to God. He wants His children to depend on Him for everything.

- Ultimately, God is the only One who truly loves us and accepts us unconditionally. His love and grace are endless, and we can enjoy His company all day every day. The problem, of course, is that He is invisible, while people who reject you are flesh and blood. Study the nature of God's grace, His presence in your life, and His tender care for you. You may want to memorize verses that will comfort you when you feel particularly lonely.

- Whether you are happy, sad, lonely, angry, or thrilled, you can share your feelings with God. He's always there for you and with you.

- Enjoy your relationship with God. He will never leave you and never disappoint you (see Heb. 13:5).

BIBLICAL INSIGHTS 6

Turn to me and have mercy, for I am alone and in deep distress. My problems go from bad to worse. Oh, save me from them all! Feel my pain and see my trouble. Forgive all my sins.

Psalm 25:16–18 NLT

When we feel alone, we're in good company. King David felt the same way, and he cried out to God to come to him, forgive him, and free him from his painful feelings.

Where can I go from your Spirit? Where can I flee from your presence? If I go up to the heavens, you are there; if I make my bed in the depths, you are there. If I rise on the wings of the dawn, if I settle on the far side of the sea, even there your hand will guide me, your right hand will hold me fast.

Psalm 139:7–10

In this beautiful psalm, David explains that we are with God all day every day, in all physical and spiritual dimensions. He holds us gently in the palm of His hand.

For we do not have a high priest who is unable to sympathize with our weaknesses, but we have one who has been tempted in every way, just as we are—yet was without sin. Let us then approach the throne of grace with confidence, so that we may receive mercy and find grace to help us in our time of need.

Hebrews 4:15–16

Jesus knows what it feels like to be abandoned, betrayed, and isolated. Whatever difficulties we experience and however awful we feel, Jesus understands because He experienced the same things when He was on earth. For that reason, we can confidently go to Him with our cares and feelings of loneliness.

PRAYER STARTER 7

Lord Jesus, You are a God of the lonely and the forgotten. Today my friend is struggling with feelings of loneliness. Reveal Your kindness and Your presence to her and draw Your child closer to You. Bring godly, encouraging friends into her life and diffuse any drama in their relationships. Use my friend to comfort others who feel lonely too. We thank You, Jesus, that You never leave us or forsake us, and that, in You, we have a best Friend forever . . .

8 RECOMMENDED RESOURCES

Clark, Chap. *Hurt: Inside the World of Today's Teenagers.* Baker Academic, 2004.

Elliot, Elisabeth. *The Path of Loneliness.* Revell, 2007.

Knoke, Derek. *God in MySpace: Answering Questions of Loneliness and Identity.* Destiny Image, 2000.

Lewis, Tracy. *God Is Always There: Past Your Sins and Circumstances.* Tate Publishing, 2000.

Parrott, Les. *Helping the Struggling Adolescent: A Guide to Thirty-six Common Problems for Parents, Counselors, and Youth Workers.* Zondervan, 2000.

Rolheiser, Ronald. *The Restless Heart: Finding Our Spiritual Home in Times of Loneliness.* Random House, 2004.

Wilson, Sandra. *Into Abba's Arms.* Tyndale House, 1998.

DVDs

Luce, Ron. *Lonely Teens and Broken Relationships/Peer Pressure: Making Wise Decisions When It Counts.* Christian Parenting DVD Series, 2009.

Obesity

PORTRAITS : 1

- Barbara had enjoyed sports when she was younger, but when she tried out for the junior high basketball squad, she didn't make the team. She tried to act as though it didn't bother her, but she lost interest in a lot of things she had enjoyed. Instead of playing club sports with some of her friends, she just sat around the house every afternoon and evening. And she ate everything she could get her hands on. Within four months, she had gained thirty pounds.

- Daniel had always been a pudgy kid, but now in high school his weight has ballooned. He is about 6 feet tall and weighs 250 pounds. As soon as he comes home each day, he sits in front of the television playing video games.

- When Robert's parents got a divorce about a year ago, his world came apart. He became deeply depressed and spent most of his time in his room. His only forays into the world of people were trips to the refrigerator, when he would sometimes pass his mother on the way. She nagged him to stop eating so much, but he just shrugged off her comments and downed another bag of cookies and another half gallon of ice cream.

DEFINITIONS AND KEY THOUGHTS : 2

- A child or adolescent is considered obese if his weight is at least *10 percent higher than the recommended weight for his height and body type*. Often the onset of obesity begins in childhood between the ages of five and six, and continues into adolescence. Studies have shown that a child between the ages of ten and thirteen who is obese has an *80 percent chance of becoming an obese adult*.

- Childhood and adolescent obesity in the United States has grown to become an epidemic. Between *16 and 33 percent of children and adolescents are considered obese*.

- Obesity is perhaps the *easiest medical condition to identify* but, because of several factors, it is one of the *most difficult to treat*.

- There are *many different elements of a person's life* that, either alone or in combination, cause obesity. These include genetics, poor eating and health habits, and cultural factors. If one parent is obese, the child has a 50 percent risk of obesity. If both parents are obese, the child has an 80 percent risk.

- *Less than 1 percent of obesity is caused by medical or physical problems.* It is generally caused by:
  — poor eating habits
  — overeating or bingeing
  — lack of exercise
  — family history of obesity
  — stressful life events or changes (separation or divorce of parents, move to a new city, death of loved one, abuse)
  — family and peer problems
  — low self-esteem
  — depression or other emotional problems

- Obesity may also be caused by *medical illnesses* (endocrine, neurological problems) or *medications* (steroids, some psychiatric medications).

- The *risks* associated with obesity include:
  — increased risk of heart disease
  — high blood pressure
  — diabetes
  — breathing problems
  — trouble sleeping
  — increased risk of emotional problems, such as lower self-esteem, depression, anxiety, and obsessive-compulsive disorder[1]

- Obesity has direct *implications in adolescent relationships.* One study reported:
  — *frequent weight-teasing* is reported by 19 percent of average-weight girls and 13 percent of average-weight boys; much higher percentages of overweight girls (45 percent) and overweight boys (50 percent) report that they have been teased frequently about their weight
  — weight teasing in adolescence appears to *affect self-esteem, body satisfaction, and depressive symptoms*[2]

3 ASSESSMENT INTERVIEW

For the Teen

1. Tell me about your weight gain. When did you begin to suspect it may be a problem?
2. How has your weight problem affected your relationships, your interest in activities, your self-esteem, and your health?
3. How do your parents feel about your weight?
4. Have they tried to help? If so, what happened?
5. Tell me about your home life. How do you relate to your parents and your siblings?
6. What are the habits that contribute to your weight problem?

7. Does your weight benefit you in any way? For instance, do certain people or coaches have lower expectations of you now than if you were in good shape?
8. What is your purpose in life? How is your weight blocking your goals?
9. What are your plans for establishing healthy habits?
10. What is your weight goal? How will you get there? What might stop you?
11. How can I help?

For the Parents

1. When did you notice your child had a problem with weight?
2. Is there a family history of this problem?
3. How have you tried to help? What happened?
4. What kinds of foods do you serve the family? What snack foods are available?
5. What kinds of activities—or more specifically, sedentary activities, like hours of video games or television—do you allow in your home each day?
6. What is your role in helping your child lose weight? What is your teen's role?
7. What is your goal for your child's weight? What is your child's goal?
8. What is your plan?
9. How can I help?

> Only 1 out of every 5 young people eats the recommended daily allowance of fruits and vegetables, and only 1 out of 7 teenagers drinks the recommended daily allowance of milk.
>
> *The Centers for Disease Control, 2007.*

WISE COUNSEL : 4

The teen should receive a *thorough physical exam* to rule out any medical cause of the obesity. Many teens and parents try to convince themselves that they can't lose weight because they have "a thyroid problem" or "low metabolism." In most cases, this is simply denial, but only a doctor can tell for sure.

Three key factors determine the *success or failure of a weight-control program: caloric intake, physical activity, and sedentary lifestyle.*

- *Caloric intake.* Simply stated, if a person consumes more calories than are burned, the person gains weight. If the person consumes 3,500 calories more than he burns, he gains one pound. Conversely, if he burns 3,500 calories more than he consumes, he loses a pound. Many of the calories in the typical diet of adolescents, which include sugary soda drinks and fat-laden snacks, are *empty of nutritional value.* Limiting caloric intake is essential and it doesn't mean the person will starve. *Delicious, low-calorie meals and snacks are readily available for anyone willing to use them.*

- *Physical activity.* Adequate physical activity is *essential for physical and emotional health.* Currently only 28 percent of high school students meet currently *recommended levels of physical activity.* Walking, running, working out, or sports activities in school or clubs can provide enough exertion to *tone muscles and burn calories.*

- *Sedentary lifestyle.* Bad habits of sedentary life contribute to obesity because they *keep the person from exercise and make it easy to snack.* One study found that time spent watching TV, videos, DVDs, and movies averaged slightly more than *three hours per day* among children aged 8–18 years.[3]

In the midst of weight loss, it is vital to establish *accountability* to develop healthy eating habits, not just hide behind a "diet." Sometimes the *faulty thinking patterns behind compulsive eating* can be more destructive than the food itself.

Almost every person who tries to lose weight gets *discouraged* at one time or another, and many *gain the weight back* fairly quickly because they *didn't change their lifestyle.* People need to be patient. The first pounds may melt off quickly, but those last ten may take a lot of effort before they disappear. And when a person meets the target weight, it's not time to celebrate with a huge hamburger, fries, and a double shake!

Losing weight isn't an end in itself. As you talk with teens and their parents, help them understand the multiplied *benefits of being physically healthy.* They'll feel better, avoid many weight-related diseases and disorders, think more clearly, and be more productive. They will be much more likely to achieve their dreams if they are physically fit.

Often weight gain results from the use of food as a means of *comfort in the midst of stress.* One of the main stress issues for teens is *low self-esteem.* Every teen, especially teen girls, struggles with low self-esteem to some extent. But *physical appearance should not define a teen's life.* The only sure foundation for identity is the truth of God's Word.

5 ACTION STEPS

1. See a Doctor

- Schedule a complete physical with your family physician to rule out any medical problem that might contribute to obesity.

2. Ask Your Parents for Help

- Ask your parents to help you solve your problem with obesity. If currently they do not have healthy eating and lifestyle habits, your working together may encourage them to change their habits as well.
- Ask your parents to help you research and then pursue good health habits, diet, and lifestyle.

3. Begin a Weight-Management Plan

- A comprehensive weight-management plan may include guidance in:

— changing eating habits (eat slowly; develop a routine)

— planning meals and making better food selections (eat fewer fatty foods; avoid junk and fast foods)

— controlling portions and consuming fewer calories

— increasing physical activity (especially walking) and having a more active lifestyle

— planning what you will eat at school and sticking to your plan

— eating meals with your family instead of while watching television or at the computer

— not using food to reward yourself

— not using food as a way of handling stress or emotion (instead, call a friend or go for a run—but don't eat when you're upset!)

— limiting snacking

— attending a support group, such as Overeaters Anonymous

4. Set a Goal

- Remember: the goal isn't a certain weight but a healthy lifestyle.
- Eat a healthy diet, get regular exercise, and avoid too much sitting around. Include these lifestyle changes and not just weight control in your plan.
- If your lifestyle doesn't change, you will probably resume previous habits after your weight goal has been reached. This will establish the yo-yo effect of weight loss and gain.
- *Advise parents not to nag, make fun of the child, or condemn him when there's a setback. Instead, they should focus on the future, talk about the benefits of being healthy, and take another step forward together.*[4]

BIBLICAL INSIGHTS 6

Like a city whose walls are broken down is a man who lacks self-control.

Proverbs 25:28

Self-control is one of the "fruit of the Spirit" in Paul's letter to the Galatians (5:22–23). In Proverbs, Solomon reminds us that not having self-control makes us vulnerable to all sorts of problems. We can see this very easily in relation to eating habits. The lack of control in this area hurts us physically, emotionally, and relationally.

"Everything is permissible for me"—but not everything is beneficial.
"Everything is permissible for me"—but I will not be mastered by anything.

1 Corinthians 6:12

There is no rigid rule about what we can eat or must not eat, but there are basic principles about what is good and right and healthy. The problem with food is that some of us use it to comfort ourselves instead of trusting God, and others simply slip into bad habits of eating too much and not exercising. When food or anything else dominates our lives, that thing has become our master.

Do you not know that your body is a temple of the Holy Spirit, who is in you, whom you have received from God? You are not your own; you were bought at a price. Therefore honor God with your body.

1 Corinthians 6:19–20

We belong to God, and our bodies are His temple, the place where heaven and earth meet. We need to respect and take care of our bodies so that God can use us in whatever way He wants. We are His, and we are glad.

7 PRAYER STARTER

Father, You care about all the intimate details of our lives—even the food we eat and our weight. I lift up my young friend to You in the struggle to achieve a healthy weight. By the power of Your Spirit, give my friend wisdom to choose healthy eating habits and the discipline to exercise even when he doesn't feel like it. Thank You for the opportunity to glorify You through what we eat and drink . . .

8 RECOMMENDED RESOURCES

Davis, Kara. *Spiritual Secrets to Weight Loss: A 50–Day Renewal of Body, Mind, and Spirit.* Siloam Press, 2008.

Halliday, Judi. *Thin Within.* Thomas Nelson, 2005.

Halliday, Judi, and Joani Jack. *Raising Fit Kids in a Fat World.* Gospel Light, 2008.

Larimore, Walt, and Mike Yorkey. *God's Design for the Highly Healthy Teen.* Zondervan, 2004.

Larimore, Walt, Sherri Flynt, and Steve Halliday. *Super-Sized Kids: How to Rescue Your Child from the Obesity Threat.* Hachette, 2005.

Sears, Barry. *Toxic Fat: When Good Fat Turns Bad.* Thomas Nelson, 2008.

CD

Larimore, Walt, and Nick Yphantides. *Combating Childhood Obesity I-II.* Focus on the Family Radio Broadcast.

Obsessions
and Compulsions

- Jade's parents fought like cats and dogs when she was a child, and they divorced when she was in junior high. When she was very young, she developed the habit of keeping her room very neat, and now she keeps her locker, her backpack, and everything else in perfect order. Her friends have stopped ribbing her about her neatness because she becomes very defensive when they kid her.

- Jeremy thinks about his complexion whenever he's not occupied with something else. Like most adolescents, he has a few pimples, but he spends lots of time in front of the mirror each day examining them, popping them, and worrying about what others think of him. Jeremy's grades are dropping fast, and his teacher has warned him that if he does not improve his concentration and focus, he could be facing a second year in the tenth grade.

- Dan cannot help it. He loves to play basketball. He used to play the occasional game but now, when he gets on the court, he feels as though he can't get off. It's almost as if his mind is paralyzed. Nobody can tell by looking at him, but he's thinking something like this: *If I can't make three shots in a row from the foul line, I am in grave danger for the next three days.* Now Dan cannot get off of the court, afraid that what his mind is telling him will come to pass.

DEFINITIONS AND KEY THOUGHTS 2

- *Obsessions* are intrusive and/or recurring *unwanted thoughts that people can't prevent or control.* They are usually associated with *fears or anxiety.*

- *Compulsions* are *repetitive, impulsive behaviors* that people can't stop doing.

- The *Diagnostic and Statistical Manual of Mental Disorders* IV (DSM-IV) describes Obsessive-Compulsive Disorder:

    A person with obsessive-compulsive disorder has either obsessions or compulsions or both. The obsessions and/or compulsions are strong enough to cause significant distress in their employment, schoolwork, or personal and social relationships.[1]

Obsessions

- Obsessions are defined by:

    1. recurrent and persistent thoughts, impulses, or images that are experienced, at some time during the disturbance, as intrusive and inappropriate and that cause marked anxiety or distress
    2. the thoughts, impulses, or images are not simply excessive worries about real-life problems
    3. the person attempts to ignore or suppress such thoughts, impulses, or images, or to neutralize them with some other thought or action
    4. the person recognizes that the obsessional thoughts, impulses, or images are a product of his or her own mind (not imposed from without as in thought insertion)[2]

Compulsions

- Compulsions are defined by:

    1. repetitive behaviors (e.g., hand washing, ordering, checking) or mental acts (e.g., praying, counting, repeating words silently) that the person feels driven to perform in response to an obsession, or according to rules that must be applied rigidly
    2. the behaviors or mental acts are aimed at preventing or reducing distress or preventing some dreaded event or situation; however, these behaviors or mental acts either are not connected in a realistic way with what they are designed to neutralize or are clearly excessive.[3]

- Some of the *most common compulsions* are:

    — repeatedly checking doors, locks, electrical appliances, or light switches
    — frequent cleaning of hands or clothes
    — strict attempts to keep various personal items in careful order
    — mental activities that are repetitious, such as counting or praying

- Seven million children and adults in the United States suffer from obsessive-compulsive disorder (OCD).
- OCD affects *men and women equally*, and appears to run in families. It is not unusual for *other anxiety disorders*, depression, eating disorders, or substance abuse to accompany OCD. People may avoid situations in which they might have to confront their obsessions or try unsuccessfully to use alcohol or drugs to calm themselves.[4]

3 ASSESSMENT INTERVIEW

1. Is there anything that consumes your thoughts each day? Tell me about that.
2. Are those thoughts connected to something you're afraid of?

3. Are there any behaviors that you often repeat [*you might list some*]?

4. Have you tried to stop them? If you have, what happened?

5. Tell me about your family relationships. In what ways do you feel safe and affirmed, and in what ways do you feel as if others are controlling you? Do you ever find yourself trying to control others in your family?

6. How are your obsessions and compulsions affecting your life—your friendships, your schoolwork, your self-esteem?

7. Would it help you if you could begin to overcome these obsessive thoughts and compulsive behaviors? How would it help?

WISE COUNSEL 4

Some studies show a *connection* between a person's present OCD and *family history*, but this connection doesn't appear to be as strong as that of *persistent family dysfunction that produces considerable anxiety*.

In many cases of OCD, the family has been experiencing *prolonged and pronounced stress*, which produces anxiety in family members. Parents may deal with their own sense of stress by *emotionally or physically abandoning the children*, or they may become rigid and strict, demanding perfection from their children. One child may blow off the parents' demands, but another may *internalize those unrealistic expectations* and develop any number of anxiety-related disorders, including OCD.

In OCD the person *feels out of control and full of self-doubt* about handling the stresses of life. The obsessive thoughts and compulsive behaviors are an attempt to carve out some semblance of stability and order so the sufferer can *feel safe*. Addressing only the behaviors and trying to control them without dealing with the *underlying fears and stresses* is usually unproductive, or at least helpful only for a short time.

Adolescents who struggle with obsessive thoughts and compulsive behaviors need *hope and handles*: hope that their lives can be better and handles on the underlying problem and steps of the solution. The Action Steps below give some ideas about how they can *retrain their minds and recondition their behaviors*.

ACTION STEPS 5

1. Have a Physical Checkup with a Doctor

- A doctor will be able to rule out any underlying medical conditions that may be affecting your obsessive thinking and compulsive actions.

- Because a psychopharmacological approach to OCD treatment has been shown to be highly effective in treating this disorder, a doctor can identify and prescribe a medication regime that can help lessen your symptoms, which will allow you time to begin to learn positive ways of coping.

2. Examine Family History and Family Causes of OCD

- Authorities aren't convinced there is a definite genetic connection in OCD, but there is no doubt that prolonged patterns of stress in a family deeply affect people, but in different ways. OCD is an attempt to create order in a world of disorder. Discuss with your counselor the family dynamics you experience. You may be able to make a connection between the stresses in the family and the anxiety you feel.

3. Understand Your Disorder

- Recognize the triggers that propel OCD thoughts and actions.
- Rituals and perfectionist behaviors promise order and predictability in a disordered world, and to some extent, they work—but at a great price. You have used your entrenched OCD patterns of thought and action to help you feel safe and secure, but they don't resolve the underlying anxiety.
- Begin journaling the moments when rituals and perfectionistic behaviors are most evident in your life. Make two columns. Write down the time of your ritualistic behavior in one column and in the other write down what is going on during that moment. Look for patterns at these times. Is there a particular activity that triggers these behaviors more than others? Are there certain people around? Do the moments happen at the same time of the day or week? Once you are aware of the triggers, you can begin to target them effectively and learn ways to counteract these thoughts.

4. Identify the Underlying Fears and Doubts

- Many, if not all, people who suffer with OCD use their behaviors to keep from having to feel the deep emotions of fear, insecurity, anger, hurt, and self-loathing. Your perfectionism and rituals provide you some sense of stability, and you may not want to give them up. As you make progress, however, you will realize that your OCD patterns are detrimental instead of productive.
- As this realization sets in, be prepared to feel long-repressed emotions. You will need to grieve your losses and rebuild your life.
- You will begin to see yourself progress in your thought processes and actions when you take steps toward change. Changing long-practiced habits is necessary but not easy.

5. Learn Thought Control

- Learn to relax, breathe deeply, and arrest the usual pattern of rituals or perfectionism.
- You have carefully constructed and tightly controlled the world you live in. Now you will need to take small steps in letting go as you gain insight and courage.

- Identify the triggers, as mentioned in step 3, first after they occur, then when they occur, and later before they occur. Your counselor will help you with this.
- Recognizing the triggers will also enable you to address the underlying fears that have caused the OCD pattern.
- Make conscious choices to think different thoughts and respond with different actions.
- To learn to relax, take a class or have your counselor teach you relaxation exercises. Learn to take breaths and use self-talk to help release the anxiety or underlying fear you have that leads to your OCD behavior. Pull out the piece of paper with a positive quote or Bible verse that will help you learn the truth about what's taking place. Remind yourself of this truth often.

20–40% of all adolescents with eating disorders will also have obsessive-compulsive disorder.

National Mental Health Association

6. Develop New Habits of Spontaneity

- Try to loosen up, be more spontaneous, and enjoy life more.
- There will be times along the way when you will want to cling to your obsessive-compulsive responses. In the past they have helped you be calm, self-soothe, and feel secure. Security is crucial for every person, and letting go of the perceived security of OCD requires persistence and patience to create new patterns of living.

BIBLICAL INSIGHTS 6

Do not be anxious about anything, but in everything, by prayer and petition, with thanksgiving, present your requests to God. And the peace of God, which transcends all understanding, will guard your hearts and your minds in Christ Jesus.

Philippians 4:6–7

Anxiety is at the root of OCD behavior. In these verses in Philippians, Paul invites us to be honest about our fears, trust God with them, spell them out to Him in prayer, and thank God for His wisdom, love, and purpose for our lives. People who struggle with OCD haven't experienced much peace, but God's peace will be theirs as they trust Him.

Therefore I tell you, do not worry about your life, what you will eat or drink; or about your body, what you will wear. Is not life more important than food, and the body more important than clothes? Look at the birds of the air; they do not sow or reap or store away in barns, and yet your heavenly Father feeds them. Are you not much more valuable than they? . . . So do not worry, saying, "What shall we eat?" or "What shall we drink?" or "What shall we wear?" For the pagans run after all these things, and your heavenly Father knows that you need them. But seek first his kingdom and his righteousness, and all these things will be given to you as well.

Matthew 6:25–26, 31–33

God is interested and involved in every aspect of our lives, and we can trust Him to protect, guide, and provide. Anxiety robs us of peace and enflames our doubts, but trusting in God's goodness and strength gives us peace and hope.

So do not fear, for I am with you; do not be dismayed, for I am your God. I will strengthen you and help you; I will uphold you with my righteous right hand.

Isaiah 41:10

God doesn't care about us from a long way off. He is as near as our breath and He supports us with His powerful hand. We can trust Him because He understands, He cares, and He is able to provide.

There is no fear in love. But perfect love drives out fear, because fear has to do with punishment. The one who fears is not made perfect in love.

1 John 4:18

Anxiety and fear thrive in times of insecurity, but God's love gives us confidence that He has wonderful plans for our lives.

7 PRAYER STARTER

Lord Jesus, You are the king and leader of our lives. I pray for my young friend as she struggles with the need to control her environment to feel safe. Surround my friend with the assurance of Your love that is not dependent on what we do or don't do. Free this teen from any bondage to empty rules, rituals, or habits. Give us wisdom in walking through this process, and teach my friend how to live in freedom. Help her give You the control of her life—even the little details . . .

8 RECOMMENDED RESOURCES

Collie, Robert. *Obsessive-Compulsive Disorder: A Guide for Family, Friends, and Pastors.* The Haworth Press, 2005.

Crawford, Mark. *The Obsessive-Compulsive Trap: Real Help for a Real Disorder.* Regal Books, 2004.

Emlet, Michael R. *OCD: Freedom for the Obsessive-Compulsive.* Resources for Changing Lives, 2004.

Osborn, Ian. *Can Christianity Cure Obsessive-Compulsive Disorder?* Brazos Press, 2007.

Peurifoy, Reneau. *Anxiety, Phobias, and Panic.* Revised ed. Hachette, 2005.

Parent-Adolescent Relationships

PORTRAITS 1

- Jaclyn's parents didn't seem to know what to do with her. As soon as she began puberty and developed physically, her father stopped hugging her and her mother saw her as somewhat of a threat. Both had been very affectionate during her early childhood, but when she reached adolescence, they began to treat her like an outsider.

- When Warren's family moved to a new city, he soon got involved with a group of friends in the sophomore class. At first, his parents were thrilled that he had connected with friends so quickly, but soon they discovered they didn't have the same influence over him that they had in the past. Within weeks Warren's disposition changed. He became distant and occasionally defiant and angry, and instead of joining in the long conversations around the dinner table they used to have as a family each night, he found excuses to avoid his parents.

- Luci seemed to be traumatized by high school. She had always been a sweet, gentle, and very compliant child. After only a few weeks as a freshman, she seemed to be depressed but didn't know how to express what she was feeling. Her mom and dad tried to get her to talk, but she always told them, "I'm fine."

DEFINITIONS AND KEY THOUGHTS 2

- *Adolescence*, a life stage defined by *transition*, is one of the most *challenging* in a person's life.

- *Adolescence* is a stage of development prior to maturity. Erik Erikson refers to adolescence as *a time of role identity versus role confusion* whereby a teenager is trying to determine who he is and how he fits into the broader world around him.

- Adolescence is a season of life, loosely defined as *between the ages of twelve and eighteen*, accompanied by *changes in physical growth, puberty, and personality development*, when a teenager is consistently and silently asking the question *How am I doing?* in everything he does. The answer the teenager receives from those around him can impact what he believes about himself and how he performs in school and relates to those around him.

- In the teen years, a child's *brain* shifts from having a concrete understanding of the world to being able to entertain an abstract, more complex conceptualization.

197

- The teen *sees the realities of life*, is forced to *create a new sense of identity*, learns to respond to a *wide array of agendas*, and begins to make *important decisions* that will affect the rest of his life.

- In this process, teens are seeking to develop a *healthy independence*, sometimes called "*individuation*," from their parents. If parents understand what's going on in their child's life, they can facilitate the process and be the child's biggest cheerleader. But if the parents feel threatened by their necessary lessened control over their child and they react by demanding compliance, smothering the child with attention and directions or withdrawing in hopelessness, a child can feel cut off from the most important support system he has.

- Parents need to grasp the fact that adolescence today is a *radically different phase* in their child's life than it was for them. Therefore they need the *skills and virtues necessary to navigate* successfully the demands of parenthood during this time. Virtues like *patience, understanding, trust, and authenticity* are important in getting their teen to listen and trust them. Skills needed to help build a strong foundation include *listening, conflict resolution, and communication*. The Golden Rule of understanding is crucial: for your teen to understand you, you first must understand your teen.

- In spite of adolescents' need and desire to discover an identity that is separate from their parents, they still look to their parents as *role models* and as *sources of encouragement and direction.*

- In blended families, adolescents are *more positive about their biological parents* than they are about their stepparents. For example, the proportion of teens aged fourteen to fifteen who agreed or strongly agreed that they think highly of their father was 82 percent for biological fathers, compared with 67 percent for stepfathers. Similar differences were found for positive youth relationships with biological mothers compared with stepmothers.

- The profound and *positive impact of good parenting* during adolescent years— treating teens with love and respect and gradually turning more responsibility for choices over to them—results in positive outcomes for teens across different ethnic groups, regions, and nationalities. These teens perform better in academics and in relationships with peers and other adults besides their parents. They exhibit *fewer problem behaviors*, including violence, delinquency, alcohol and drug use, tobacco use, premarital sex, gang involvement, and mental and social disorders.

- Studies show that *strong, loving, supportive parent-adolescent relationships have dramatic effects on people as they enter adult relationships and responsibilities*, such as lower levels of stress and higher quality of mental health, overall physical health, and higher quality of self-esteem, happiness, and confidence.

- Teens who regularly eat meals with their parents have *higher levels of literacy and academic achievement*, which are predictors of future success. Similarly, teens who *discuss social issues and politics* with their parents also show *higher levels of academic success.*[1]

- Adolescents who engage in *high levels of physical exercise*, like running, biking, weightlifting, aerobics, and basketball, have better relationships with their parents than those who exercise little or not at all. They also enjoy *higher levels of intimacy and family support.*[2]

ASSESSMENT INTERVIEW : 3

For the Teen

1. Tell me about your relationship with your mother and with your father [or with your stepparent].
2. How do you feel when you are around them? How do they feel when they are around you? How can you tell?
3. When did you relate to them most positively? What was going on during that time?
4. In your view, what has changed?
5. It's normal for adolescents to want to make more of their own decisions. How have you expressed this desire to your parents? How have they responded?
6. In what ways do you feel that you have done enough to earn their trust? In what ways is it understandable that they may not trust you completely?
7. What would it take for trust to be built or rebuilt between you and your parents [stepparent]?
8. What do you want your relationship with them to become? What can you do to take steps toward this kind of relationship?

For the Parents

1. Tell me about your relationship with your teen.
2. How do you feel when you are with your teen? How does your teen feel? How can you tell?
3. Describe a time when your relationship was most pleasant and positive. What was going on in the family at that time?
4. In your view, what has changed?
5. It's normal for an adolescent to develop his own sense of identity that is separate from his parents. How can you help to guide that process?
6. Are you afraid of what might happen to your child during this process? Explain the reasons you are or are not afraid.
7. What would you like your relationship to become?
8. What steps can you take toward this kind of relationship? What will build or rebuild trust?

WISE COUNSEL : 4

Psychologist Erik Erikson observed *eight stages* in a person's development from birth to old age. He identifies the fifth stage, *the stage of adolescence, as the most crucial to a person's future.* It is a time when he moves out of the dependency of childhood and must prepare himself for the *interdependency needed for successful adulthood*. During this time, which is by definition a time of great isolation and incongruity, the teen must discover who he is (*identity*), what gifts and uniqueness he has (*autonomy*), and how to find an adult community that wants them (*belonging*). These three key tasks of the process of becoming a unique individual (*individuation*)—identity, autonomy, and belonging—are what *motivate the entire adolescent journey*.

During the process of adolescence, from age twelve to as late as the midtwenties, parents need to expand their child's "sandbox" of responsibility so that *the child gradually gains confidence to make his own choices* and becomes a successful young adult. During the child's early years, parents have protected the child and given firm and clear directives about virtually every aspect of life, but even during these childhood years there *must be opportunities for the child to explore his own sense of voice and person*. As the child grows from childhood through adolescence, parents need to allow the child to make more *choices*.

Learning how to own one's own choices earns an increasing size of the sandbox, so to speak, meaning that more and more *trust is being built* in the relationship and the parent can therefore give *more responsibility and leeway* to the teenager; repeated or severely irresponsible choices, however, reduce the size of the sandbox because the parent cannot trust the teenager with any more freedom until he demonstrates that he both understands and can handle increased responsibility. The *issues in the sandbox* are many and varied, including respect for others, awareness of consequences for one's actions, academics, participating in family work and life, television and media time and choices, and use of money.

In any endeavor, giving increased responsibility almost always involves a growth curve of *confidence and success*. Parents of teens need to stay involved, expanding and clarifying the sandbox, enjoying being together, and celebrating successes. But like parents, every teen is going to fail from time to time. Parents need to *distinguish between a failure and intentional distancing or even defiance*.

During adolescence there are many *conflicting* agendas, expectations, desires and longings, and adolescents need to know that *their parents are stable enough to be compassionate, understanding, and fair*.

5 ACTION STEPS

For the Teen

1. Know That Your Parents Love You

- Whenever your parents set boundaries or curfews or they discipline you for something that seems really dumb to you, know that they really do have your best interests in mind. Sometimes their actions may not make sense to you, but give them grace. They really do love you.

2. Help Your Parents Understand You

- Whether you realize it or not, parenting teenagers is one of the toughest jobs in the world, and many parents have a very hard time understanding or connecting with their teens. But deep down that's what they really long for—a relationship with you. Though you don't have to share your deepest, darkest secrets with your parents, make it a point to start sharing parts of your day with them, things you liked or disliked, people you interacted with, and perhaps concerns you have about school, family, or friends. You may find that your parents have some wisdom that can help you.

3. Do Something Every So Often to Honor Your Parents

- The Bible says that we are to honor our parents. Every few weeks do something for them to show your love for them. Wash the car, clean the house, make dinner, or schedule a lunch date or a day together hiking, shopping, or going to the movies.
- Make a card expressing your appreciation to them. Be creative with it. The Bible says we reap what we sow. When you honor your parents, you in turn will be blessed.

4. Find a Godly Adult Mentor

- If you have a difficult relationship with your parents or are split up from them due to divorce or separation, it's important to find a mature adult who can walk with you through life's difficulties and guide you spiritually in your relationship with God and others.
- We all need older, wiser people who can have an influence on our lives and help us with choices, decisions, and interpreting our experiences. Find a godly person you can trust, like a youth pastor, teacher, or grandparent, and ask him to be a mentor in your life.

5. Seek God's Guidance

- Building a relationship with our parents doesn't happen overnight. In fact some teenagers and parents have grown so far apart that even thinking about developing a better relationship is not easily done. Seek God's guidance as you reach out to honor your parents.

For the Parents

1. Remember Your Adolescent Years

- Parents may have more understanding and compassion for their teen children if they take some time to reflect on the challenges they faced during their adolescent years. Today's stresses and struggles are exponentially more difficult than in the world parents grew up in. Become familiar with the world of your adolescent and try to understand the challenges he faces.

> Teenagers are people who act like babies if they're not treated like adults.
>
> MAD *magazine*

> Adolescents are not monsters. They are just people trying to learn how to make it among the adults in the world, who are probably not so sure themselves.
>
> *Virginia Satir, The New Peoplemaking, 1988*

2. Understand the Stage of Adolescence

- The goal for a child in adolescence is to create a strong, healthy sense of identity that is separate from his parents' identity. This is the way children become adults. Remember the purpose of this stage so you don't react to every change in your growing child by clamping on the controls even tighter or giving up in despair.
- Teenagers are constantly striving to find where they fit in this world. Every teenager at this stage of life is asking the question, "How am I doing?" And whether you know it or not, you as a parent are answering that question every day by the words you speak to him.
- To understand more about this stage of development, learn to listen to your teen. Try to appreciate the challenges he faces and get to know who his friends are. As you begin to engage his world, be observant and humble and keep an open mind.

3. Allow Your Teen to Have More Responsibility

- You need to have a clear plan for gradually turning over more responsibility and decision making to your maturing teen.
- You will probably need help in knowing how to do this. A counselor or a trusted friend who has grown children can offer expert advice.
- Include your teens in the discussion and listen to what they have to say.

4. Discipline Seldom—Celebrate Often

- Children become successful, confident, competent adults as they are increasingly treated like adults. As your teen matures, he will be more likely to follow your discipline principles if he has helped define them.
- Celebrate often your teen's successes. Your teen feels tremendous fear of the future and he needs a lot of love and reinforcement.
- When you must impose discipline for defiance, it should be targeted and dispassionate. Be sure to provide a way of rebuilding damaged trust as well.

5. Treat Your Child Like an Adult

- In the vast majority of cases, people become what they are expected to become. When you treat your teen with increasing respect and trust, he will thrive.
- When you show your teen that you trust him, which he desperately needs to know, he will develop confidence.

6. Seek God's Guidance

- Deuteronomy 6:5–9 says:

    Love the LORD your God with all your heart and with all your soul and with all your strength. These commandments that I give you today are to be upon your hearts. Impress them on your children. Talk about them when you sit at home and when you walk along the road, when you lie down and when you get up. Tie them as symbols on your hands and bind them on your foreheads. Write them on the doorframes of your houses and on your gates.

- Though living by His commands is not always easy for us, God does promise to help us when we ask. Make it a point to begin praying every day with your spouse about your relationship with your teenager. In addition, ask your child to pray with you. Seeking God's guidance with your teenager models to him your dependence on God.

BIBLICAL INSIGHTS 6

Fathers, do not exasperate your children; instead, bring them up in the training and instruction of the Lord.

Ephesians 6:4

Parents exasperate their kids by being too harsh, too controlling, or uninvolved. Instead, they need to be involved, equipping their kids with skills and confidence to take on more responsibility. When emotions run high in a parent-child conflict, the parent must take the lead to reduce the tension.

Fix these words of mine in your hearts and minds; tie them as symbols on your hands and bind them on your foreheads. Teach them to your children, talking about them when you sit at home and when you walk along the road, when you lie down and when you get up.

Deuteronomy 11:18–19

This Deuteronomy passage is one of the most misinterpreted texts in Scripture. The *your* is plural, meaning that it is the entire community's responsibility to teach children. Parents, of course, have the great privilege of imparting character and wisdom to their kids—and they're watching like hawks! But it is all the adults within the community who are called to collectively impart the faith to all the children.

Honor your father and your mother, so that you may live long in the land the LORD *your God is giving you.*

Exodus 20:12

Every teen should give respect, love, and obedience to his parents. It is a biblical mandate to honor our parents for bringing us into the world and raising us as teenagers. Though some teens have grown up with either abusive or otherwise bad parents who were not worthy of the honor due them, God tells us to walk above reproach and honor them anyway. When we do, God promises that ultimately we will be blessed.

7 : PRAYER STARTER

Lord Jesus, I thank You today for these parents [and this teen], and for their desire to strengthen their relationship. Give these parents wisdom in supporting, guiding, correcting, and listening to their teenager. Give this teen patience and grace to be open about what he is feeling and experiencing. Conflict is part of any relationship, but Jesus, You are bigger than our frustrations and misunderstandings. Shower the relationship of the parents and their child with Your grace and mercy, and show them how to build a healthy, respectful, trusting bond . . .

8 : RECOMMENDED RESOURCES

Clark, Chap, and Dee Clark. *Disconnected: Parenting Teens in a MySpace World.* Baker Books, 2007.

Cline, Foster, and Jim Fay. *Parenting with Love and Logic.* NavPress, 2006.

Gage, Rodney. *We Can Work It Out: Creative Conflict Resolution with Your Teen.* B&H Publishing Group, 2002.

Smalley, Gary, and Greg Smalley. *The DNA of Parent-Teen Relationships: How to Forge a Strong and Lasting Bond with Your Teen.* Tyndale House, 2005.

Townsend, John. *Boundaries with Teens: When to Say Yes, When to Say No.* Zondervan, 2007.

White, Joe, and Jim Weidmann. *Parent's Guide to Spiritual Mentoring of Teens.* Tyndale House, 2001.

Parents' Divorce

- Karen's parents finally got a divorce when she was a sophomore in high school. For years they had fought almost every day. Her dad was very controlling, demanding that her mom report her every move. When they split up, Karen thought her life would finally be free of the drama, but she found that she was angry with her mom for giving up on the marriage.

- Luke was shocked when his father announced that he was leaving. He thought his parents loved each other. His dad is a successful businessman who travels a lot. For the past two years, he has been having an affair with a woman in another city. Luke feels that his whole world has collapsed. He doesn't think he can trust anybody any more.

- Rebecca's parents divorced just last year, a month before her fourteenth birthday party. Though her parents said they were going to try to work things out, the day after her party, her dad moved three hundred miles away to live with another woman. Confused and feeling as if he has left her too, she battles with mixed feelings of anger and sorrow, hating her dad for leaving her and her mom and missing the wonderful times they shared together.

DEFINITIONS AND KEY THOUGHTS 2

- The Centers for Disease Control states:

  Virtually all children of divorce spend some time in a single-parent household until the mother remarries. Even when the mother does remarry, studies suggest that children in stepfamilies have similar risks of adverse outcomes as children in single-parent families: both groups of children do worse than children living with two biological parents in terms of academic achievement, depression, and behavior problems such as drug and alcohol abuse, premarital sexual intercourse, and being arrested.[1]

- *Children of divorced parents are at risk to:*

  — drop out of high school
  — have lower grades and attendance in school
  — fail to graduate from college
  — fail to graduate from high school

— experience unemployment or underemployment
— become single parents
— suffer from social incompetence
— experience long-term health problems[2]

- Children and teens in a *single-parent home* experience *higher levels of anxiety, emotional problems, and hyperactivity disorders.*[3]

- Approximately 20 percent of parents who divorce continue to experience high levels of conflict. Their continued fighting causes the children to suffer:

— tension, anxiety, and regression
— feelings of confusion and embarrassment
— feelings of responsibility and self-blame
— withdrawal or clinging behavior at transitions
— long-term emotional and behavioral wounds
— feelings of disillusionment, fear, insecurity, or vulnerability
— temper tantrums, school problems, or self-destructive behaviors[4]

3 ASSESSMENT INTERVIEW

For the Teen

1. When and under what circumstances did your parents divorce?
2. How would you describe their relationship in the years before they divorced?
3. How would you describe it now?
4. How did you initially feel and respond when you heard they were getting a divorce?
5. How has the divorce changed your relationship with each of them?
6. Has it changed your relationship with your siblings?
7. How has it affected your life (where you live, your financial stability, your emotional health, and so on)?
8. How would you describe what you've lost because of the divorce? What do you miss? What do you wish you had back?

For the Parent

1. When and under what circumstances did you and your spouse divorce?
2. How would you describe your relationship with your spouse in the years before the divorce?
3. How would you describe it now?
4. How have the separation and divorce affected you and your ability to be the parent you want to be?
5. How have the separation and divorce affected your child?
6. Did you remarry? If so, how do your child and your spouse relate to one another? How do the stepchildren get along? How would you describe the level of harmony or tension in the stepfamily?

7. How have you tried to help your child through this difficult time? How effective were your efforts?
8. How would you describe your child's difficulties today related to the divorce and any conflict between you and your former spouse?
9. What do you hope for your teen?
10. How can I help?

WISE COUNSEL : 4

When a teenager is put into a new environment and asked to begin a relationship with a new parent, either a stepfather or stepmother she did not choose, *mixed emotions* will result.

A teenager who has difficulty accepting influence from or trusting her biological parent will probably find the presence of a total stranger in her life totally unwanted and unacceptable. Understand, as the counselor, that *every teenager is different and that the emotions they experience will vary based on the gender, age, personality, and quality of relationship* they currently have with their biological parents. For example, a teenage girl who trusts her biological mother a lot may have no problem trusting a stepfather if she sees that her mom trusts him. It is important to consider all the factors before making any assumptions in counseling the teen.

Adjustments Take Time

A teen who is entering a new situation needs to understand that her parents' divorce is *not* her fault and getting used to a new adult in her life will take time. *Trust is never built overnight.*

If the teen wants her new stepparent to understand her and get to know her, *the teenager must help the stepparent* in this process, as well as make an effort to get to know the stepparent.

Help the teenager understand that though the divorce is not her fault, and the new situation is not necessarily something she asked for or wanted, *cooperation and respect* are required of everybody involved.

The Family's Loss

Quite often parents who get divorced become *preoccupied with their own pain, anger, and financial problems,* and the children feel as though they *must cope on their own.* There may have been years of open hostility in the family, or the decision to divorce may have been announced unexpectedly. However it happened, children and teens feel devastated because *the stability of their world has come to an end.* Undoubtedly they feel many different emotions, and their assignment of blame may change from day to day. Parents shouldn't demand that their kids make it on their own. Instead, they need to *have compassion for their sense of loss.*

Parents who endure separation and divorce need to be *honest about their own hurts and hopes,* and then they can provide an environment for their children and

Divorce and the decline of the two-parent, married-couple family result in poverty, poor health, problems for children in school, despair, risky and anti-social behavior, isolation, and social exclusion for thousands of women, men, and children.

Rebecca O'Neill, "Experiments in Living," 2002

teens to be *honest about their emotions*. Parents need to brace themselves when their children express *anger*, perhaps at them, for the divorce and all the damage caused by it. They should avoid quick emotional fixes or anger with the teen for being honest, and they must *listen, ask questions, and invite the teen to explain and share her feelings. Emotional honesty* is the beginning of healing.

> Adolescents benefit when both parents (custodial and non-custodial) remain involved with them in positive ways during and after the divorce. Both adolescents and younger children cope with divorce more effectively when parents can put their own relationship differences aside, keep conflicts to a minimum, and agree on policies and strategies for dealing with the young.[5]

Blended Families

Remarriage and blended families are a real challenge for everyone involved. It can be difficult to show *respect, love, understanding, and patience* with new siblings and a stepparent. Too often these families are full of *unresolved hurt and anger*, and these *painful emotions get more intense* with each new perceived and real offense.

Parents need to face the complexity of the new family relationships and the risk of adding more pain to each person. With *honesty, patience, empathy, and respect*, each person can experience peace, gratitude, and joy.

The adolescent years are full of risks and threats to the *teen's sense of identity*, and when family disruption is thrown into the mix, it can be explosive. Despite what is happening in the parent's life, he or she needs to invest plenty of time and energy in *affirming the teen*, focusing on strengths and the future, and providing assurance that the child is loved and accepted.

5 ACTION STEPS

For the Teen

1. Be Honest

- No matter how the divorce happened, no matter who is to blame, and no matter what the current situation may be, be honest about your feelings.

- Bottling up your feelings or denying the reality of the pain will cause emotional disaster for you—either an explosion of anger or an implosion of depression and despair. Though being honest and expressing what you're feeling now may be difficult to do, it's essential for you to begin to process the emotions you have about the situation and those involved. Being honest now can bring about forgiveness, reconciliation, and even understanding to a situation that otherwise is confusing. When we express our feelings honestly, it can prevent bitterness, rage, and resentment from brewing inside.

2. Ask for Peace

- If you are living with the pressure of divorced parents who are continuing to quarrel, ask if you can sit down with them and express the hurt they are causing you. Be respectful and let each parent know you love him or her.

- Ask your parents to call a truce on any hurtful behavior. At the very least, parents should maintain peaceful interaction when children are visiting.

3. Talk to God about the Way You Feel

- God says in Malachi 2:16 that He hates divorce. The reason He hates divorce is because He knows that it tears apart families and relationships. He understands what you are going through right now. He understands what it's like to feel forsaken, abandoned, and alone because He went through it when He died on the cross. He cried, "My God, my God, why have you forsaken me?" (Matt. 27:46). In the Greek text, the word *forsaken* literally means that Jesus felt abandoned by His Father, yet He called out to Him in His pain. He asks us to do the same.

4. Grieve

- When our parents divorce, we lose not only the security of what we had but the future we expected. Family get-togethers and celebrating important occasions, such as holidays and even our wedding, won't be the same. It is important to grieve these losses and enlist the support of friends, grandparents, and other loved ones.

5. Find a Trusted Friend or Mentor

- Find somebody you can trust who can walk through your parents' divorce with you. It could be a youth pastor, a friend who has also been through a similar situation, or another trusted adult in whom you could confide.

- Surround yourself with positive social support.

For the Parent

1. Make Your Teen a Priority

- Divorced parents, and especially those who are dating or remarried, quite often suffer from a host of compounded worries: relational, emotional, physical, financial, and spiritual. The natural tendency is to become self-absorbed at a time when your children need your help processing their own heartache and confusion. Carve out time to spend with your teen (even though she may be as prickly as a porcupine) to talk about her life, hopes, struggles, ambitions, and relationships.

2. Keep the Peace

- Often parents get caught in the "heat of the battle" without even thinking about the consequences the conflict has on their children, who are usually nearby

- Each year, more than 1.5 million children in the U.S. experience their parents' divorce.
- Approximately half of children will see their parents divorce before the children turn 18.
- Only 42% of teenagers live in a "first marriage" family—a home in which their two biological parents are still married.

http://www.heritage.org/research/family/bg1373.cfm

watching. Avoid arguing, blame casting, and overreacting, especially in the presence of the children. This can cause even more confusion and feelings of insecurity for them.

- You must understand the importance of keeping the peace for the sake of the emotional safety of your children.

3. Be Patient about Making New Relationships Work

- Parents in stepfamilies almost always feel caught in a triangle between their children and the new spouse. They want to please everyone, but sooner or later they realize this is impossible. If you choose to please your new spouse, your children feel abandoned again. But if you choose to please your children, you run the risk of another devastating divorce. Be honest with your spouse about how you need to support your children and help them deal with the changes in their lives and invite feedback on how you are doing.

- You may want to show love to your children and stepchildren equally, but your children may feel offended if you show equal attention to the stepsiblings. It's a tangled web requiring a delicate balance, but it's best to wade in, be honest about what you want to accomplish, and invite honest feedback.

- Realize that suffering people are far more easily hurt than strong, stable people, and everyone in the family is probably suffering—at least at the beginning of the new arrangement. Be patient with each one and try to understand how each member of the family is struggling.

4. Help Your Teen Grieve, Learn, and Move On

- Seldom does divorce provide the joy and freedom spouses expect, though it may give some temporary relief. Be aware that your teen is suffering just as much as you are, and she is at a vulnerable time in her development.

- Enlist the help of grandparents and other caregivers to show your teen compassion and acknowledge her sense of loss, which will allow her to grieve.

- Make this a time of teaching your teen important lessons about marriage, commitment, resolving conflict, and love. These lessons are hard-won in the context of a divorce, but they provide a wonderful platform for the teen to make good choices later in life.

5. Forgive Your Former Spouse

- The Bible says, "Love covers over a multitude of sins" (1 Peter 4:8), and in cases of divorce, there are plenty of hurts and wrongdoings that need God's love and forgiveness. Each spouse is, to some degree, both victim and sinner. Refusing to forgive keeps a person locked into the bitter spiral of despair and resentment and can have negative effects on the teenager and the way she relates to you and your former spouse.

- Remember, your former spouse is your child's dad or mom. Though your relationship with your former spouse may be broken, she is still your teenager's parent. To help your teen cope with the divorce, you must be an agent of healing to help her walk through the life changes in a healthy way. Demeaning or badgering your former spouse in front of your teen is not healthy. Working toward a healthy resolution with her is, and could be the difference between whether your teenager grows bitter or finds peace and reconciliation with you and the situation despite the circumstances.

- To prevent a destructive process, you need to give your teen a wealth of love and support, offering genuine affirmations, spending plenty of quality time with her, and listening, really listening, to her heart.

6. Seek God's Guidance

- In Matthew 6:33 Jesus says, "Seek first [God's] kingdom and his righteousness, and all these things will be given to you as well." When we seek God's guidance and obey Him, He promises to come through and help us in the midst of our circumstances.

- God promises that "everyone who *asks* receives; he who *seeks* finds; and to him who *knocks*, the door will be opened" (Matt. 7:8, emphasis added). Though this doesn't mean that relationships will magically be restored and all will be well, it does mean that God hears our heart and is working on our behalf.

BIBLICAL INSIGHTS 6

Who shall separate us from the love of Christ? Shall trouble or hardship or persecution or famine or nakedness or danger or sword? . . . in all these things we are more than conquerors through him who loved us. For I am convinced that neither death nor life, neither angels nor demons, neither the present nor the future, nor any powers, neither height nor depth, nor anything else in all creation, will be able to separate us from the love of God that is in Christ Jesus our Lord.

Romans 8:35, 37–39

When everything in our life seems to be coming unraveled, there is one thing we can absolutely count on: God's undying love for us. Teens and their parents need to think often about God's love and forgiveness during troubled times.

Though my father and mother forsake me, the Lord will receive me. . . . I am still confident of this: I will see the goodness of the Lord in the land of the living. Wait for the Lord; be strong and take heart and wait for the Lord.

Psalm 27:10, 13–14

When divorce happens, teens naturally want to assign blame. First, they may be angry at one parent, then later at the other—or at a person who had an affair with one of the parents or maybe at herself for somehow causing the conflict. Assigning blame may have some value as we grieve, but ultimately we need to turn to and depend on God's love, wisdom, and purpose for our lives.

How great is the love the Father has lavished on us, that we should be called children of God! And that is what we are!

1 John 3:1

Even when teens feel that their parents have abandoned them, they can be confident in God's constant faithfulness and compassion.

When I am afraid, I will trust in you. In God, whose word I praise, in God I trust; I will not be afraid.

Psalm 56:3–4

Trust isn't the absence of fear; it is confidence in God in the face of our fears. God never asks us to lie about how we feel. We can be completely honest with Him about our deepest emotions and trust Him for wisdom and direction.

7 PRAYER STARTER

Heavenly Father, we are Your children, and You will never leave us or forsake us. As my young friend struggles with the divorce of her parents, I pray that You will make Your presence very real and reassure her of how big Your love is. Teach her to run to You and be honest with You when she is upset instead of becoming bitter or angry. Jesus, You promise to take care of us. Thank You that nothing—not even divorce—can separate us from You . . .

8 RECOMMENDED RESOURCES

Burgen, Jim. *What's the Big Deal?: About My Parents*. Standard, 2001.

Butterworth, Jesse. *Six String Rocketeer: Holding Life Together When Your Parents Spilt Apart*. Random House, 2005.

Chase, Emily Parke. *Help! My Family's Messed Up*. Kregel, 2008.

Hart, Archibald D. *Helping Children Survive Divorce: What to Expect, How to Help*. Thomas Nelson, 1997.

Hill, Kim, and Lisa Harper. *Hope No Matter What: Helping Your Children Heal after Divorce*. Regal, 2008.

CDs

Butterworth, Jesse. *Surviving Your Parents' Divorce*. Focus on the Family Radio Broadcast.

Hart, Archibald D. *Children of Divorce: Hope and Healing I-II*. Focus on the Family Radio Broadcast.

Peer Pressure

PORTRAITS : 1

- Edward had been a model child—kind, responsible, and relatively successful in school and sports. His parents were thrilled when he got into the church's youth group. A few months later Edward and four others were arrested. After youth group one Sunday night, they broke into a warehouse and stole some things. "It was kind of an initiation," Edward told his parents.

- Anne had always been an attractive girl with lots of friends. She began dating Bill, one of the star players on the basketball team, and they began staying out later and later on weekends. Her mom talked to her openly about the dangers of premarital sex. Anne insisted that her mom had nothing to worry about, but a few weeks later, her mom found spermicide hidden behind the toilet paper in her bathroom closet. When she confronted her daughter, Anne exploded, "Do you think Bill would date me if I didn't have sex with him?" she yelled.

- Ivan just wanted to fit in. In high school he had a hard time finding a group of friends. After a while he became desperate and was willing to do anything to be accepted. He began drinking and smoking weed with a bunch of loners who had banded together, and before long he was thinking about using the coke some of them had bought. He felt as if he needed to keep up or he'd be left behind—again.

DEFINITIONS AND KEY THOUGHTS : 2

- *Peer pressure* is social pressure on somebody to adopt a type of behavior, dress, or attitude so that the person will be accepted as part of a group. It is the *way of life in junior high* and, while not having the same power it used to have, is still *a continual pull for most kids in high school*.

- Students *can't avoid it* but they can *learn to identify it, resist it, form more healthy alliances* (positive peer pressure), and navigate their way through it toward healthy adulthood.

- A study of the *differences in resistance* to peer pressure at different ages showed the following:

- Being observed by peers during risk taking *doubled the amount of risky behavior* among *middle adolescents*, increased it by 50 percent among *college undergraduates*, and had no impact at all among adults.
- In mid-adolescence the susceptibility to peer pressure is most consistently seen in *antisocial behavior*, such as cheating, stealing, or trespassing, and this is especially true among boys.
- In early adolescence teens have not yet established their own sense of identity, so they are *less able to resist peer pressure*. During this time, they express the desire for emotional autonomy most strongly, which ironically makes them more vulnerable to peer pressure.
- In late adolescence, *teens have developed more of their sense of identity*, which enables them to resist the real or perceived demands of their friends.[1]

• In sexual behavior among teens, 24 percent report engaging in *sexual acts* that they really did not want to do—*pressured more often by their partner* than their friends. Teens may also feel that they need to become sexually active to *demonstrate their love and commitment*.

• Today young people feel tremendous *pressure to look sexy* and be sexual, which leads not only to *sexual behaviors* but also to *underage drinking and drug use*.

• The *more time a girl spends with her boyfriend*, the more likely she is to use alcohol and drugs. Substance abuse increases the incidence of *unprotected sex*, which can lead to *sexually transmitted diseases*.

• Adolescents who are sexually experienced are *more likely to engage in delinquency*. When teenage girls engage in violence against other girls, they are often fighting over boys, to protect their status in the peer community as an attractive, desirable person.[2]

3 ASSESSMENT INTERVIEW

For the Teen

1. Tell me why you came to see me today. Do you perceive that you have a problem, or do your parents think you have a problem?
2. How would you describe your relationships with your friends? How do you help each other? What are some ways you have a positive impact on each other?
3. Every relationship has positives and negatives. What are some negative effects of these relationships?
4. Every group has its own culture and set of behaviors. What does it take to fit into your group of friends?
5. What are some things you're expected to do that you really haven't wanted to do (maybe at first)?
6. If you say no to any of the expectations of the group, what happens? How do you know this will happen?
7. If you continue to respond to your friends in the same ways, what does the

future look like for you? In other words, how will the influence of the group shape your life for years to come?

8. Do you want to learn how to resist the pressure to do what the group expects?

For the Parents

1. What was your teen like when he was a child?
2. Describe your relationship over the years from childhood until now.
3. Tell me about your teen's peer group. How did he get involved? What concerns do you have?
4. When you've tried to talk to your child about the influence of the group on his life, what happened? How did your teen respond? How did you then respond?
5. What do you like and appreciate about your teen? What are his strengths and talents?
6. Out of ten messages you send your child each day (verbal and nonverbal), how many of them are positive? How many are negative? What kind of impact does this ratio have on your teen?
7. The ability to resist peer pressure is a function of self-confidence and a strong sense of identity. What can you do to help your child have confidence in who he is and feel good about his future?

WISE COUNSEL 4

Adolescents in their early teen years are more vulnerable to peer pressure because they *haven't developed the identity and confidence* to chart their own course. It's ironic that *popular students are more vulnerable* than those who are less popular. Joseph P. Allen, a professor of psychology at the University of Virginia, says, "Popular kids tend to be the most vulnerable. They pay attention to what their peers value. And at fourteen or fifteen, when their peers value experimenting with alcohol, they're going to be right there."[3]

Adolescence is an *awkward age*, full of starts and stops, successes and failures, and changes in desires, emotions, friendships, and physiology. Often teens feel *insecure*, which compounds their *fears*. Instead of trying to control and manage every activity and relationship or giving up and not being involved at all, parents need to be *their kid's main source of stability, support, and encouragement*.

Teens may act like they don't want their parents' input, but most of them do. In a *positive, supportive environment*, when parents talk about things that matter—in their life, the teen's life, the school, and the world—teens will be interested. This means that parents should *talk about important issues*, like drugs, smoking, sex, and other risky behavior, before problems arise when the child is in early adolescence and throughout the teen years.

Parents need to overlook most if not all of their teen's mistakes, offering only to help in any way they can. They should save any correction for genuine defiance.

5 ACTION STEPS

For the Teen

1. Find a Positive Group of Friends

- It's difficult to fight peer pressure when you're involved with people who do things you don't want to do that can get you in trouble.
- Friends who encourage you to drink, do drugs, engage in premarital sexual activities, steal, bully, and participate in other delinquent activities can lead you down a path you otherwise wouldn't choose to go. Remember, the Bible says, "Bad company corrupts good character" (1 Cor. 15:33). Though it may be one of the most difficult things for you to do, you must find a positive group of friends who will build you up, not tear you down.

2. Confide in a Mature Adult Mentor

- You will need someone in your life to give you wisdom, understanding, and support, especially when you are feeling strong pressure from your friends.
- Go to your parents, youth pastor, teacher, coach, or another mature adult and ask the person to help you through your difficult situation. We all need somebody wiser and older than we are to speak truth and be a support network for us.

3. Join a Youth Group or Club

- A youth group, sports team, or school club can be a safe haven where you will find influential friends and discover skills, hobbies, and activities you like and are good at. When we're connected with influential people and doing things we're good at, we can find a healthy identity that helps us discover who we are. When we have a healthy sense of who we are, fighting off peer pressure is easier.

4. Seek God's Guidance

- Pray about what you are going through and ask God to give you strength and courage to face peer pressure.
- Doing daily devotions is a great way to help you get through the struggles at school or with peers. Spend time praying, reading the Bible, and writing down how you feel about what happens throughout the day.
- Ask God and a godly mentor to help you walk through these situations so that you develop confidence in who you are and in the decisions you make.

For the Parents

1. Share Your Hopes, Not Just Your Fears

- Parents need to focus on the positives and paint a verbal picture of a hopeful future for the teen. You can voice your fears, but sparingly, unless there is a legitimate concern.

2. Listen

- Everyone wants to feel heard, and teens especially need to know that their parents respect them enough to listen to their point of view. You may not agree with your child's thinking on every issue or concern, but you can show respect by really listening.

- Your teen will know you are really listening intently if you ask follow-up questions or say, "Tell me more."

3. Be Honest about Your Struggles

- Too often teens feel that they are their parents' projects, things to be managed instead of people to be loved. Treat your teen with respect by sharing your life with him, including talking with him about your hopes and fears.

4. Celebrate More than Punish

- Many teens feel their parents are always on the lookout to catch them doing something wrong. Turn the tables: always look for things to affirm and celebrate.

- Be genuine but be liberal. When you have to correct, it should never be assumed that your teenager understands the reason he is being disciplined. The guidelines and expectations must be clear, fair, and mutually agreed on. Then the teen will more readily accept the correction.

5. Build Trust

- With your adolescent your goal should be trust, not control. Think of the things that build trust between people and treat your child that way, with honesty, fairness, respect, and open communication.

- Trust isn't built in a day, and in some relationships there is a lot of damage to resolve. The process of resolution, though, is a great way to begin building a loving, respectful relationship.

The 2004 Child Trends opinion poll found that only 28% of adults think that parents have more influence on a teen than an adolescent's peer group. One-half of adults think that peers and parents have equal influence, while only 25% think that parents have a greater influence than peers. However, well-adjusted teens may interact with mature, well-adjusted peers and also have quality relationships with their parents.

http://www.childtrends.org/files/parent_teenRB.pdf

BIBLICAL INSIGHTS 6

He who walks with the wise grows wise, but a companion of fools suffers harm.

Proverbs 13:20

It's not rocket science: we become like those with whom we spend time. Parents of teens can't dictate every moment of their kids' day, but they can talk openly and honestly about wisdom, trust, and the impact of today's relationships on tomorrow.

Do not conform any longer to the pattern of this world, but be transformed by the renewing of your mind.

Romans 12:2

The battle for someone's heart is waged in the mind. The pressures of the world to fit in and belong aren't seen only in adolescence. All of us feel this pressure. As examples to their children, parents can share their own struggles and their commitment to walk with God and please Him above all else.

But he said to me, "My grace is sufficient for you, for my power is made perfect in weakness." Therefore I will boast all the more gladly about my weaknesses, so that Christ's power may rest on me. That is why, for Christ's sake, I delight in weaknesses, in insults, in hardships, in persecutions, in difficulties. For when I am weak, then I am strong.

2 Corinthians 12:9–10

Parenting an adolescent is one of the most challenging roles in a parent's life. We sometimes feel confused, alone, and disappointed—in our teen, in ourselves, and maybe in God. But we can always turn to the Lord and trust Him to be our strength in times of weakness. Those are the times when we really learn to depend on Him.

7 PRAYER STARTER

Heavenly Father, even when we are tempted, You never leave our side. You understand our weaknesses, Lord, because You too were tempted! Give my young friend wisdom and strength to fight peer pressure, rather than just conforming to the norm. I thank You that our identity is not defined by our friends but by You, Jesus, and Your sacrifice to set us free. Bless this teen with affirming, godly friendships. Teach him to say no to his sinful desires and find his delight in You . . .

8 RECOMMENDED RESOURCES

Covey, Sean. *The 6 Most Important Decisions You'll Ever Make: A Guide for Teens.* Fireside, 2006.

Hersh, Sharon A. *"Mom, Everyone Else Does!" Becoming Your Daughter's Ally in Responding to Peer Pressure to Drink, Smoke, and Use Drugs.* Random House, 2005.

Meyer, Joyce, and Todd Hafer. *Battlefield of the Mind for Teens.* FaithWords, 2006.

Tripp, Paul David. *Peer Pressure: Recognizing the Warning Signs and Giving New Direction.* New Growth Press, 2008.

Welch, Edward T. *When People Are Big and God Is Small: Overcoming Peer Pressure, Codependency, and the Fear of Man.* P&R Publishing, 1997.

Pornography and Masturbation

PORTRAITS : 1

- Randy is a handsome, outgoing young man in the church's youth group. One night he confided to one of the adult volunteers, "I have a problem I can't seem to get over. Every night when my parents have gone to bed, I go downstairs and get on the computer to look at porn. And every night I masturbate. I've tried to quit, I've promised God I'd quit, and I've tried a bunch of techniques I found online, but nothing works."

- Susan has heard her friends talk about sexual encounters and she has mixed feelings. She knows it's wrong, but it sounds so exciting. Recently a friend told her about a vibrator that would give her an incredible orgasm. She found that it does exactly that. She bought one of her own, and she keeps it hidden in the back of her closet so her parents can't find it.

- Zach has been looking at porn since he was ten, when his father gave him his first magazine. By the time he was thirteen, he was paying to look at sites online and masturbating several times a day. That's a habit he has never broken or even wanted to break. He has tried to date some girls, but they soon realize he only wants sex with them. A few have complied, but one threatened to call the police when he was too pushy. He's thinking about looking for prostitutes.

DEFINITIONS AND KEY THOUGHTS : 2

- *Pornography and masturbation* often go together.
- *Pornography* is any depiction of *erotic behavior* intended to create sexual excitement. This may come in the form of writing, pictures, movies, and even phone conversations.
- Pornography promotes "sex without consequences" and serves as an aid to self-gratification. It is sometimes called "the victimless sin," but this perception doesn't account for the damage done to the person's soul and the erosion of relationships.
- *Misogyny*, the hatred of women, is portrayed in *violent pornography* with the harsh treatment or torture of women, usually by men.
- More often pornography is defined as *images that exploit people and dehumanize sexual experiences*, treating people as objects.

- *Masturbation* is sexual self-stimulation resulting in sexual pleasure and orgasm.
- The heart of the debate on masturbation comes down to two primary issues: fantasy and self-control.
- We agree that self-sex in and of itself is not wrong. But when people masturbate in conjunction with pornography or sexual fantasies, which is often the self-absorbing case for maturing teens, it is wrong. In addition, masturbation usually leads to chronic behavior, and Paul challenges each of us to let nothing master or control us (1 Cor. 6:12; 1 Thess. 4:3–5).
- *Women and men of all ages* practice masturbation for the purposes of *pleasure, self-exploration, and/or escape.*

3 : ASSESSMENT INTERVIEW

1. Tell me why you came in to see me today. How can I help?
2. When did you first begin viewing pornography and/or masturbating? Are the two connected in your experience very often?
3. What about your sexuality is good and healthy? What do you think may be out of bounds in some way?
4. How do you feel about yourself after you've looked at porn or masturbated?
5. Have you tried to quit? If you have, what happened?
6. How much do you think about sex? How does this thinking pattern affect other areas of your life, like schoolwork, friendships, relationships with the opposite sex, and your parents?
7. Do you look at porn online? If so, when and where?
8. How would you describe the kind of healthy sex life you want in the future with a faithful spouse?
9. Do you want to take steps toward being that person for your future spouse?

4 : WISE COUNSEL

God's Creation

Once puberty sets in, *sexual desires*, expectations, and needs take a *prominent role* in the adolescent's life. The teen years are a time of change and exploration. New worlds are opening up to the young person to experience, and sex is perhaps the most alluring and exciting. While hormones begin surging in the adolescent's body, and the urges can feel overwhelming, especially for young men, young people (and *all* people) need to know that *sexual desire is directly related to our longing to be known and loved.* Because adolescence can be a lonely and disconnected time of life, the *combination of hormonal changes and loneliness* creates a volatile cauldron of desire.

God made us sexual beings, and He delights in our understanding and expressing that aspect of our lives—in the right time, with the right person, and in creative ways. But He also wants us to realize our sexuality is one of the ways we *express and celebrate our promises to each other*. Sex is about *connection and intimacy*.

When talking with teens, you'll relate to them far better if you affirm that *sexuality is a good and natural aspect of being human, created by God*. Be sensitive to not only the teen's actions but also the motivation behind them. *The reason* a teen is masturbating is just as important as the fact that he is engaging in the behavior. *Sexual exploration is part of adolescent development*, but an all-consuming drive for sexual release is not how God designed us.

Pornography and Masturbation

Most authorities report that there is a strong link between *porn, fantasy, and masturbation*, and those who masturbate with pornography can easily become *sexually addicted*. If a teen is willing to talk about one of these issues, explore the others as well.

God created people in a beautiful way, male and female, but a line is crossed when they are viewed as *objects to gratify sexual urges* instead of people of inherent value. By its nature, *pornography degrades people* and makes them objects for another's pleasure. When we regularly allow ourselves to objectify another person so we can have a sexual release, we will have a difficult time treating others with respect and care.

A wise counselor needs to assess the person's inherent view of the subject of masturbation to assess any level of defiance or resistance—even to communicating about the subject.

The key question, we believe, is whether or not a "tipping point" has been passed; masturbation can easily become an *unhealthy obsession* in today's sex-crazed culture. Teens who can't stop thinking about masturbation and schedule their day around this behavior need help related to *obsessive-compulsive behaviors* and in facing the sin it has become. When a teenager's thoughts and life revolve around masturbation, and he begins to *rely on it more than God*, an addictive pattern has set in, and *masturbation becomes an idol*.

In talking with teens, look for the *progression of the addictive process*, from exploration to absorbing thoughts to a consuming lifestyle. The farther down this path the teen has gone, the more difficult the healing path will be.

ACTION STEPS 5

1. Talk About and Explore Perceptions of Masturbation

- What were you taught in your past to believe about masturbation? By talking about and exploring your perceptions and belief system regarding masturbation, you will be able to identify any underlying issues that may be present and causing distress or confusion. You may believe that God is angry and condemning and that your parents would be horrified. (You may be right on the second count but not on the first.) Be assured that your sexual urges are completely normal and God still loves and forgives you.

2. Take Practical Steps to Fight Temptation

- The temptation to view pornography is not going to go away by merely willing it away or hoping you can just quit cold turkey. First, find an accountability partner to help you stay grounded, somebody you feel safe enough with to confess when you view pornography yet will be strong enough to hold you to your conviction.
- At the same time, install a software program that will block pornographic sites or send a listing of the sites you visit to an accountability partner. If you really want to quit, join a program like Covenanteyes.com and have the list of your Web activity sent to your parents.

3. Identify the Triggers

- Identify the triggers that propel your viewing of porn and/or your desire to masturbate.
- Ask yourself, *what is going on inside that is causing me to want to do this? Am I bored, lonely, tired, sad, upset, angry?*
- Discovering how you feel at that moment can help you understand what urges you to turn to pornography and/or masturbation.

4. Work on Building Healthy Relationships with Others

- Healthy relationships can help alleviate feelings of loneliness and isolation by fueling the affection, intimacy, and acceptance you are looking for in pornography.
- Get connected in athletics, drama, choir, band, civic clubs, or other activities that will help you connect with people and prevent you from sitting around being bored.

5. Learn New Skills

- Learn new skills for controlling your thought life and behaviors. Your counselor can help you with this.
- Ask your counselor to teach you cognitive reframing skills that will help with positive self-talk.
- Read the Bible and memorize verses that teach you about God's acceptance, love, and desire for a relationship with you as well as verses on how sin, such as lust, inhibits our ability to relate to God.

6. Normalize Healthy Sexual Desires

- Sexual urges are explosive and powerful, but they are completely normal. Think about healthy relationships and make a plan for building such relationships and avoid thinking of people as sexual objects.

- Train your eyes to see differently. Learn to see others as God sees them—as His daughters and sons and our sisters and brothers.

- Remind yourself that your normal sexual desires are to be acted on in a monogamous relationship with your spouse. Any sexual acts prior to your marriage can later create real intimacy issues with your marriage partner. Learn the importance of protecting your eyes and body for the spouse God has designed specifically for you.

BIBLICAL INSIGHTS : 6

No temptation has overtaken you but such as is common to man; and God is faithful, who will not allow you to be tempted beyond what you are able, but with the temptation will provide the way of escape also, so that you will be able to endure it.

1 Corinthians 10:13 NASB

At our time of need, God is there. He doesn't take away our struggles, but He gives us a path through them so that we honor Him every step of the way. Temptations around porn and masturbation are powerful, but God can provide wisdom, strength, and accountability from trusted people who will help the adolescent make better choices.

You were taught, with regard to your former way of life, to put off your old self, which is being corrupted by its deceitful desires; to be made new in the attitude of your minds; and to put on the new self, created to be like God in true righteousness and holiness.

Ephesians 4:22–24

The choices we make affect our lifestyle and relationships. As though we were changing our clothes, we can "put off" sinful, defeating thoughts and behaviors and "put on" healthy thoughts and behaviors that honor God and build relationships with people.

Finally, brothers, whatever is true, whatever is noble, whatever is right, whatever is pure, whatever is lovely, whatever is admirable—if anything is excellent or praiseworthy—think about such things.

Philippians 4:8

The struggles of life are fought in our minds. We have the power to choose what we think about. Lustful, negative thoughts may drift into our minds, but we can arrest them and replace them with thoughts that reflect the goodness and grace of God.

Flee the evil desires of youth, and pursue righteousness, faith, love and peace, along with those who call on the Lord out of a pure heart.

2 Timothy 2:22

God has a wonderful plan for each of our lives, and every day He gives us wisdom about the path toward His will. As we pursue Him, He leads us, purifies our hearts, and gives us blessings to enjoy.

7 PRAYER STARTER

Father, thank You for my young friend's concern about his sexuality. Thank You for the beautiful gift of sex that You have created. We understand, Lord, how fragile this gift truly is and how easily it can be abused and misused. Give this teen wisdom about his sexuality. Make him strong to resist sexual temptation of every type. Lord, may this teen be controlled not by his passions but by Your Holy Spirit . . .

8 RECOMMENDED RESOURCES

Arterburn, Stephen, Fred Stoeker, and Mike Yorkey. *Every Young Man's Battle: Strategies for Victory in the Real World of Sexual Temptation*. Random House, 2002.

Ethridge, Shannon, and Stephen Arterburn. *Every Young Woman's Battle: Guarding Your Mind, Heart, and Body in a Sex-Saturated World*. Random House, 2004.

Kern, Jan. *Eyes Online—Eyes on Life: A Journey Out of Online Obsession*. Standard, 2008.

Maier, Bill, and Jim Vigorito. *HELP! Someone I Know Has a Problem with Porn*. Focus on the Family Resources, 2006.

Parrott, Les. *Helping Your Struggling Teenager*. Zondervan, 2000.

Speck, Greg. *Sex: It's Worth Waiting For*. Revised and expanded ed. Moody, 2007.

CDs

Hart, Archibald D. *Christian Men and Sexuality I-II*. Focus on the Family Radio Broadcast.

Pregnancy

PORTRAITS : 1

- Jen had been feeling nauseated for a few days. She tried to convince herself that she had the flu but she suspected there might be a different cause. She took a home pregnancy test, and it was positive. Hoping it was wrong, she took another one, and it was positive too. She didn't want to tell her parents, so she began searching for a way to have an abortion with nobody knowing.

- Leslie and her boyfriend had been having oral sex for a long time, but one night in the heat of passion, they had vaginal sex. It was only one time but it was enough—Leslie was pregnant. Her mom noticed some changes in her, and Leslie told her the truth. When her dad got home, the lid came off! He insisted that she get an abortion because a baby would ruin her future, but her mom advised her to marry her boyfriend immediately.

- Juanita was from a large, loving family. When she became pregnant at sixteen, her family was a mass of mixed emotions. One thing was sure: she would keep the baby and raise it in her parents' home. A few months before delivery, Juanita dropped out of school. With no high school degree and no prospects for a good job, her future looks bleak. She daydreams of a young man falling in love with her and adopting her baby, but she fears she'll wind up like many young women in her neighborhood who are alone with their children, living on welfare.

DEFINITIONS AND KEY THOUGHTS : 2

- *Government programs* spend billions of dollars taking care of teenage mothers and their children, and these families are more likely to be in the poverty bracket. But a relatively small amount of money, millions of dollars, is *spent on prevention programs.*

- *Teen births have dropped by almost a third since 1990* because of the relative success of *pregnancy prevention programs.* In 2002 the abortion rate among teen girls was 50 percent lower than in 1988.[1]

- Often teenage sex leads to pregnancy and *children having children* while still living at home with their parents. While many teens now abort their baby, many more give birth and *commit to raising the child with or without the father.* Some give the child up for *adoption.*

225

- *Single parenting*—and most teen parents are single parents—involves *taking responsibility for parenting one's children* without the benefit of (and sometimes the direct sabotage of) the other parent, who may have abandoned the child because of the parent's immaturity.

- Nearly *half of all teenage moms receive welfare* but, even with government assistance, raising a child on your own is very difficult. Often single teen parents have *unmet social and emotional needs*—it's tough to develop friendships when a fussy baby demands so much attention.

3 ASSESSMENT INTERVIEW

For the Teen

1. How do you feel about your pregnancy?
2. What options are you considering?
3. Have you seen a doctor? What counsel has your doctor given you?
4. What do your parents want you to do?
5. What does your boyfriend want now in the relationship? What does he want you to do with the baby?
6. How will you determine the best course of action? What factors weigh the most in your consideration?
7. How can I help you?

For the Parents

1. How did you learn about your daughter's pregnancy?
2. How is she handling it? How are you handling it?
3. Are you and your spouse in agreement about your advice to your daughter? If not, how are you resolving the disagreement?
4. What are the options your daughter is considering?
5. How will she make her decision?
6. Are you willing to be supportive no matter what she decides? Explain your answer.
7. What factors about her future and the future of the baby weigh most heavily in your thinking?
8. How can I help?

4 WISE COUNSEL

Most pregnant teens realize they have *three options*: to have the baby and raise it as their own, to put the baby up for adoption, or to have an abortion. Another set of *options relates to the baby's father*. The pregnant teen and the father may choose to *get married or they may choose not to*. He may *relinquish parental rights or he may continue to claim his rights*.

Too often, when girls discover they are pregnant, they *panic* and try to make *quick decisions*, often to end the pregnancy. After the initial shock has worn off, parents, counselors, and other responsible adults need to offer *reasoned, wise advice about the options*. A local *crisis pregnancy agency* can provide a wealth of information, videos, and referrals to doctors who value the life of the unborn child. At this time of shock, girls need help sorting out their options, so parents need to *rein in their anger and grief* to provide the wisdom their daughter needs.

An unwanted pregnancy threatens the stability of the young woman, her relationship with her boyfriend, her relationship with her parents and siblings, and perhaps even her relationship with her friends. A few girls genuinely celebrate an unplanned pregnancy, but most experience *a real sense of loss*. And the *process of grieving* has just begun when many major changes and demands enter the girl's life.

Parents may be *angry and deeply disappointed*, but this is a time in their daughter's life when she needs their love and support more than at any other time. She is probably scared about the future and she feels unsure about any of the options she's considering. Even after the decision, she needs plenty of love and care during the pregnancy and beyond.

The role of parents and other caregivers is to offer *wisdom, information, and sound advice* during the crucial first days after the realization of pregnancy. *Quick fixes*, such as an abortion, may seem like an option at the moment, but the girl and her parents need to consider carefully *the sanctity of life and the sovereignty of God*. Even if the girl doesn't want informed advice, the parents can talk to a counselor at the local crisis pregnancy agency to gain insight. The teen needs to *consider the options* of keeping and raising the child or putting the child up for adoption.

ACTION STEPS 5

1. Recognize the Reality of Change, Loss, Anger, and Sadness

- In an unplanned teen pregnancy, everything in life changes for you and your family. Every option you consider will involve a measure of heartache and struggle. During this time, you will feel a full range of emotions, often all at the same time, including the numbness of shock, anger, blame, and deep sadness. Be honest about what you are feeling, begin the process of grieving, and also work on creating a new normal.

2. Focus on Your Relationship with Your Parents

- As a pregnant teen, getting the support and encouragement from your parents is important to your own mental and emotional health. While your parents may not agree with the circumstances under which your baby was conceived, your child is a gift from God—a child to be cherished and loved.

- Everyone in the family may be feeling a deep sense of hurt or loss, and you all may be taking out your frustrations on one another when everyone needs unconditional love and support. If your parents are angry about the choice you make concerning the baby, work on forgiving them.
- Take your parents' advice seriously. If they are not willing or are unable to help you during your pregnancy, find another adult you respect, such as a grandparent, aunt, uncle, or family friend, who is willing to help you through this time.

3. Prepare for the Future

- Every option you and your family consider is a door to a future for you, the baby, and everyone else involved. Carefully prepare emotionally and financially.
- Plan a way to finish school when time permits. Getting your GED, high school diploma, and/or college education are critical to your future financial stability.
- Look to God and the church for help. Asking a pastor or church leader to mentor and walk with you through your pregnancy and first few years of motherhood can be a big help to you.

4. Develop a Parenting Plan

- Your parenting plan will depend on your age and other issues involved, including the flexibility of your parents, whose house everyone lives in. Ask the whole family to talk together and share ideas to be incorporated into the plan. Even the youngest members can have input, but you and your parents must cooperate and come up with a final decision.
- *If you sense that the grandparents or teen parents are immature enough that they won't be able to develop a good plan together, follow up after they have had their family meeting to look over the plan they develop. You may need to help them make the plan more realistic.*

5. Consider Adoption

- You may feel that your only option is an abortion, or you may be feeling extremely overwhelmed with the prospect of having to raise a baby on your own. Throughout the United States, there are nearly three thousand crisis pregnancy centers staffed by volunteers who want to give you true alternatives to abortion, such as adoption, and who will lovingly help educate you about what options are available.
- Look in the Yellow Pages under the heading "Abortion Alternatives" or call, toll-free, 1-800-848-LOVE.
- *Provide a list of crisis pregnancy centers.*

BIBLICAL INSIGHTS : 6

The LORD is merciful and compassionate, slow to get angry and filled with unfailing love.

Psalm 145:8 NLT

In times of our deepest heartache, God is there. No matter what we've done, no matter how far we've gotten off track, God is "filled with unfailing love." Unwed teens and their parents need to remember this truth during their struggle to come to grips with the reality of the pregnancy.

For you created my inmost being; you knit me together in my mother's womb. I praise you because I am fearfully and wonderfully made; your works are wonderful, I know that full well. My frame was not hidden from you when I was made in the secret place. When I was woven together in the depths of the earth, your eyes saw my unformed body. All the days ordained for me were written in your book before one of them came to be.

Psalm 139:13–16

Every person is created and shaped by God, a wondrous work of His hand, and with a good purpose in His plans. Some of the most notable leaders in history were men and women whose birth wasn't planned. God has plans for every child.

You intended to harm me, but God intended it for good.

Genesis 50:20

God is willing to use every circumstance in our lives for good—if we'll trust Him.

He is the God who made the world and everything in it. Since he is Lord of heaven and earth, he doesn't live in man-made temples, and human hands can't serve his needs—for he has no needs. He himself gives life and breath to everything, and he satisfies every need.

Acts 17:24–25 NLT

From our point of view, some pregnancies are unplanned "accidents," but God doesn't see any child as an accident. He is the Lord of heaven and earth, and He loves every child, no matter what the circumstances of her conception and birth.

88% of teens say it would be easier for them to postpone sexual activity and avoid teen pregnancy if they were able to have more open, honest conversations about these topics with their parents, yet 23% of teens say they have never discussed sex, contraception, or pregnancy with their parents.

http://parentingteens.about.com/od/teensexuality/a/teen_sex7.htm

7 PRAYER STARTER

Lord Jesus, thank You for the gift of life. We praise You that no life is an accident, even an unplanned pregnancy. I ask You today to surround my young friend with Your peace and the reassurance that even when our lives seem out of control, You are always in control. Give her wisdom in making decisions about the future of her baby. Lord, we know that this little life is no surprise to You and that You have a beautiful plan for her. Regardless of circumstances, You are this baby's kind and loving God. Wrap this mother and her baby in Your strong arms. Protect them and bring wise and supporting people into their lives to help them in this journey . . .

8 RECOMMENDED RESOURCES

Goyer, Tricia. *Life Interrupted: The Scoop on Being a Young Mom.* Zondervan, 2004.

Graham, Ruth, and Sara Dormon. *I'm Pregnant . . . Now What? Heartfelt Advice on Getting through Unplanned Pregnancy.* Gospel Light, 2004.

Schooler, Jayne. *Mom, Dad, I'm Pregnant: When Your Son or Daughter Faces an Unplanned Pregnancy.* NavPress, 2004.

Speck, Greg. *Sex: It's Worth Waiting For.* Revised and expanded ed. Moody, 2007.

Promiscuity and Sexually Transmitted Diseases

PORTRAITS 1

- Darrell tried to tell himself that it was jock itch, but the condition gradually got worse. He had some bumps on his penis, and no matter how much over-the-counter medicine he put on it, the bumps seemed to be getting larger.

- Amy, a beautiful eighteen-year-old junior in high school sat crying with her friend Janise after she had been dumped yet again. "I just can't figure it out," cried Amy. "I have had six boyfriends in the past three years. I felt connected to all of them. The relationship is great at first. We have sex. And after a few months they dump me. I thought that's what they wanted." Amy sat confused and lonely, wondering what else she could do to get a guy to love her. Two weeks later, she was overjoyed, sharing with Janise once again that she had found "the love of her life" after meeting another guy at a party and sleeping with him later that night.

DEFINITIONS AND KEY THOUGHTS 2

- *Promiscuous sex* is usually *casual, indiscriminate* sexual relations between people who do not necessarily have an emotional attachment.

- *Sexually transmitted diseases (STDs)* are described as any disease characteristically *transmitted by sexual contact,* such as gonorrhea, syphilis, genital herpes, and chlamydia.

- The Kaiser Family Foundation partnered with *Seventeen* magazine to conduct national telephone surveys of teens about sex. Of teens between the ages of fifteen to seventeen, more than *50 percent indicated that they practiced abstinence from sexual intercourse.* Most of those surveyed believed that abstinence in high school was a good idea and reportedly wanted to wait until they were "more mature" and in a "committed relationship" before having sex. Many factors weighed heavily on their decision, including:

  1. unwanted pregnancy
  2. concern about acquiring a sexually transmitted disease
  3. their parents' views
  4. sex education

5. religion
6. moral values
7. concerns about their reputation
8. having friends who had not had sex.[1]

- In a typical class of thirty high school students, *fifteen have had sexual intercourse at least once.* Five have had four or more sex partners, and eleven have had sex in the past three months. Of those latter eleven, five *did not use a condom* the last time they had sex, nine *did not use birth control pills,* and two had been *drinking* or *using drugs.*

- In 2008 when teens were tested for four STDs by the Centers for Disease Control, it was found that human papillomavirus, or HPV, which can cause cervical cancer, was the most common, with chlamydia, trichomoniasis, and genital herpes found to a lesser extent.

- The following factors *increase the chances* of a teen getting an STD:

  — *Sexual activity at a young age.* The younger a person starts having sex, the greater his chances of becoming infected with an STD.
  — *Lots of sex partners.* People who have sexual contact—not just intercourse but any form of sexual activity, including vaginal, oral, or anal sex—with many different partners are more at risk for STDs.
  — *Unprotected sex.* Latex condoms are the only form of birth control that reduce the risk of getting an STD. Spermicides, diaphragms, and other birth control methods may help prevent pregnancy, but they don't protect a person against STDs.[2]

- Some *genital inflammations,* such as yeast infections in girls and infected hair follicles in boys, aren't caused by STDs.

- Too often sex is a *substitute for healthy communication.* Many teenagers are still learning how to engage and live in mature, healthy adult relationships. Therefore, very few have learned that *nonsexual touch and communication are the foundation for true intimacy and trust.* Instead, they have learned, either through the media, their friends, or past relationships, that intimacy is based on sex and not the unconditional love of the persons in the relationship.

3 ASSESSMENT INTERVIEW

For the Teen

1. I'm glad you came here today. How can I help?
2. Tell me about your relationship with your girlfriend.
3. Are you having unprotected sex?
4. Do you suspect that you might have an STD? If so, what are your symptoms?
5. Have you seen a doctor for an exam?
6. Do your parents know about the problem? Does your partner know?
7. How are you feeling about the relationship, sexual activity, and your future?

For the Parents

1. What is your concern about your teen?
2. Describe your previous conversations with your teen about sex.
3. Do you suspect (or know) that your child has an STD? If so, what symptoms have you noticed?
4. Has your teen seen a doctor? If so, what was the diagnosis?
5. How can you help your teen make better choices in the future?
6. How can I help?

WISE COUNSEL 4

Promiscuity and STDs are *easier to prevent than stop or cure.*

Parents may feel uncomfortable talking with their children about sex, but most authorities say that *these conversations are the most important* in educating children and steering them in the right direction. *Kids hear their friends talking about sex by the time they are ten years old,* so parents should begin these conversations at that time, or perhaps even a little earlier. Parents need to be *honest, set appropriate boundaries, and focus on the future.*

Some parents give their kids free rein to choose any behaviors they want, but others go to the other extreme, reacting violently to any suspicion their teen may be sexually involved. Parents need to avoid these extremes. They should *be involved* in their teen's life, *talking candidly* about important issues like sex, and giving *clear guidelines* about what behavior they expect. The focus, though, isn't just to control present behavior; it is to provide a platform for a future of good relationships for a lifetime.

Teens need good information about the *risks of promiscuity.* Many teens don't understand that they can *transmit STDs through oral and anal sex* and then carry the disease into marriage. Also, many don't understand the risk of an unintended pregnancy.

The *rates of STDs* in 2008 were as follows:

Syphilis: 46,277 cases: a rate of 15.3 per 100,000 people.

Chlamydia reached a twenty-year high with 1,210,523 cases: a rate of 401.3 per 100,000 people.

Gonorrhea: 336,742 cases: a rate of 111.6 per 100,000 people.

The risk of getting an STD is *higher with multiple partners*, a common trend among teenagers. Although some STDs can be cured or medicated, HIV/AIDS cannot. Unfortunately, there is no cure and the number of cases has increased 26 percent from 2004 to 2007.[3]

God calls us to holiness, to recognize that sexual intimacy outside of a committed relationship (marriage) will bring pain, brokenness, and heartache. Having sexual activity before marriage causes emotional, spiritual, and sometimes physical wounds that eventually need to be repaired and restored.

5 : ACTION STEPS

For the Teen

1. Stop Having Sex

- Nobody has ever died from not having sex. If you are currently in a relationship and being told that you don't love the person if you're not having sex with her, then get out of the relationship because she is not treating you with respect.

- Sex is not a means to intimacy. Sex is a by-product of intimacy and is only to be practiced in the context of marriage. If you do not stop having sex, you are risking acquiring an STD and/or getting your girlfriend pregnant.

2. Find Same-Sex Peers to Help Hold You Accountable

- Get involved in a youth group or in a positive group of same-sex peers to hold you accountable to biblical standards for romantic relationships. Remember, you are who you spend time with.

3. Get a Physical from Your Family Doctor

- If you have had sex, especially with multiple partners, you will want to see a doctor to be tested for STDs.

- If you have an STD, be sure to heed your doctor's advice for treatment.

4. Make a Commitment of Purity to God

- One of the most incredible results of Jesus's death on the cross was that He took your sins and paid the penalty you deserved. That means He took away your debts and paid the price to restore your innocence and purity. It was a very painful act yet so beautiful and selfless. He did it because He loves us and respects us. Ask God to show you how much He loves you so that you in turn can love others in the same way He loves you.

- When you sense how much God loves you, you can make a commitment of purity that will last until your wedding day. Once you make this commitment, tell a mentor or friend who can help hold you accountable and disciple you along the way.

For the Parents

1. Talk Openly about Sex and STDs

- Some parents are hesitant to talk about sex, but their teens talk about it all the time. Have candid conversations with your teen. Discuss (don't just preach) the benefits of abstinence and healthy relationships.

2. Schedule Regular Doctor Visits

- Your teen may be embarrassed by the prospect of a doctor examining his genitals, but regular medical exams are essential for his health—especially if you suspect he may have contracted an STD.

3. Focus on Abstinence

- Find examples of programs and people who are actively engaged in abstinence programs and encourage your teen to get involved. This will help prevent the pain that comes with promiscuity and the physical problems of STDs.

4. Teach Impulse Control

- Talk with your teen about practical techniques to avoid sexual temptation (for example, not spending time alone with a girlfriend in isolated places or lying down together).
- Talk about and teach healthy ways to respond in sexual situations.

5. Encourage Healthy Relationships

- Beyond the topic of sex and the prospect of disease, talk to your teen about the value of strong relationships based on trust and respect and how to build those relationships.
- If currently you have a broken relationship with your teenager and have a hard time trusting one another, ask him to go to counseling with you so you can work on your relationship together. If he is unwilling to do that, ask another adult or youth pastor to help mentor your teen in healthy peer relationships that are honoring to God and those in the relationship.
- Too often sex is a substitute for good communication, so teaching and modeling good communication skills can go a long way in helping your teen relate to young women in healthy ways.

6. Focus on the Future

- The choices your teen makes today will affect his future for better or worse. Talk optimistically with your teen about his prospects for the future and put conversations about today's sexual choices in that context. What would happen if his girlfriend became pregnant? Do they have a plan? Does he understand how that would affect his ability to go to college and start a career? Would he be able to support a child? What happens if he acquires an STD? What would that mean for his future health and the health of his future spouse and their children? How would he tell his future spouse that he has an STD?
- If your teenager has engaged in premarital sex or any sexually intimate behavior, encourage him to make a commitment now before the Lord to remain chaste and pure until marriage.

An estimated 25% of sexually active teens have a sexually transmitted disease by the time they graduate from high school.[4]

Teenagers reporting first sex as unwanted are more likely than others to report that their first partner had been 3 or more years their senior. In 7th grade, 6% of males and 18% of females reported having had a boyfriend or girlfriend 2 or more years their senior.

http://www.thefreelibrary.com/Boyfriends%2c+girlfriends+and+teenagers'+risk+of+sexual+involvement.-a0147012631

6 : BIBLICAL INSIGHTS

No temptation has overtaken you but such as is common to man; and God is faithful, who will not allow you to be tempted beyond what you are able, but with the temptation will provide the way of escape also, so that you will be able to endure it.

1 Corinthians 10:13 NASB

A teen's hormones, loneliness, and the pressure of peers to engage in sexual activity can seem unbearable, but God promises that He always provides a way to follow His will. It may not be easy, and we may have to fight hard to stay on track with Him, but He always opens a door so we can do His will.

Flee from sexual immorality. All other sins a man commits are outside his body, but he who sins sexually sins against his own body. Do you not know that your body is a temple of the Holy Spirit, who is in you, whom you have received from God? You are not your own; you were bought at a price. Therefore honor God with your body.

1 Corinthians 6:18–20

One of the most important truths in the Christian life is the realization that we don't belong to ourselves. We have been created by God and bought back from our slavery to sin by Christ's payment on the cross. Everything we are and everything we do is now dedicated to honor and please Him.

Be imitators of God, therefore, as dearly loved children and live a life of love, just as Christ loved us and gave himself up for us as a fragrant offering and sacrifice to God. But among you there must not be even a hint of sexual immorality, or of any kind of impurity, or of greed, because these are improper for God's holy people.

Ephesians 5:1–3

Many people want to see how close they can get to sin without crossing the line, but that's a recipe for disaster. God wants us to focus on His love and grace, and then to stay as far away from sin as possible. We live in the world, but God has called us to live for Him.

If we confess our sins, he is faithful and just and will forgive us our sins and purify us from all unrighteousness.

1 John 1:9

Confess means to agree with. No matter what we've done wrong, we can agree with God that it's sin and that He has completely forgiven us. We may have to live with some of the consequences, but we can be assured of God's complete forgiveness.

For I am convinced that neither death, nor life, nor angels, nor principalities, nor things present, nor things to come, nor powers, nor height, nor depth, nor any other created thing, will be able to separate us from the love of God, which is in Christ Jesus our Lord.

Romans 8:38-39 NASB

Sexual sin is serious business, but it's not the end of the world. We are forgiven if we repent and trust God for the future. Nothing, not even sexual sin and disease, can separate us from God's great love.

PRAYER STARTER : 7

Lord Jesus, thank You for the beautiful gift of sex. I pray for this teen as he struggles for physical and emotional purity. We praise You for Your unconditional love and forgiveness when we mess up. Make this young man strong in the face of temptation through the truth of Your Word. Lord, You are the only One who can truly satisfy our heart's desires. Satisfy us with Your love . . .

RECOMMENDED RESOURCES : 8

Alcorn, Randy. *The Purity Principle: God's Safeguards for Life's Dangerous Trails.* Multnomah, 2003.

Arterburn, Stephen, Fred Stoeker, and Mike Yorkey. *Every Young Man's Battle: Strategies for Victory in the Real World of Sexual Temptation.* Random House, 2002.

Chirban, John. *What's Love Got to Do With It: Talking Confidently with Your Kids about Sex.* Thomas Nelson, 2007.

Clark, Chap. *Next Time I Fall in Love.* Wipf and Stock, 2004.

Elliot, Elisabeth. *Passion and Purity: Learning to Bring Your Love Life under Christ's Control.* Revell, 2002.

Ethridge, Shannon, and Stephen Arterburn. *Every Young Woman's Battle: Guarding Your Mind, Heart, and Body in a Sex-Saturated World.* Random House, 2004.

Meeker, Meg. *Your Kids at Risk: How Teen Sex Is Killing Our Sons and Daughters.* Regnery, 2007.

Speck, Greg. *Sex: It's Worth Waiting For.* Revised and expanded ed. Moody, 2007.

Schoolwork

1 PORTRAITS

- Hannah's father has big plans for her. He's a corporate attorney and he envisions his daughter joining his law firm someday. She is a very good student, but her grades aren't high enough to get her into the best colleges. Her dad has good intentions, but Hannah feels that he pushes her way too hard.
- Doug doesn't seem to be motivated to do well in school. "I'm just not smart," he shrugs. His parents are concerned that he seems to be drifting through high school and doesn't have the desire or confidence to go to college.
- Isaac makes good grades, and his test scores show that he is brilliant. In school he just skates by, seldom studying but always doing well enough to escape notice. His mother and a couple of his teachers see his potential but they can't get through to him that he needs to apply himself to do his best.

2 DEFINITIONS AND KEY THOUGHTS

- There are *many causes* for teens not doing well in school. Some are simply *not motivated* to excel. Some have simply *never learned how to study*. They did well in elementary school, but as the homework load increased, they have gradually fallen behind. Others may be motivated and disciplined but have a *learning disability* that blocks their ability to learn. And some are simply so *tired from endless activities* that they fall asleep in class.
- A report on child trends found:

  — Teens who have *positive relationships with their parents generally do better academically*. These adolescents are also less likely to have been suspended from school than their peers with less positive parent-adolescent relationships, even after taking into account other social and economic influences.
  — When there is *parental involvement* with teens fourteen to eighteen years old, the teens will make *higher grades and have higher academic expectations*. Positive connections between parents and adolescents lessen the likelihood that teens will exhibit problem behaviors.
  — A study of more than twelve thousand teenagers found *a link between positive parent-child relationships and fewer violent behaviors*.[1]

- It has been shown that the *quality of adolescents' diet affects their success in school.* Going without a healthy diet causes *irritability, distractibility, or emotional changes,* which affect children's achievement scores or psychosocial behaviors. Homeless children are more likely than low-income children to be anxious and have behavior and academic functioning problems.[2]
- *Exercise also affects academic success.* Students who exercise or engage in sports tend to have higher grade point averages.[3]
- Compared with teens who abstain from sex, *sexually active adolescents* are more likely to have *lower academic achievement* and aspirations.[4]

ASSESSMENT INTERVIEW 3

For the Teen

1. Tell me how school is going for you. What do you enjoy? What is frustrating?
2. What are your plans after graduation? How do your grades and academic success fit into these plans?
3. In which classes are you succeeding? Which ones are problems?
4. How do you feel before big tests? Do you typically do well on tests or do you sometimes go through brain lock just before you begin?
5. Do you need help with study skills, anxiety relief, or finding time to study?
6. How do your parents feel about the quality of your schoolwork?
7. Do you want their help? Why or why not?
8. How can I help?

For the Parents

1. What is your chief concern about your teen's academic success?
2. Does she have good study habits?
3. Has your teen's attitude about school changed recently? If so, how?
4. Does your child lack confidence, motivation, or good study skills?
5. Is there a chance there's a learning disability? If you suspect this, have you had your child tested?
6. What are your hopes for your child's education and future career?
7. Does your child share your hopes? Explain your answer.
8. How can I help you today?

WISE COUNSEL 4

For the Teen

When a teen is doing poorly in school, it most likely means she has *lost the motivation* to succeed. This could be the result of a variety of reasons, such as *laziness,* the *influence of friends,* or *other things having higher priority* for her.

A teenager has a hard time thinking long term, so to *help her regain her motivation,* ask her to think about what she wants to do after high school and if and where she wants to go to college. Then begin working backward to where she is now, helping her to understand *what it will take to achieve her goals.* This method can help the teen see how the path she is on and her actions now in school are or are not leading her to where she wants to be in the future.

Change will not happen immediately. Help the teen *set realistic goals* that will increase her intrinsic motivation to do well. Such goals could include trying to bring her GPA from a 1.5 to a 2.0, for example, or having her develop good study habits by setting aside a couple hours a day to focus on schoolwork. Help her *recognize and celebrate small successes.*

Many times the reason a teenager is doing poorly in school is because she is bored, probably because she is *not being challenged.* This is often the case for teenage boys who respond best to challenges.

For the Parents

Parents tend to make one of *two mistakes* about their kids' school performance. They either *demand too much or expect too little.* It's a balancing act, but parents need to work hard to find *the right blend of involvement without being domineering.*

Some parents think they're helping by organizing their kids' homework and doing much of their homework for them. Actually, these *overinvolved parents are stealing confidence away from their kids.* Teens need to learn how to manage their own lives. Certainly, they need help from time to time, but parents need to show confidence in them—and let them fail occasionally so they learn important lessons.

Adolescents are in the *stage of experimentation.* The things that excite them one day bore them the next. That's not a character flaw; it's a natural product of *their developmental stage.* Parents need to *look for patterns* in the things that interest and involve their teens. As they notice, name, and nurture talents and interests, they *help guide the teen to a lifetime of success*—even if it's in a field that the parents have never pursued.

5 ACTION STEPS

For the Students

1. Think Long Term

- The decisions you are now making in school will most likely determine what you will be doing for the rest of your life. If you have plans to attend college, you need to do well in school now. Think about what you want out of life and ask yourself if and how your behavior and study habits are preparing you for future success. Patterns of studying and good grades are developed early and carried on into adulthood.

2. Work on Study Habits

- Look at your daily schedule and begin building good time-management strategies so you will use your time most effectively. Then you will be able to meet the requirements of school and still have time built in for socializing with friends and extracurricular activities.

- Good study habits include setting aside time to study during the hours when you are mentally at your best and finding a quiet place away from anything that will distract you. (And by the way, working with your iPod in your ear or in front of the TV are not good habits.)

- Once you have a quiet place to study, consider how long you need to study to comprehend the material and finish the assignment.

- Consider what study methods to use. There is not one right study method. Some people like studying in groups. Others like to study by themselves. Sometimes students read the book to study, whereas others write out a study guide or use note cards. You will soon find out what works for you and can adapt it to every study need.

- The last thing that will greatly improve your ability to study is listening in class. Most teachers test from their lectures; therefore if you listen well and take good notes, you will know where your focus should be when you study.

3. Ask for Help

- If you are having a difficult time staying focused in class or understanding the material, consider finding a tutor to help you in a particular subject. If you are having trouble concentrating, you may need to get more sleep or eat a more nutritious breakfast.

- When concentration is a big issue, it is advisable to see a professional counselor or your family doctor to determine if you have ADHD. If this is the case, you can take steps to learn your particular learning style and ways you can do well in school.

For the Parents

1. Determine the Nature of the Problem

- Take time to talk to your teen to uncover the nature of the problem she is having with school. Try to determine if the problem is lack of time, fatigue, or perhaps a learning disability.

- Don't assume it's a motivation issue.

2. Discover Your Teen's Interests

- Watch your teen carefully and see what makes her eyes light up. It may be drama or sports or engineering or helping disadvantaged people or many other things.

In 2006, 88% of young adults ages 18–24 had completed high school with a diploma or an alternative credential such as a General Educational Development (GED) certificate. At the same time, 66% of high school graduates enrolled immediately in a 2-year or 4-year college.

http://childstats.gov/americaschildren/edu.asp

- Don't expect, and certainly don't demand, that she follow in your footsteps. Allow your teen to become a woman with her own dreams.

3. Build a Healthy, Productive Environment for Study

- Unless teens have a learning disability or are mentally challenged, virtually all of them can do well in school if they develop good study habits. Work with your teen to set up some healthy ground rules for studying.

  These could include:

  — Eliminate distractions (though audio doesn't distract some teens).
  — Designate times and places for study.
  — Develop a plan for completing homework and projects on time.
  — Use good study practices, like underlining, highlighting, and taking notes.
  — If studying in a group, have a clear goal of what is to be accomplished.

- Stay involved with your teen, show interest in her work, have an idea of when she has tests or papers due, and check her report card.

4. Set Goals

- It's been said, "If you aim at nothing you are sure to hit it every time." Help your teenager set realistic goals about the future.
- Dream with her about what she can achieve and set a plan to help make it become a reality.
- Set goals for your teen to improve her grades in small steps. When realistic goals are set, your teen will feel that she can accomplish them.
- Help your teen see how the decisions she makes now will greatly affect her future when it comes to applying to colleges and for jobs.
- Talk to your teen about her plans for college. Where does she want to go? Has she thought about trying to get a scholarship?

5. Encourage but Don't Push

- Adolescents are under enormous pressure to measure up socially, physically, and academically. Your child may not be performing as well as you want, but probably the problem isn't a lack of motivation. Encourage, support, and affirm your teen when she tries to do well.
- Don't make excessive demands and apply too much pressure. Ask yourself what your motives are for your teen's success. Is it because you want to feel good or is it because you genuinely want your teen to do well? Is the love you show your child based on her performance?
- Celebrate every success, and help the teen learn lessons from every setback.

BIBLICAL INSIGHTS : 6

Let us not lose heart in doing good, for in due time we will reap if we do not grow weary.

Galatians 6:9 NASB

Studying is hard work, but sooner or later students will see the fruit of their labor.

Whatever you do, work at it with all your heart, as working for the Lord, not for men.

Colossians 3:23

Whatever we do, it is the Lord we serve, not our parents, not a teacher. Our top priority is not even getting a grade. It is to please the One who loves us.

He who has been stealing must steal no longer, but must work, doing something useful with his own hands, that he may have something to share with those in need.

Ephesians 4:28

We are all called to use our gifts and talents to care for the needs of others. When we neglect our opportunities to develop ourselves and our talents, we actually limit our ability to help others down the road.

PRAYER STARTER : 7

Lord Jesus, we praise You today for the opportunity to go to school and learn. Thank You for placing us in an environment where this is possible. Give my young friend motivation to apply herself to her studies. Even when the work is difficult, teach her to rely on Your strength rather than giving up. By the power of Your Spirit, guide her in developing determination, focus, and a positive attitude toward school. Teach her to be grateful for the opportunity to learn rather than complaining about having to study. May her desire be to worship and honor You, Lord, through her willingness to learn and be used for good . . .

RECOMMENDED RESOURCES : 8

Morgenstern, Jessi, and Julie Morgenstern-Colon. *Organizing from the Inside Out for Teens*. Henry Holt, 2002.

Palmer, Adam. *The High School Survival Guide: Making the Most of the Best Time of Your Life*. Think, 2008.

Sax, Leonard. *Boys Adrift: The Five Factors Driving the Growing Epidemic of Unmotivated Boys and Underachieving Young Men.* Basic Books, 2008.

Swenson, Richard. *Margin: Restoring Emotional, Physical, Financial, and Time Reserves to Overloaded Lives.* NavPress, 2004.

Vuko, Evelyn Porreca. *Teacher Says: 30 Foolproof Ways to Help Kids Thrive in School.* Perigee, 2004.

Sexual Abuse

PORTRAITS 1

- When Sharon was a freshman in high school, her demeanor and personality changed. She had been a happy, outgoing young girl, but slowly she became sullen and withdrawn. Her parents thought it was just a phase of adolescence, so they didn't ask too many questions. Two years later, though, she had become an angry young woman. When they probed, she was initially defiant, but then she blurted out that her dad's brother had sexually molested her several times on summer vacation before she started high school.

- Rhonda loved to have fun with her friends, and they often had parties at homes when the parents were out of town for the weekend. At one of these a boy mixed a drink for Rhonda. The next thing she knew, she woke up nude in the bedroom. She had been the victim of a date rape drug.

- Frank wanted to play football his freshman year, but he didn't have much hope of making the team. Though he tried hard, other guys on the team picked on him for his lack of skill. One day after practice, two of the biggest boys grabbed him, stripped him, and forced him to bend over for anal sex. For days after, he felt like his insides had been torn apart, but they threatened him with a severe beating if he told anyone. *I thought only girls got raped*, Frank thought. *No one can ever know.* He kept quiet as long as he could, but a few days later he fainted from blood loss.

DEFINITIONS AND KEY THOUGHTS 2

- Sexual abuse is seeking *sexual gratification* by taking *unfair advantage of someone with less power*. It includes *rape, incest, fondling, indecent exposure, voyeurism, and verbal innuendo*.

- Sexual abuse is often perpetrated by an adult who has access to a minor by virtue of *real or imagined authority or kinship*. In child and adolescent sexual assault, the victim usually knows and often loves the abuser, making the victim vulnerable.

- By eighteen years of age, *one in three girls* and *one in six boys* will have been sexually abused by someone they know, love, and trust.[1]

- The internet has become a valuable tool for a sexual predator. Approximately one in five teens received a sexual solicitation or approach over the internet in the last year. Many of these were aggressive sexual solicitations. The predator wanted to meet them somewhere; called them on the telephone; and/or sent them regular mail, money, or gifts.[2]

- Sexual abuse may result in *significant complications* for the victim, including:

  — *physical problems*, such as chronic pelvic pain, premenstrual syndrome, gastrointestinal disorders, and sexually transmitted diseases, as well as pregnancy

  — *psychological problems*, such as chronic anxiety, depression, denial, sleep disturbances, emotional detachment, and flashbacks, as well as post-traumatic stress disorder, suicidal ideation, sexual dysfunction, and flashbacks

  — *social problems*, such as withdrawal, a compulsion to engage in risky behavior, and delinquency

3 ASSESSMENT INTERVIEW

For the Teen

1. Tell me why you came to see me today. How can I help?
2. When and where did the abuse take place?
3. How do you feel about what happened to you?
4. Do you feel responsible at all for what happened? If so, tell me about that.
5. How does the abuse make you feel about yourself?
6. How do you feel about the person who violated you?
7. Have you tried to stop the abuse? If you have, what happened?
8. What kind of boundaries do you need to have to protect yourself in the future?
9. Who else knows about this? How did she [or he] respond?
10. Are there people who understand and provide encouragement and support for you?

For the Parents

1. When and how did you learn about your teen being a victim of sexual abuse?
2. Do you know how often this has happened?
3. How do you think your child is coping with this?
4. How are you coping with it?
5. Has your child seen a doctor?
6. What boundaries are needed to protect her?
7. What is your role in helping put these boundaries in place and reinforcing them?
8. How are you and your child relating to the abuser now?
9. Have any authorities been notified?
10. What will it take to rebuild your child's sense of safety and learn to trust more wisely?

Note: Sexual abuse is a crime. If the victim is a minor, the abuse must be reported, usually between one and seven days, to the appropriate agencies, such as the police or Child Protective Services.

WISE COUNSEL 4

Deeply wounded people find ways to protect themselves from harm and establish a new identity. Sometimes these paths are positive, but quite often victims of abuse create roles that promise *relief from the pain* but actually *prevent genuine healing*. In his book *The Wounded Heart*, Dan Allender identifies three common profiles for victims of sexual abuse: *the tough girl* who hardens herself from ever being vulnerable again, *the party girl* who tries to find love in anyone's arms and other forms of risk taking, and *the good girl* who tries to win approval by pleasing those around her.[3] As you talk with a victim of sexual abuse, male or female, look for these patterns.

Some victims immediately share their deepest, strongest emotions about the event and the perpetrator, but many struggle with feelings of shame. They aren't sure who to trust anymore, and they are slow to trust even those who genuinely want to help. Be patient and kind in asking questions, and show that you will respect their feelings, no matter how painful or mixed up they may be.

Empathy is essential in caring for hurting people, but *be careful not to let your anger at the perpetrator become too intense* and color your conversations with the victim and your ability to offer good counsel.

Some victims were emotionally healthy before the abuse, but many were victimized because they were vulnerable, "easy marks." Sexual abuse is a violation of a person's boundaries and inherent personal rights. *Counseling will help the person reestablish these boundaries* and teach her to respect her personal rights to her body and her dignity, or in the case of fragile, vulnerable people, it will *help them establish boundaries for the first time in their life.*

Many victims conclude that the abuse was somehow their fault. Instead of feeling righteous anger, they feel terribly guilty and ashamed. One of the goals in caring for these victims is to help them assign appropriate responsibility for the abuse.

ACTION STEPS 5

For the Teen

1. Be Honest

- You may find it difficult to talk about what happened to you and struggle with feelings of shame. It is important to talk about the abuse and get the help you need.

- Talk with your counselor about your experiences. There are many people who are afraid to discuss what happened to them because someone they love or trust was the abuser. Talking it over with the counselor will help you heal. You are not the only one who struggles with the effects of abuse, and there are support groups that your counselor can recommend that will help you realize you are not alone.

2. Assign Responsibility

- You may think that you did or said something that caused the abuse, but it is important for you to know that you are not responsible for it.
- Your counselor will help you assign responsibility for the events to the appropriate person. This will help you deal with your emotions, take necessary steps to grieve, set boundaries, and eventually forgive.

3. Establish Boundaries

- Every person has the right to self-protection. You have been severely violated and need to establish or reestablish strong, healthy boundaries, including:

  — speaking the truth to the perpetrator and to proper authorities about the perpetrator
  — saying no to any further manipulation or abuse
  — establishing a safe distance between you and the perpetrator

- Your boundaries should make you feel strong, secure, and confident.
- If the perpetrator refuses to comply, legal action may be required, such as a restraining order.
- If you decide to seek help, which is highly recommended, your counselor will help you set the proper boundaries and guide you through them.

4. Be Hopeful

- Sexual abuse is one of the deepest wounds a person can endure, but God knows, understands, and cares. Take the time needed to heal and expect that during this process you will learn some of the deepest lessons of life about wisdom, love, and purpose.
- Remember, you aren't alone. Rely on the people who care about you and allow them to help you through the healing process.
- Know that God has a plan for you and He can help you get through this difficult time. In Jeremiah 29:11 He says, "For I know the plans I have for you . . . plans to prosper you and not to harm you, plans to give you hope and a future." Sometimes things happen in life that we do not understand, but if we have faith and trust in God, we know He will be with us and will lead us.

5. Grieve

- Sexual abuse is one of the biggest losses a person can experience. You have lost your innocence, a sense of safety, and part of your identity. To resolve your hurt and anger, you need to grieve these losses.

- You grieve when you are honest about the pain, anger, and loss you feel, and when you express your sadness to those who really understand and care. This will take a while. Grieving isn't a smooth or quick process.

6. Forgive

- At some point in the healing process, you will need to think about forgiving the offender. This may be one of the hardest things you have ever had to do.
- Before you can forgive the one who has hurt you, it will be necessary to focus first on God's forgiveness of *your* sins. Ultimately, we can forgive others only to the extent we have experienced God's forgiveness.
- Forgiving doesn't mean you have to trust the person. It means you won't take revenge and you don't delight in his pain.
- The person who abused you may not ask to be forgiven or even feel sorry for what he's done. Your act of forgiveness is your response to God's love for you, and it's part of the healing process. It keeps you from becoming consumed with resentment and bitterness.

For the Parents

1. Stay Calm

- As hard as this can be for you personally, you have to stay calm, at least in your teenager's presence. She is already having to deal with extreme emotions and doesn't need any added stress. If you become angry, this could make your child feel as if you are angry at her.

2. Listen

- It is extremely important to listen to your teen as she tries to deal with what happened to her. You want to try to comfort your daughter as much as possible and show her that you are there for her. Your teen may feel ashamed or guilty, especially if the perpetrator was a close family member. Therefore it may take a while for your teenager to get the story out.

3. Find Help

- If your teen tells you about sexual abuse that has just happened to her, remain calm and get help. Your child may have been physically injured, so you need to go to the hospital immediately. When you arrive at the hospital, have someone there contact your local rape crisis center. You can also call Childline at 1-800-932-0313.

In 2008 a national survey by the Centers for Disease Control found:

- 60.4% of female and 69.2% of male victims were first raped before age 18.
- 10.8% of girls and 4.2% of boys from grades 9 through 12 were forced to have sexual intercourse at some time in their lives.

Girls between the ages of 16 and 24 are most at risk for nonfatal dating violence.

6 BIBLICAL INSIGHTS

He heals the brokenhearted and binds up their wounds.

Psalm 147:3

Sexual abuse victims naturally wonder, *Why me? Why did God let this happen?* There are no answers to some questions, but we can be sure that God's heart breaks for those whose hearts are broken. He knows, He cares, and He loves us deeply.

A bruised reed he will not break, and a smoldering wick he will not snuff out. In faithfulness he will bring forth justice.

Isaiah 42:3

Instead of insisting on revenge, a victim can allow God to take care of her perpetrator. Sooner or later God will bring forth justice in that person's life. We can count on it so we don't have to be the instruments of God's wrath.

For I am convinced that neither death, nor life, nor angels, nor principalities, nor things present, nor things to come, nor powers, nor height, nor depth, nor any other created thing, will be able to separate us from the love of God, which is in Christ Jesus our Lord.

Romans 8:38–39 NASB

No matter what has happened to us, God's love is one constant we can always count on. As important as this truth is, however, to a victim of sexual abuse it may sound like a "typical Christian pat answer." We must be careful in using Bible verses with victims of severe trauma, as this may feel like trivializing their pain. At the same time, God's message of mercy and power must be at the heart of all of our counsel.

But I say, love your enemies! Pray for those who persecute you! In that way, you will be acting as true children of your Father in heaven. For he gives his sunlight to both the evil and the good, and he sends rain on the just and the unjust alike.

Matthew 5:44–45 NLT

At some point in the healing process (not too early, not too late), victims need to address the issue of forgiveness. But one must be careful here not to push or force the person into something she is not ready or willing to do. It will be gut-wrenching for the victim, and she will need help eventually to forgive the one who has hurt her so badly. The abuser may not care if he is forgiven, but when the victim forgives, she is protected from harboring resentment, which poisons the soul and makes us bitter.

PRAYER STARTER :7

Lord Jesus, You cry with us in our pain. Nothing can separate us from Your love. Wrap this hurting teen in Your arms today and reassure her of Your amazing love. Give my young friend wisdom in this journey of healing from abuse. I thank You that no matter what anyone else has done to her, You are a loving and safe refuge to whom she can always run. Take the brokenness in this teen's life and create something beautiful. Give Your child grace to forgive and wisdom to know how best to move forward . . .

RECOMMENDED RESOURCES :8

Alcorn, Nancy. *Violated: Mercy for Sexual Abuse*. WinePress, 2008.

Allender, Dan. *The Wounded Heart: Hope for Adult Victims of Childhood Sexual Abuse*. NavPress, 2008.

Kearney, R. Timothy. *Caring for Sexually Abused Children: A Handbook for Families and Churches*. InterVarsity Press, 2001.

Langberg, Diane. *On the Threshold of Hope: Opening the Door to Healing for Survivors of Sexual Abuse*. Tyndale House, 1999.

Morrison, Jan. *A Safe Place: Beyond Sexual Abuse*. Random House, 1990.

Sands, Christa. *Learning to Trust Again: A Young Woman's Journey of Healing from Sexual Abuse*. Discovery House, 1999.

Tracy, Steven R. *Mending the Soul: Understanding and Healing Abuse*. Zondervan, 2008.

Van Pelt, Rich, and Jim Hancock. *A Parent's Guide to Helping Teenagers in Crisis*. Zondervan, 2007.

_____. *The Youth Worker's Guide to Helping Teenagers in Crisis*. Zondervan, 2007.

Sexual Orientation

1 PORTRAITS

- Jeremy was very confused. He had always been attracted to girls, but lately, seeing a boy in his gym class in the shower has been turning him on. When he made a veiled hit, the guy responded. After school that day, they performed oral sex on each other. Jeremy really enjoyed it, but he wonders if he's now completely gay.
- Carla is the oldest of three children. When her father walked out a few years ago, her mother started depending on her for emotional support, cooking, and taking care of her younger brother and sister. Some people kidded that she had become "the man of the house," but they had no idea how right they were. For the past year, Carla and a girlfriend have been giving each other orgasms when they get together to study.
- From the time he was a little boy, Rick enjoyed dressing up in his mother's clothes, putting on makeup, and fussing about his appearance. No one had much doubt about his sexual orientation, but in high school, he took a lot of abuse from the other boys. He's thinking seriously about having a sex-change operation.

2 DEFINITIONS AND KEY THOUGHTS

- *Sexual orientation* is an *enduring emotional, romantic, and sexual attraction toward another individual.*
- Sexual orientation is different from sexual behavior because it refers to *feelings and self-concept.*
- There are three categories of sexual orientation, *classified with regard to the gender* to which an individual is sexually attracted: *heterosexual, homosexual, and bisexual.*
- Probably no other topic elicits such *powerful emotions* and *entrenched and conflicting perspectives* as same-sex attraction, especially in the Christian community.
- Many hold to the biblical view that *homosexuality is not God's design for intimacy and is a distortion of human identity.* Others argue that *homosexuals "don't have a choice"* about their sexual preference, and they lobby for acceptance of the people and their behavior.

- Forty percent of homosexual teens report having attempted suicide. *Homosexuals are more likely than heterosexuals to have mental-health concerns,* such as eating disorders, personality disorders, paranoia, depression, and anxiety.
- Homosexual relationships are *more violent* than heterosexual relationships.[1]
- Many experts think *young women are much more likely than young men to go back and forth between sexual identities* and that the line between a close friendship and a romantic relationship is less clear between women than it is between men.
- Some teens consider themselves *fully bisexual.* Others prefer the terms "heteroflexible" or "polyamorous." Still others just say they are "questioning." Some authorities believe that on issues of sexuality, *all teens are, to some extent, questioning.* They're becoming aware of their attractions and trying to determine how attraction translates into behavior and identity.[2]
- *Identifying the causes of homosexuality* has proven to be a difficult and explosive issue. At this point no definitive study has proven the etiology, but there seem to be *several contributing factors.*

  — A person's *family background,* and especially the relationship with the same-sex parent, can shape emerging sexuality in adolescence.
  — *Social interactions,* especially in formative years, teach and reinforce sexual norms.
  — *Early sexual experiences*—and particularly seductive, abusive, and homosexual experiences—can shape a child's self-concept and perception of sexuality.
  — *Biological causes* have received the most attention in recent years, but ambiguous research results have been offered as "proving a biological or genetic cause" for homosexuality. Of course, finding a biogenetic cause for homosexuality is desirable to those who espouse a gay lifestyle because it could no longer be considered a choice but rather a biological reality and, therefore, not a sin requiring repentance.

- The American Psychological Association states:

  There is no consensus among scientists about the exact reasons that an individual develops a heterosexual, bisexual, gay or lesbian orientation. Although much research has examined the possible genetic, hormonal, developmental, social, and cultural influences on sexual orientation, no findings have emerged that permit scientists to conclude that sexual orientation is determined by any particular factor or factors. Many think that nature and nurture both play complex roles.[3]

- The *passionate and risky nature of homosexual encounters* makes anyone involved vulnerable to many different kinds of sexually transmitted diseases, including HIV/AIDS. Young men who have sex with men (MSM) with high numbers of different partners are at extremely high risk for contracting a sexually transmitted infection. According to the Centers for Disease Control, the number of MSM thirteen to twenty-four years old who are diagnosed with HIV is increasing each year. The number has nearly doubled

During the adolescent years, teens often engage in sexual behavior as a means of establishing their identity. Our culture views sexual activity—with either gender—as a normal "rite of passage" into adulthood.

In the past, the average age people used to "come out" as a homosexual was in their mid-20s; however, over the last two decades the average has dropped to the mid-teen years.

Nearly 6 in 10 young people say "homosexuality is a way of life that should be accepted by society," according to a survey released by the Pew Research Center.

http://www.pbs.org/newshour/generation-next/demographics/gayteens_08-10.html

since 2000. The number infected increased by 11 percent in 2001 and by 18 percent in 2006.

3 ASSESSMENT INTERVIEW

For the Teen

1. Tell me why you have come to see me today.
2. Tell me about your sexual desires.
3. Are these only feelings, daydreams, and urges, or are you acting out these desires?
4. If you've been acting them out, how long and how often has this pattern been going on?
5. When did you first realize your sexual orientation was different from what was expected? How did you handle it then?
6. Do you feel any anxiety or distress over your orientation? Tell me about that.
7. Have you ever been sexually abused, afraid of the opposite sex, seduced by same-sex peers, or engaged in exotic forms of sex?
8. If you are engaged in sexual activity, are you practicing safe sex?
9. Do you notice any physical symptoms of STDs or other medical problems that might be associated with sex?
10. How can I help you?

For the Parents

1. When did you first suspect your child might have a different sexual orientation?
2. Have you talked about it? If so, what happened?
3. Tell me about your relationship with your child when he was little. What has it been like more recently?
4. How does your child want you to respond to his sexual orientation? How do you know this?
5. Is your child experiencing emotional difficulties or social problems because of his sexual orientation?
6. Do you notice any physical symptoms of STDs or other medical problems that might be associated with sex?
7. How can I help?

4 WISE COUNSEL

In the controversial realm of homosexuality, the *professional counselor's role* is easily compromised by demonstrations of *shock or extremes of judgment and disapproval*. The teen has come to you for help (or perhaps has been brought to you by someone else) and is most likely in a very vulnerable emotional state. Any teen confused about his sexual orientation is already dealing with a huge amount of shame and guilt. It is essential that you help him *feel safe* so he can be honest about hurts, fears, and hopes for the future. You must let your client know you accept him as *fully deserving of God's love.*

Empathy and understanding are essential tools at the outset of counseling. If it is determined that there is a clear conflict of values in the counseling relationship (for example, the client wants to continue in homosexual behavior and you believe that it is not biblical), then you need to make a responsible referral. Making such a referral is a professional ethic and demonstrates your commitment to client self-determination and to sound professional counseling.

Conflicting Thoughts

Many teens feel deeply conflicted and ashamed about their sexual orientation. Provide a *safe, calm, nonreactive environment* where the teen can surface hidden feelings and share experiences and perspectives. Without this kind of safe, supportive relationship, there is little chance of helping the teen.

Adolescence is a time of *powerful but conflicting thoughts and desires*, none stronger than those related to sex. Quite often teens need someone who can help them sort out what they feel. *Many adolescents consider same-sex attraction secretly and briefly.* Similarly many authorities on the issue aren't overly concerned if an adolescent engages in *brief sexual experimentation* with same-sex partners.

Most Christian parents would be horrified to learn their child has had these thoughts and experiences. *Parents would be wise to avoid overreacting* if they find that their teen has same-sex urges. They need to *help the teen process his feelings* and listen before they give advice about healthy, God-honoring relationships.

The Issue of Identity

Explore the teen's feelings and attitudes about sexual urges and behavior, rather than trying to deny them or shut them down. In many cases, teens come for counsel because they *feel confused and ashamed*. (Those who feel satisfied and justified in their homosexuality rarely, if ever, come for help.) In the process of sexual development, every teen experiences anxiety, and their fears may easily cloud their thinking processes. Therefore, one of the first tasks is to *help the teen resolve his identity confusion* and discover who he is. *The ultimate issue is usually identity, not sexual orientation.*

Challenge the teen to answer this *crucial question* first, a question that will help *clarify the identity puzzle*: Am I gay or lesbian—which is the embrace of a sexual identity—or am I instead a man or woman (or Christian) who is struggling with homosexual attractions and desires?

Distinguish between sexual orientation and sexual sin. Many authorities believe that changing sexual orientation is often a difficult journey, however, a person always has the ability through the power of God's Spirit to *choose not to sin sexually.*

Even if a teen's parents want him to change, he won't make any progress unless *self-motivation* is present. The teen may express remorse and promise to change just to get mom and dad off his back, but that commitment lasts only until he walks out the door. As we just mentioned, *even those who want to change their sexual orientation need to understand that the process is long and difficult.* Some argue that their sexual orientation may not change, but they can *learn to live a full, meaningful, and God-honoring life by abstaining from same-sex or bisexual behavior.* The choice to obey pleases God.

It takes tremendous *courage and wisdom*, and a lot of *support* from those who understand the struggle, for people to choose to follow God in spite of their sexual "bent," but in reality, it's the same struggle for all of us. *Each believer is responsible to "put off" the old nature and "put on" love for God and obedience to Him every moment of every day.*

5 ACTION STEPS

For the Counselor

1. Determine the Severity of the Problem

- *A teen's fleeting homosexual thought or a single act doesn't constitute a lifestyle, and he may well self-correct, especially in an environment of love and support. Look for patterns of behavior, established same-sex or bisexual relationships, the use of pornography, any incidence of violence, and obsessive thinking about sex.*
- *Take a thorough history, including:*
  — *relationships with parents, siblings, and near relatives*
  — *the specific nature of the relationships with the same-sex parent and opposite-sex parent*
  — *the history and nature of any sexual confusion*
  — *any seduction by same-sex peers or opposite-sex abuse*
  — *violence or intimidation by peers*
  — *the teen's perspective on homosexuality or bisexuality*
  — *his present sexual practices*
  — *physical problems associated with sexual activity, such as STDs*

2. Provide Tenacious Support

- *Throughout the process of discovery and counseling, teens who are confused about their sexual orientation need a lot of love, encouragement, and support. If the problem isn't severe, some grace and truth can put them back on the right track. If their homosexual or bisexual orientation is well established, however, the struggle for change may be a long one, especially if they are unwilling to address the root issues of identity. In such cases, prayer can be one of the most powerful influences. Our God never gives up pursuing His children—even in sin.*

3. Identify Personal Goals of Client

- Determine if your goals and the client's goals are compatible with your faith and practice. If clients feel affirmed in their homosexual identity and lifestyle and want help to have better relationships with same-sex partners, as one who does not believe that same-sex behavior is right before God, that really constitutes a values conflict we referenced earlier. Remember, however, that clients may assume that a Christian counselor is rigid and condemning, and they may be defensive until you demonstrate empathy and understanding. Help your client clarify their life goals.

For the Teen

1. Identify Personal Goals

- Think about goals you would like to achieve through counseling. What would you like your life to be like at the end of the counseling process?

2. Find Accountability

- The Bible speaks specifically against the homosexual lifestyle. Therefore, if your attraction to someone of the same sex is leading you into sinful behavior and causing significant distress or conviction, it is important to seek accountability from a trusted peer, mentor, professional counselor, or pastor.

3. Explore Your Current Beliefs regarding Sexuality

- Focus on discussing what you have been taught in the past about homosexuality and how this has contributed to your current belief system. What do you consider "normal" and "abnormal"?
- Many who experience homosexual urges and behaviors come to counseling with a wealth of misinformation about causes, diseases, the definition of "normal" sexuality, and a host of other topics related to the problem. Some have been taught that they've committed a sin God won't forgive, and they feel not only ashamed but hopeless as well. Help the client understand God's design for sexuality, as well as His willingness to forgive and pardon all sin.

4. Uncover Your Fears and Hopes

- Be honest about your emotions. This is an important step in feeling understood, building trust in your counselor, and moving forward.
- Many people hope that a counselor will give them a quick and easy solution and make them feel better right away. This, of course, won't happen. Homosexuality requires rugged realism about the process and goals for change. Change is possible but often requires hard work and time, and even then, the urges sometimes won't completely go away.
- Homosexuality can be as emotionally explosive in treatment as it is in society, full of raw passion and dark fears. Be transparent about the full range of your feelings.

5. Realize the Importance of Mental Self-Control

- Be open to learning how thoughts and feelings dictate actions. Practice new ways of interpreting and analyzing destructive thoughts and feelings prior to acting on them.

- *The combination of sexual passion and shame causes many homosexuals to be preoccupied, even obsessed, with their sex life and identity. For some, their sexuality is primarily a fantasy world, but this world consumes their lives. It becomes an obsession, and they can't stop thinking about sex. Teach clients to identify thoughts, songs, passages of Scripture, and inspiring messages to focus on and confess aloud, using them to replace their unwanted or intrusive fantasies.*

6. Be Encouraged by Each Step Forward

- Changing identity and a lifestyle is a monumental task. People with other complex issues such as alcoholics, drug addicts, compulsive gamblers, and those with eating disorders have successfully taken steps out of their darkness toward hope and health, and you can do the same.

- Celebrate each step forward you make. Even if you slip, all is not lost. God loves you and He is in the process of helping you change. You can begin to move forward again by repenting, receiving the Lord's forgiveness, and focusing on biblical goals.

- *Provide strong encouragement that the benefits of progress are worth the struggle of moving forward.*

7. Consider Participating in Group Support

- The encouragement you will receive in a Christ-centered support group can make a tremendous difference. In an environment of mutual support and accountability, you will hear from others who struggle with similar problems as they make courageous decisions and experience the joys of real change.

- *Provide a referral to a support group in the area for your client or start one yourself.*

8. Surround Yourself with Good Company

- When struggling with same-sex attraction and homosexual acts, it is important to cut off all relationships that you have had with another homosexual. You also need to stay away from places where homosexual activity is present or could be encouraged.

- Choose friends who are committed to a godly lifestyle and will support your efforts to resist falling into sin.

9. Confess, Seek Forgiveness, and Repent

- Completely surrendering your struggle to God is the most important step you can take.

- Confess to God all of your past sinful behavior and ask for forgiveness. Repent and turn from acting out on your desires and trust that God has forgiven you as He promised.
- Remember, this is going to be a daily battle, something you will have to pray about and constantly surrender to God perhaps even multiple times throughout the day. Make sure you are staying connected to godly mentors and social support.

For the Parents

1. Don't Judge

- God does not consider one sin more heinous than others. We have all sinned and fall short of God's glory.
- Examine your own heart before God and be aware of your own personal struggles and temptations so that you are prepared to show your teen the same love and forgiveness God has shown you.

2. Avoid Lecturing

- Avoid lecturing on all the risks and problems associated with homosexuality. Rarely does a person respond positively when being told what he shouldn't do.

3. Maintain Your Relationship

- Let your child know that you want to maintain a relationship with him.
- When you show your daughter acceptance, it does not mean you agree with her choices.

4. Dig Deep

- Talk with your teen and listen. It may be tough but try to get your teen to share the reasons behind his choices.
- As you dialogue, you will become more comfortable sharing your concerns about the gay lifestyle. And after you have listened to her, your teen may be more willing to listen to you.

5. Give It to God

- It is always best to give your burdens to God. Believe His promises and that He has a plan for your teenager.
- Pray that God will use this difficult situation to bring glory to Himself.

BIBLICAL INSIGHTS 6

Therefore if anyone is in Christ, he is a new creature; the old things passed away; behold, new things have come.

2 Corinthians 5:17 NASB

The real hope for all of us, no matter what our fears, desires, or past, is that Jesus Christ changes lives, even ours.

Flee from sexual immorality. All other sins a man commits are outside his body, but he who sins sexually sins against his own body. Do you not know that your body is a temple of the Holy Spirit, who is in you, whom you have received from God? You are not your own; you were bought at a price. Therefore honor God with your body.

1 Corinthians 6:18–20

Sexual pleasure is one of the most attractive and powerful forces in our lives, and it's easy to let it take control. For those who are Christians, however, the truth is that we belong to God—body, soul, mind, and spirit. And it should be our goal to please Him in everything we do.

Because of this, God gave them over to shameful lusts. Even their women exchanged natural relations for unnatural ones. In the same way the men also abandoned natural relations with women and were inflamed with lust for one another. Men committed indecent acts with other men, and received in themselves the due penalty for their perversion. Furthermore, since they did not think it worthwhile to retain the knowledge of God, he gave them over to a depraved mind, to do what ought not to be done.

Romans 1:26–28

There comes a point when God "gives people over" to their passions and lets them experience the painful consequences of their choices. When we talk to teens about the importance of their decisions, we can lovingly and honestly speak the truth about the destination of the path they are on.

7 PRAYER STARTER

Lord Jesus, we praise You for the beautiful gift of sex that You have created. I ask You today for wisdom for my young friend as he [she] struggles with sexual orientation. You promise, Lord, that the truth will set us free. Show my friend the truth from Your Word about sexuality and clear up any confusion. Lord, You know each of us intimately, down to the deepest desires and longings of our hearts. Give my friend wisdom in sorting through all the sexual talk, images, temptations, and pressures. Surround him [her] with the blessing of deep and godly friendships . . .

8 RECOMMENDED RESOURCES

Arterburn, Stephen, Fred Stoeker, and Mike Yorkey. *Every Young Man's Battle: Strategies for Victory in the Real World of Sexual Temptation.* Random House, 2002.

Chambers, Alan. *God's Grace and the Homosexual Next Door: Reaching the Heart of Gay Men and Women in Your World.* Harvest House, 2006.

_____. *Leaving Homosexuality: A Practical Guide for Men and Women Looking for a Way Out.* Harvest House, 2009.

Chase, Emily Parke. *What Do I Say to a Friend Who's Gay?* Kregel, 2006.

Chirban, John. *What's Love Got to Do With It: Talking Confidently with Your Kids about Sex.* Thomas Nelson, 2007.

Haley, Mike. *101 Frequently Asked Questions about Homosexuality.* Harvest House, 2007.

Speck, Greg. *Sex: It's Worth Waiting For.* Revised and expanded ed. Moody, 2007.

Internet Resource

Exodus Youth: Finding True Freedom. www.Exodusyouth.net.

Spiritual Doubt

1 PORTRAITS

- Mark grew up in a strong Christian family. From the time he was a baby, his parents took him to church. In high school studying biology and history, he began to ask questions about creation and evolution, and he was fascinated with the Protestant Reformation. He asked his parents about evolution, but they barked back that he just needed to trust God and not fill his head with those "lies" his teacher was telling him. Their response, though, didn't answer his questions. Gradually his doubts grew, and by the time he was a senior, he had abandoned the faith.

- Helen trusted in Jesus at youth camp. Her youth pastor and her parents were thrilled. A few weeks later, however, she realized that she still struggled with the same fears she had endured before that night at camp. She had assumed they would go away, and for a while they did. But then they came back stronger than ever. *I must not really be a Christian*, she assumed. But she didn't want to tell anybody. Several months later her doubts overwhelmed her, and she told a friend that she was now sure she had never trusted in Jesus at all.

- Randy had attended his church's youth group and he was a regular in a Christian group that was part of his high school basketball team. Everybody looked up to him as a shining example of a fine young man of faith. When his parents announced they were getting a divorce, Randy's world crumbled. "Why did God let this happen?" he growled at his youth pastor. "Couldn't He have stopped it?" Gradually his anger turned to bitterness—at his parents, at himself, and at God.

2 DEFINITIONS AND KEY THOUGHTS

- *Doubt is a fundamental distrust, fear, or lack of confidence in personal belief.* Questioning one's beliefs is a healthy part of the growing-up process, but for many teens, fear of being judged keeps them from actually asking the hard questions. Yet asking hard questions—of parents, of friends, of faith—is a*n important part of coming to own one's faith.*

- The *questions of faith are an integral part of the adolescent search for identity.* The *normal teen tendency to question* her parents' authority and beliefs leads her also to question what she's been taught about faith. For many this questioning is soon resolved by *good teaching and patient listening*, but for some, unanswered (or poorly answered) questions can erode their faith.

- There's *nothing wrong with teens asking hard questions* about the character of God, the authority of the Bible, and the meaning of faith. Adults who are threatened by these questions drive teens away from the faith. Instead, we need to validate their questions, avoid simplistic answers, value them for their courage and interest, and enter the process of discovery with them.

ASSESSMENT INTERVIEW : 3

1. Tell me how you're thinking and feeling about God these days.
2. Has there been a time when you felt your faith was strong? If so, tell me about that time in your life.
3. When did your doubts begin to surface?
4. Was there any particular event in your family, difficult questions at school, or disappointments that caused you to doubt God's goodness or even His existence?
5. Do you have concerns about your security as a believer? Do you wonder if you've done enough to go to heaven?
6. Have you tried to talk to your parents or youth pastor about your questions, fears, and doubts? If so, how did it go?
7. If you could identify your chief question or doubt, what would it be?
8. Do you expect God to answer all of your questions so that you never doubt Him or His purposes?
9. How can I help you today?

WISE COUNSEL : 4

Adolescents are on a search: for truth, for where they fit in, for their purpose in life, for people they can trust, and for real answers about God. If they believe the authorities in their life—mainly parents, teachers, and pastors—feel threatened by their questions, they are more likely to turn to others who will validate their search. Instead, *we need to affirm their search*, affirm them for having the courage to ask hard questions, and support them all along their journey.

In many cases, *teens simply want to feel that someone cares enough to listen*. They need to vent their frustrations, fears, and doubts. If we respond by being threatened and demand they just trust God, we shut them off from truth, from God, and from future conversations with us. But if they feel that we are really listening, they relax and may enter into *genuine dialogue*. And then they can learn whatever we feel they need to know.

Questions Are Normal

The adage is true: "People don't care what you know until they know that you care." No matter how flaky the questions, no matter how defiant the anger, and no matter how convoluted the teen's thinking pattern may be, *build a relationship of love, honesty, and respect*. In many cases, that's what they were looking for anyway.

Some adults have harbored secret doubts for years but haven't had the courage or the opportunity to resolve them. All of us have questions, and none has all the answers to life's deepest problems. If we're honest with ourselves, we may be completely convinced that God is sovereign, good, and strong, but the intricacies of His will remain, to some degree, a mystery to all of us.

Sometimes teens are struggling with spiritual doubt because they believe wrong theology. They may have heard that God demands they never sin, so they quickly realize they can't meet that standard. They may think they have to beat themselves up when they sin to prove they are repentant. In many cases, *opening the Bible and showing people the truth of God's Word about the grace, love, and forgiveness of God will help dissolve the doubts.*

What Are They Asking?

It's important to *explore adolescents' thoughts and emotions* to determine the cause and nature of spiritual struggles. Sometimes the issue is primarily theological, sometimes it's an ethical challenge, and often teens are simply trying to reconcile what they've been taught with the realities they see in their family, at school, and in the world. *Make sure you are answering the question they are really asking.*

Naturally many teens and adults *ask questions about God when their world gets turned upside down by a tragedy or disappointment*. A death, divorce, failure, or betrayal can cause them to conclude that God doesn't care or isn't powerful enough to protect them. The "*problem of pain*" isn't easily answered, but it's important to let people wrestle with these issues. *Our encouragement during these times is more important than the wisdom of our words.*

Some questions are far more difficult. Job wanted to ask God why He allowed him to experience such loss. God answered, but not in the way Job expected. Many students want to reconcile the teaching of creation in the Bible with their biology and geology textbooks. If we tell them, "Just believe," we cut off some of the most wonderful conversations we can have with them. *A far better answer is, "Let's look at that together."* There are many excellent resources on issues of creation, ethics, the problem of pain, and other important topics. *Encourage teens to read, study, and talk with you about them* (see Recommended Resources at the end of the chapter).

Christ's Grace When We Question

You can't give what you don't have. Any teen struggling with doubt needs to see the grace and truth of Jesus Christ, first and foremost in you, the counselor. The teen needs to know that *Jesus invites honest questioning*, and promises that He will reveal Himself to those who seek Him. *Especially because the church tends to discourage questioning, it is essential that the teen realize that doubting is not a sin.* To blindly hold beliefs without knowing why is a sin.

ACTION STEPS 5

1. Be Honest about Your Beliefs

- Be honest about your belief in God. Many people believe there is a God in heaven but doubt whether He can really help them in their daily life struggles. Do you believe God exists? If so, do you believe He is powerful enough to be there for you when you are hurting, when a friend betrays you, when a trusted adult lets you down, when you're struggling in school, when life doesn't seem fair, when you are fighting with your parents?

- Make a list of things you believe about God. How do you view Him? Is He judgmental, always looking down to see whether you are doing right or wrong? Is He ready to slap your wrist or punish you for being bad, or is He compassionate and loving and with you no matter what you're going through?

2. Talk to a Trusted Pastor or Bible Teacher

- Once you have journaled about your beliefs, take your ideas to somebody you trust who can help you correct any false ideas you have about God. Doubts are important. In fact Henry David Thoreau once said, "Faith keeps many doubts in her pay. If I could not doubt, I should not believe."[1] Doubting leads to questions that lead to foundational answers that will help you build your faith. Find somebody to disciple you and help you find answers to your questions.

3. Surround Yourself with Faithful Christians

- While it's important to talk with a pastor or Bible teacher, you should also talk over your struggles and doubts with your peers, who will probably better understand where you're coming from.

- Friends in your church and youth group may have also struggled with doubt and they may have insights that will help you.

4. Read the Word

- Reading your Bible is a great way to find and renew your faith.

5. Take Your Doubts to God

- Ask God to help you with your doubts. Jesus said, "Everything is possible for him who believes" (Mark 9:24). As soon as He said this, the father of a boy who was possessed said to Jesus, "I do believe; help me overcome my unbelief!" (v. 25). Seek God and ask Him to help you overcome your unbelief. He will.

6 : BIBLICAL INSIGHTS

If any of you lacks wisdom, he should ask God, who gives generously to all without finding fault, and it will be given to him. But when he asks, he must believe and not doubt, because he who doubts is like a wave of the sea, blown and tossed by the wind. That man should not think he will receive anything from the Lord; he is a double-minded man, unstable in all he does.

James 1:5–8

From time to time, all of us hit a brick wall spiritually. We don't know where God is and we don't know the path we should take. When this happens, we can turn to God for direction, trusting Him to lead us—in His way and in His time—but we have to stand firm in our faith and know that God has not disappeared even though it may feel as though He has.

Immediately the boy's father exclaimed, "I do believe; help me overcome my unbelief!"

Mark 9:24

Throughout the Scriptures, we see people wrestling with doubt and faith. God never condemns anyone for asking hard questions. He invites those who doubt, like this father or Thomas or us, to engage Him with our deepest, hardest questions. He can handle any of them and He will lead us to trust Him even more.

You will seek me and find me when you seek me with all your heart.

Jeremiah 29:13

God promises us that our search for truth will eventually lead us to Him. We may not have all our questions answered, but we can rest in the fact that God understands even when we don't.

Yet [Abraham] did not waver through unbelief regarding the promise of God, but was strengthened in his faith and gave glory to God, being fully persuaded that God had power to do what he had promised.

Romans 4:20

In Abraham's long wait for God to provide the promised son, he doubted from time to time. In the end, his life was a pattern of tenacious trust in God's goodness, His plan, and His ultimate provision. In the same way, all of us experience doubts. As we trust in God instead of turning away, we'll find Him faithful.

PRAYER STARTER 7

Lord Jesus, You welcome our questions and You aren't intimidated by our doubts. We are grateful that in You, there is no condemnation. Your unconditional love sets us free! I pray that You will give my young friend wisdom to seek out Your truth in the midst of confusion. Give courage to grapple with the hard questions and study Your Word. Even when we don't understand, we can rest in knowing that You will never leave us or forsake us, even when we doubt . . .

RECOMMENDED RESOURCES 8

Clark, Chap. *Hurt: Inside the World of Today's Teenagers.* Baker Academic, 2004.

Clark, Chap, and Dee Clark. *Disconnected: Parenting Teens in a MySpace World.* Baker Books, 2007.

DeMoss, Nancy Leigh, and Dannah Gresh. *Lies Young Women Believe: And the Truth That Sets Them Free.* Moody, 2008.

Matlock, Mark. *Freshman: The College Student's Guide to Developing Wisdom.* Think, 2005.

McDowell, Josh. *The New Evidence That Demands a Verdict.* Thomas Nelson, 1999.

Smith, Christian, and Melina Denton. *Soul Searching: The Religious and Spiritual Lives of American Teenagers.* Oxford University Press, 2009.

Strobel, Lee. *The Case for Christ.* Student ed. Zondervan, 2001.

_____. *The Case for Faith.* Student ed. Zondervan, 2002.

Yaconelli, Mark. *Downtime: Helping Teenagers Pray.* Youth Specialties, 2008.

Stress

1 : PORTRAITS

- Wilson had heard that his sophomore year would be tougher academically than his first year of high school, but he had no idea how much more demanding his classes would be. His homework load doubled from the previous year, and he was struggling to maintain his GPA. After a few months the strain began to show in many different ways. Some nights, he didn't take time to eat dinner, he snapped at his mom when she offered to help, and he had a hard time going to sleep every night. At school the activities he used to enjoy became a nuisance.

- When Marjorie entered junior high, she had a hard time fitting into the right group. Girls she had enjoyed only a year before didn't want her around, and when she tried to make friends with some other girls, they didn't pay any attention to her at all. She felt alone, confused, and angry.

- Rob had been a very happy child, but as a freshman, he struggled with almost every aspect of life. Now he had to study to keep up, so he didn't have as much time for his friends. He felt embarrassed in gym class because he wasn't as developed as some other boys his age and he felt very awkward around girls. His parents were putting a lot of pressure on him to get good grades, and he thought he was going to explode!

2 : DEFINITIONS AND KEY THOUGHTS

- *Stress is the body's reaction to a change* that requires a physical, mental, or emotional adjustment or response. It can come from any situation or thought—critical or chronic—that *makes a person feel frustrated, angry, nervous, or anxious.*

- *Mild levels of stress inspire us to be creative, take action, and solve problems. Higher levels, however, debilitate our energy, erode confidence, and create discouragement.* Prolonged, severe periods of stress can create *physiological symptoms*, such as chronic headaches and gastrointestinal disorders. Also, severe stress negatively affects our mood and relationships.

- *Common causes of stress* for adolescents include:

  — school demands and frustrations
  — negative thoughts and feelings about self
  — changes in their body

- problems with friends and/or peers at school
- unsafe living environment or neighborhood
- separation or divorce of parents
- chronic illness or severe problems in the family
- death of a loved one
- moving or changing schools
- taking on too many activities or having expectations that are too high
- family financial problems

- Physical and/or mental changes can occur when determining that *a situation is dangerous.* This response will vary depending on the personality of the person and the situation. The commonly known phrase describing this response is "*fight, flight, or freeze,*" which may mean faster heart and breathing rates, increased blood to the muscles of the arms and legs, cold or clammy hands and feet, upset stomach, and/or a sense of dread. *Anxiety, withdrawal, aggression, physical illness, or poor coping skills,* such as drug and/or alcohol use, are some of the most common ways people deal with life when they are not managing their stress appropriately.

- Two reasons for *suburban students' stress are inordinate pressure to achieve* and *isolation from adults.* Junior high students from upper-income families are often alone at home for several hours a week. Isolation may be caused by the demands of the affluent parents' career obligations and the children's many after-school activities.[1]

- A study of stress in high-risk teens discovered:

  - Physiological development, cognitive differences, puberty, immaturity, slower recovery from stressful events, and lack of coping skills may *intensify the stressful events* experienced by adolescents.
  - Stress has been associated with a variety of *high-risk behaviors,* including smoking, suicide, depression, drug abuse, behavioral problems, and sexual behaviors.
  - Teens have identified *schoolwork* "as the most frequent and important source of stress" in their lives. Homework, tests, learning disabilities, a conflict with teachers and other students, or simply not liking school represented common areas of stress.
  - Teens with a *low self-esteem* were reported to seek "acknowledgment and acceptance by teachers and peers," which was also extremely stressful.
  - *Poor student-teacher relationships* were noted to have a profound impact on learning, success in school, and overall stress levels.
  - Teens described *family stress* as including "worrying about the well-being of family members," "being nagged," and "conflicts over family responsibilities with siblings."
  - Teens noted that *not getting along with a sibling or parents* was an important indicator of stress. *Hearing or seeing their parents fight* with each other and worrying about the outcome of these altercations was a frequent stressor.

— The most frequently cited *stressors among inner-city adolescents* were the pressure to join a gang and "being offered sex by drug addicts for money."
— The most frequently noted stressor was *school,* followed by *money, relationships, and parents.*[2]

3 ASSESSMENT INTERVIEW

1. How would you describe the level of stress in your life today?
2. What are the things (school, home, work, relationships with friends, and so on) that contribute to your stress?
3. Tell me how each of these affects you.
4. How do you normally try to cope with all the stress you experience?
5. Does it affect you physically? Do you have headaches, stomachaches, sleeplessness, or other physical symptoms?
6. How does stress affect your moods and your relationships?
7. What are the things you really enjoy? When do you get to do them?
8. What activities and challenges energize you and stimulate your creativity?
9. What have you tried to do to manage your stress? How have these attempts worked out?
10. How can I help you today?

4 WISE COUNSEL

New challenges often bring out the best in us. They cause us to think more creatively and act decisively to solve problems. That's the good, healthy side of stress. *Negative, debilitating stress* has an opposite effect. Teens who feel overloaded by the demands of life:

- feel depressed, angry, guilty, and tired
- experience headaches, stomachaches, trouble sleeping
- laugh or cry at odd times and for no apparent reason
- instinctively blame other people for their troubles
- see only the negative side of people and situations
- no longer enjoy things that used to be fun
- feel that nothing will ever change
- establish unrealistic expectations

One of the *biggest challenges* of adolescence is learning how much can be done in a day and what each person is responsible for accomplishing. Most teens need help figuring out these *important limits and responsibilities.* Through healthy dialogue, help the teen make choices. Teens soon discover on their own if they've bitten off more than they can chew. *Self-discovery is an essential part of learning to manage stress.*

Adolescents are under tremendous *pressure to figure life out*. They face enormous new challenges and threats in virtually every area of life. A *safe, supportive home environment helps them feel comfortable* handling situations at school and with friends, but sadly, *the stress levels of many teens are multiplied by their relationships at home*. Teens may feel more comfortable talking about the stress they feel at school, but don't neglect to uncover the possible pressures they feel at home.

Parents probably won't be much help in assisting their kids to handle stress unless they learn those skills themselves. We can't give away something we don't possess. *Parents should follow the recommendations in Action Steps to address their own stresses*.

ACTION STEPS 5

1. Determine What Causes Your Stress

- Think about the expectations that are made on you at school, by friends, and at home.
- Do you often have changes in mood, feel hopeless, or burst out in anger? Is your achievement in school declining? These are signs of stress. Making a list of these reactions and when they happen will help you understand what is causing your stress.

2. Take Steps to Reduce Stress

- Exercise and eat regularly.
- Do not use drugs, alcohol, or tobacco. Keep caffeine to a minimum.
- Learn relaxation and calming exercises.
- Determine realistic expectations. Your counselor will help you with this.
- Learn to say no to additional responsibilities.
- Practice positive assertions instead of negative self-talk. Do this by telling yourself with confidence that you are capable of doing things. Writing encouraging notes and putting them around your house is a good way to gain positive energy throughout the day.
- Try to avoid being a perfectionist and worrying.
- Spend time with friends who handle stress well.[3]

3. Relax

- Find something fun to do with your family or friends. Spend time in pleasure-filled activity that focuses on relationship building, not performance.
- Having fun is vital to stress reduction. A time to let loose and enjoy the company of others can do wonders for the brain and relationships that matter most.

4. Decrease "Stinking Thinking"

- Negative thinking and false beliefs about oneself and environment are often at the root of stress and anxiety. Learn to identify areas of negativity and false belief systems that are present in your current thought life. Talk with your counselor or other adult about your negative thinking.

- Replace your false beliefs with the truth of God's Word and learn positive ways of coping from Scripture. This will reduce your pain, stress, and self-defeating behaviors. Proverbs 12:25 says, "An anxious heart weighs a man down, but a kind word cheers him up."

5. Don't Give Up

- You may feel that your situation is hopeless. You've tried to make life work, but for some reason, the demands, failures, and disappointments have only increased. Talk with your counselor or another adult about your feelings of hopelessness.

- Remember that no matter how discouraged you feel, God offers wisdom, peace, and a clear direction for the future. He is with you. You don't have to walk through life alone.

- *As you help a teen handle stress, look for signs of depression and, if appropriate, refer him to a physician or professional counselor.*

6 BIBLICAL INSIGHTS

Do not fear, for I am with you; do not anxiously look about you, for I am your God. I will strengthen you, surely I will help you, surely I will uphold you with My righteous right hand.

Isaiah 41:10 NASB

Inordinate stress and unrealistic expectations produce anxiety. We can be sure that God understands. He cares and He will lead us to find workable solutions.

Peace I leave with you; My peace I give to you; not as the world gives do I give to you. Do not let your heart be troubled, nor let it be fearful.

John 14:27 NASB

Jesus promises a different kind of peace. Most of us think of peace as the absence of struggles, disappointments, and stresses, but Jesus promises us His presence and His peace in the midst of life's difficulties. The situations may not change, but He changes us from the inside out.

Do not be anxious about anything, but in everything, by prayer and petition, with thanksgiving, present your requests to God. And the peace of God, which transcends all understanding, will guard your hearts and your minds in Christ Jesus.

Philippians 4:6–7

When we feel stressed and anxious, we don't have to deal with things on our own. We can bring our requests to God, trusting Him and thanking Him that He will show us the way forward.

Come to me, all you who are weary and burdened, and I will give you rest. Take my yoke upon you and learn from me, for I am gentle and humble in heart, and you will find rest for your souls. For my yoke is easy and my burden is light.

Matthew 11:28–30

We can handle life's difficulties best when we are walking in tandem with Jesus. He doesn't take the load away completely, but He walks beside us and shoulders most of the load as we trust Him for wisdom, direction, and peace.

PRAYER STARTER 7

Father, today my young friend feels tired, worn out, and stressed. Give him rest in Your presence and calm the anxiety. You tell us, Lord, not to worry, and we thank You that we can rest in Your promises, even when life is stressful. Give my friend wisdom in setting healthy boundaries and not over-committing himself. Guide Your child in learning to say no and making wise decisions. You are in control of everything, Jesus. Teach us to trust You rather than trying to control life on our own . . .

RECOMMENDED RESOURCES 8

Burns, Jim. *Tough Problems, Real Solutions.* Gospel Light, 2002.

Floyd, Scott. *Crisis Counseling: A Guide for Pastors and Professionals.* Kregel Academic, 2008.

Hart, Archibald D., and Catherine Hart Weber. *Is Your Teen Stressed or Depressed? A Practical and Inspirational Guide for Parents of Hurting Teenagers.* Thomas Nelson, 2008.

Ortberg, John. *When the Game Is Over, It All Goes Back in the Box.* Zondervan, 2007.

Swenson, Richard. *Margin: Restoring Emotional, Physical, Financial, and Time Reserves to Overloaded Lives.* NavPress, 2004.

Suicide

1 PORTRAITS

- Alisha had been distraught since her twin sister died in a car accident four months ago. They had been sitting next to each other in the car, talking and laughing like they did most of the time. Her parents have been too wrapped up in their own pain to see how devastated Alisha is. She told a friend that she misses her sister so much she's thinking of going to see her soon.
- Marvin has been using drugs since his older brother introduced him to Ecstasy when he was nine. Soon he was smoking joints before and after school and shooting coke on the weekends. His father gave up on the family and left, and his mother focused her attention on Marvin's little sister. In the past few months the police have busted Marvin four times and he's always in detention at school. He has only one friend in the world and he announced to his friend that he just bought a gun and intends to use it. His friend isn't sure whom he plans to kill.
- Suzanne has dated Ike for two years, but throughout that time her parents have told her again and again how much they disapprove of their relationship. Suzanne stands up for Ike every time, but in the past few months, Ike has been violent, hitting her in places where the bruises don't show. Her friends plead with her to end the relationship, but she thinks she can make Ike a better person. And she sure can't tell her parents! One night, Ike gets drunk and beats her, breaking her teeth. Suzanne runs home and sneaks in the back door, grabs a bottle of pills from her parents' bathroom, and takes them all.

2 DEFINITIONS AND KEY THOUGHTS

- *Suicidal behavior* is any deliberate action that may have *life-threatening consequences*, such as taking a drug overdose or deliberately crashing a car.
- A person may attempt suicide *to escape* intense and chronic emotional pain, *to punish* herself, *to inflict pain* on survivors, *to be reunited* with a loved one who died, *to prove affection, to avoid being a burden, or to get attention.*
- It is estimated that more than 90 percent of teen suicide victims have a *mental disorder, such as depression, and/or a history of alcohol or drug abuse.*[1]
- Suicide is the third-leading cause of death for teens.

ASSESSMENT INTERVIEW :3

For the Teen

1. How are you feeling about life today?
2. Have you thought about hurting yourself? Have you ever thought of suicide?
3. How often or how long have you felt this way?
4. Have you thought about how you would end your life? Do you have the resources at hand to do it?
5. Have you tried to hurt yourself in the past? If so, what happened?
6. Tell me about the stresses and losses in your life. What has happened that makes you feel hopeless?
7. Have you been using drugs or alcohol? If so, what and how much?
8. Tell me about your family life. Does your family understand the stress you're under, or are they a chief cause of the stress?
9. Who really cares about you? What do these people think of your plans to kill yourself?
10. Where do you think God is in all of this?

For the Parents

1. Why are you concerned about your child's safety?
2. What are the symptoms of hopelessness in your child?
3. Does she have a plan to end her life? Does your child have the resources to make it happen?
4. Has your child recently experienced a significant loss? How did she respond at the time?
5. Describe your home environment. How might this contribute to a sense of hopelessness?
6. Is your child using drugs or alcohol?
7. Have you noticed that your child no longer enjoys things she used to enjoy?
8. Do you think the danger to your child's life is imminent?
9. Have you talked with your child about suicide? If so, how did the conversation go?

WISE COUNSEL :4

To understand the depth and seriousness of the *teen's hopelessness*, look at:

- the family environment, including divorce, abuse, drugs, and rage
- her success or failure in school
- changes in her circle of friends
- outbursts of anger or tears
- signs of depression
- any mention of wanting to die

We may assume that all suicidal people are simply hopeless, but the reasons people consider ending their life are varied and *based on a particular set of perceptions, desires, and fears.* Talk with the teen openly about these issues.

Talk Openly

Some people are reluctant to *talk candidly* with a hopeless person about suicide because they think they are putting the idea into her mind. That's almost never the case. It's much *more productive to talk openly* about a person's thoughts of suicide, plans, and resources, like a gun, rope, knife, or pills, than to ignore the subject. If the teen has a plan and has gone to the trouble to get the necessary resources to carry it out, the *threat is very serious.*

In the first conversation with a suicidal person, *safety is the paramount objective.* Protecting her life is the first priority. If you think the teen is in imminent danger, *call 911 or get her to an emergency room* for help.

After the immediate threat subsides, and in cases when the person is only considering suicide and hasn't formulated a plan, *focus on the causes of hopelessness.* Discuss problems at home and at school. Invite the adolescent to talk about what she enjoys and the things that feel hopeless.

Suicide is seldom a simple, impulsive decision. In most cases, feelings of despair have been building for months if not years, and the slide into hopelessness has been a long process. Help the teen look back at that process to see what *current, desperate feelings have evolved over time.* Encourage the teen to trust that there is a *path back toward hope,* even though it may be long and gradual.

Reasons for Hope

When imminent danger has passed, help the teen *broaden the scope of her perception to see that life is worth living.* Depression causes people to see only the negative, discouraging, and hopeless things about life. In counseling and in conversations with friends and family members, teens can discover new reasons to get up each day.

Avoid simplistic or overly spiritualized answers. Yes, Jesus saves, but often He leads us through a long path of insight and growth so that we learn valuable lessons from the suffering we endure. *Most of the time He rescues us through our pain, not out of our pain.*

People who are hopeless see the negatives in life. People around them may see plenty to enjoy, but these people see only *pain and emptiness.* Gently challenge the teen with your reasoned optimism and the truths from *God's Word about His love, faithfulness, and plan for all of us.* You can share stories about people like David and Elijah, men who had bouts of depression and heartache, but who found God not only to be with them in the midst of their pain but to be the strength they relied on to overcome their pain.

Refer the Teen to an Expert

Depression is a serious mental disorder, one that usually needs professional care. Certainly, when teens express the intention to end their life, they need counseling to uncover the root causes of the problem, identify the sense of loss, and *learn to grieve, forgive, and find hope again.*

Refer the teen who is depressed and/or hopeless to a medical doctor and to a professional counselor who has expertise in dealing with people who are suicidal.

ACTION STEPS 5

For the Teen

1. Sign a Contract with Your Counselor

- Sign a contract stating that you will not attempt suicide for twenty-four hours.
- If you sign a contract, try to remain with somebody you trust for the next twenty-four hours so that person can help you through this critical period. If possible, spend this time with your parents. Do something together at home. If you cannot be with your parents, ask somebody you like to be with to spend this time with you.
- *Follow up with the teen the next day to reassess her condition. If she has not improved, seek help immediately.*

2. Talk to Your Counselor

- With your counselor, begin working through the reasons behind your suicidal thoughts.
- If you have suicidal thoughts that you cannot get rid of, seek help immediately.

3. Refocus

- Refocus your thoughts on your strengths, your abilities, and what you have to offer the world.
- Refocus your attention on things you like to do. What hobby or activity do you love the most? How long has it been since you have done it? Make plans to pursue this favorite hobby or activity as soon as possible.
- Isolation will only make depressive symptoms and suicidal thoughts worse. Begin spending time with friends or join an after-school activity or club.

4. Get Involved in Exercise and Physical Activity

- Physical activity is a great way to let off steam. If you do it with a friend or a sports team, the time spent with others will also strengthen you emotionally.

Firearms account for the most commonly used suicide method among youth ages 15–19, accounting for 49% of all completed suicides. Males complete suicide at a rate 4 times that of females. However, females attempt suicide 3 times more often than males. There is a relationship between alcoholism and suicide; the risk of suicide among alcoholics is 50–70% higher than in the general population.

suicidology.org

For the Parents

1. Get Help Immediately

- If your child has a plan and the means to commit suicide, call the police or paramedics immediately. She must be protected.
- Inpatient psychiatric units are locked because of the need to protect people from their desire to harm themselves. Every attempt is made to remove from the unit any means of causing harm. You need to protect your child in the same way.
- Do not try to transport a suicidal person, especially your teenager, to the hospital by yourself. It is too dangerous.
- If your suicidal teen is under the influence of drugs or alcohol, arrange for her to be supervised constantly while detoxing or becoming sober. Then the suicidal ideation should be reassessed. If she is no longer suicidal, you should definitely consider seeking treatment for her substance abuse.

2. Follow Up and Supervise

- Ask your child to sign a contract stating that she will not attempt suicide for twenty-four hours. Of course, this contract is only as good as your teenager's word. It is not a legal document.
- If your teen is willing to sign a contract, try to remain with her for supervision. Do something with her at home.
- Reconnect with your child the next day to see if the suicidal thoughts remain.
- If she has not improved, seek help immediately.

3. Be Gentle but Persistent

- Be sure to offer support in a gentle but persistent manner. Teenagers are not necessarily comfortable talking about depression or suicide and therefore may not want to talk initially. Stay with your child and show your unconditional love and support.
- Do not lecture your teen. She is not likely to be receptive to a lecture at this time. Just listen and offer your support in a way that acknowledges the seriousness of her situation.

4. Investigate the Tunnel Vision

- Sometimes the problem that is causing your child to consider suicide can actually be solved rather simply, but she has tunnel vision and cannot see any way out of her predicament.
- Ask your teen to sign a contract that she will not harm herself while you investigate the circumstances for three days. In that time, work to find the beginning of some solutions.
- During the three days be sure that your teenager is supervised.

- If you have not made substantive progress in finding a solution at the end of three days, find a professional therapist or a hospital that will treat your child.

5. Take Care of Your Family

- Seek support networks for you and everybody affected by these circumstances. Be open with one another and do not blame yourselves. Blaming yourself or your teenager is not helpful for anybody. Seek ways to grow together through this crisis.

BIBLICAL INSIGHTS : 6

Do not fear, for I am with you; do not anxiously look about you, for I am your God. I will strengthen you, surely I will help you, surely I will uphold you with My righteous right hand.

Isaiah 41:10 NASB

Hopeless people have given up on finding meaning, purpose, and love in their lives—but God hasn't given up on them. If we turn to Him in our grief and sadness, He will uphold us, strengthen us, and lead us to a path of peace.

When my heart was grieved and my spirit embittered, I was senseless and ignorant; I was a brute beast before you. Yet I am always with you; you hold me by my right hand. You guide me with your counsel, and afterward you will take me into glory.

Psalm 73:21–24

In this passage, the psalmist was at his worst—bitterly disappointed, furious, and hopeless—but even at his worst moment, God reached out in love to take his hand. When we feel completely hopeless, we aren't alone. God takes our hand and leads us.

I waited patiently for the LORD; he turned to me and heard my cry. He lifted me out of the slimy pit, out of the mud and mire; he set my feet on a rock and gave me a firm place to stand. He put a new song in my mouth, a hymn of praise to our God.

Psalm 40:1–3

About 4,500 young people between the ages of 10 and 24 die by suicide each year.

National Center for Injury Prevention and Control, 2008

Suffering is a part of this life. Often people who are contemplating suicide are burdened by a myriad of unresolved issues, feelings, and pain—problems that can mostly, if not always, be resolved. The one thing they lack, and we as believers must help them regain, is faith in the sovereignty of God. A biblical understanding of God and all that He has promised for those who love Him inspires hope and diminishes despair. Suffering is never without purpose. Choosing to live by faith that God is in control is the only path toward complete healing and strength to overcome our pain.

For though we live in the world, we do not wage war as the world does. The weapons we fight with are not the weapons of the world. On the contrary, they have divine power to demolish strongholds. We demolish arguments and every pretension that sets itself up against the knowledge of God, and we take captive every thought to make it obedient to Christ. And we will be ready to punish every act of disobedience, once your obedience is complete.

2 Corinthians 10:3–6

The struggle with depression, despair, and rage is in our minds, and often our perceptions about God and life are flawed. God's truth helps us sort out what is really true so that we can base our choices on reality instead of wandering in confusion and hopelessness.

7 PRAYER STARTER

Lord Jesus, we thank You for the gift of life. Every day and each breath is a gift from You. I lift up my young friend as she struggles with thoughts of suicide. Reassure her of how wide and high and deep and long your love is and how precious she is to you. Give Your child hope and reveal the purpose You have for her life. Lord, You are bigger than depression, loneliness, and pain. Your grace and mercy are more powerful than the greatest evil. No matter how difficult life is, there is always hope in You . . .

8 RECOMMENDED RESOURCES

Fresonke, Cherie. *Go in Peace for Teens*. WinePress, 2009.

Gerali, Steven. *What Do I Do When: Teenagers Deal with Death*. Youth Specialties, 2009.

Luce, Ron. *"It's Only a Tattoo!" And Other Myths Teens Believe: A Parent's Response Book*. David C. Cook, 2006.

Nelson, Richard E., and Judith Galas. *The Power to Prevent Suicide*. Updated edition. Free Spirit Publishing, 2006.

Rowatt, Wade G. *Adolescents in Crisis: A Guidebook for Parents, Teachers, Ministers, and Counselors*. Westminster, 2001.

Trollinger, Sara. *Advanced Triage Counseling: Counseling That Heals Teenagers & Parents*. HigherLife Press, 2009.

Van Pelt, Rich, and Jim Hancock. *A Parent's Guide to Helping Teenagers in Crisis*. Zondervan, 2007.

_____. *The Youth Worker's Guide to Helping Teenagers in Crisis*. Zondervan, 2007.

Trauma

PORTRAITS : 1

- Mindy was having a great time on the youth group's mission trip to Honduras. They were working with children in an orphanage, and Mindy felt they were making a difference in the children's lives. One afternoon as she and a friend were walking through town, a little boy ran out into the street. The bus driver never saw the child and didn't even stop. Others stood frozen as the boy lay in the street, but Mindy ran to him and held him in her arms. In less than a minute, he died. For days she couldn't get the event out of her mind, and months later she still wakes up in the night screaming in terror.

- Aaron and his family had been working outside all day. In the afternoon a storm was brewing in the west, but that wasn't unusual for that time of year. Soon the sky got dark and the rain began to fall. Suddenly they heard a roar that sounded like a freight train. Aaron looked in the distance and could see a tornado coming straight for him. The family ran into the bathroom and his dad grabbed a mattress to put over them. The tornado blew the roof off and they were cut by some of the broken windows, but they were alive. Since then, Aaron has panic attacks whenever he hears the wind in the trees.

- Catherine thought the party would be lots of fun. All her friends were going, and she heard that a new boy in school would be there. Early that night, they struck up a conversation. After a few drinks, he asked if she wanted to have sex. She said, "No, I don't think so." After midnight when most people were wasted, he found her in the kitchen, dragged her into a bedroom, and raped her. He told her he'd beat her to a pulp if she told anybody. Weeks later Catherine became deeply depressed.

DEFINITIONS AND KEY THOUGHTS : 2

- *Trauma is any physical or emotional injury.*
- In medical terms, *trauma* refers to a *serious or critical bodily injury, wound, or shock*. This definition is often associated with trauma medicine practiced in emergency rooms and represents a popular view of the term.
- In psychiatry, *trauma* has assumed a different meaning and refers to *an experience that is emotionally painful, distressful, or shocking*, which often has lasting mental and physical effects.[1]

- A child may experience *trauma as a result of abuse*. The American Academy of Pediatrics (AAP) defines childhood abuse as:

  > a repeated pattern of damaging interactions between parent(s) [or, presumably, other significant adults] and child that becomes typical of the relationship. In addition to physical, sexual and verbal abuse, this can include anything that causes the child to feel worthless, unlovable, insecure, and even endangered, or as if his only value lies in meeting someone else's needs. Examples cited in the report include "belittling, degrading or ridiculing a child; making him or her feel unsafe [including threat of abandonment]; failing to express affection, caring and love; neglecting mental health, medical or educational needs.[2]

- Adolescents twelve to seventeen years old may exhibit *responses to trauma* that are similar to those of adults, including flashbacks, nightmares, emotional numbing, avoidance of any reminders of the traumatic event, depression, substance abuse, problems with peers, and antisocial behavior. Also common are withdrawal and isolation, physical complaints, suicidal thoughts, school avoidance, academic decline, sleep disturbances, and confusion. The adolescent may feel extreme guilt over his failure to prevent injury or loss of life and may harbor revenge fantasies that interfere with recovery from the trauma.[3]

- *Posttraumatic stress disorder* (PTSD) is an emotional illness that develops as a result of a terribly frightening, life-threatening, or otherwise highly unsafe experience. PTSD sufferers reexperience the traumatic event or events in some way; tend to avoid places, people, or other things that remind them of the event (*avoidance*); and are exquisitely sensitive to normal life experiences (*hyperarousal*).

3 : ASSESSMENT INTERVIEW

1. Tell me what happened to you.
2. How did you feel and respond in the hours and days after the event?
3. How do you feel emotionally and physically in recent days?
4. Do you have any recurring symptoms, such as nightmares, flashbacks, panic attacks, sleep disturbances, problems with eating, or depression?
5. Have you talked to people about your struggles? How did they respond? How did you feel after talking with them?
6. When do you feel safe? When do you feel threatened?
7. How can I help you?

4 : WISE COUNSEL

The *first hours, days, and weeks after a traumatic experience* are crucial for the mental health of the adolescent.

In the early stage after the event, *parents and caregivers* can:

- *Talk to the teen about exactly what happened.* Shock can easily cloud a person's memory, so an accurate description is essential.

- Invite the teen to share the full range of emotions, from numbness to panic and rage. Don't try to "fix" the young person's pain at this point. Just listen and ask follow-up questions to show you really care.

- Avoid rushing the healing process. Some parents are so traumatized they don't have the emotional energy to help their children process their pain, and they just want their kids to get over it as quickly as possible.

- Validate the teen's feelings and fear responses. Many people, including teens, have trouble sleeping after a traumatic event. Leave a light on in the room or in the hall, and reassure him that he is safe. Don't criticize him for needing more reassurance during this time.

- Reassure the teen that he isn't to blame for the trauma.

- Build confidence by helping the teen make decisions, even small decisions, for himself.

Quite often *caregivers are also traumatized*, trying their best to cope with their own heartache, shock, and loss. This is certainly true for natural disasters, but *parents also feel traumatized by violence or accidents that happen to their children*. In these cases, the whole family needs immediate care.

Teens react to trauma in different ways: stuffing the pain, talking incessantly about the event, getting really busy, withdrawing from interactions with people, blaming themselves, blaming the victims, and many other ways. Some experience severe reactions immediately, but *the response may be delayed* in others for several weeks. Many of them now feel unsafe. *They don't trust parents, themselves, or God.*

If teens get attention and help in the first hours and days after a traumatic event, most of them recover from the initial shock within a few weeks. They still, however, need to do the *work of grieving* the losses they experienced from the event. *This process takes months.*

After a few weeks, some victims may continue to demonstrate significant emotional damage and need *professional help*. They may exhibit:

- *avoidance behavior*, refusing to go places that remind them of the traumatic event,

- emotional numbing, a diminished emotional response or lack of feeling toward the event,

- reexperiencing the trauma, including nightmares and disturbing memories during the day, and

- hyperarousal, being easily startled and suffering sleep disturbances.[4]

Once the person has been exposed to a traumatic event whereby feelings of intense fear, helplessness, or horror are experienced, three groups of symptoms are required to assign the *diagnosis of PTSD*:

- *a persistent reexperiencing of the traumatic event* (for example, distressing recollections of the event that include images, thoughts, feelings, or even perceptions of the event, flashbacks, or reliving the event in the moment, that are usually

PTSD statistics in children and teens reveal that more than 40% have endured at least one traumatic event, resulting in the development of PTSD, up to 15% of girls and 6% of boys. On average, 3–6% of high school students in the United States and as many as 30–60% of children who have survived specific disasters have PTSD. Up to 100% of children who have seen a parent killed or endured sexual assault or abuse tend to develop PTSD, and more than one-third of youths who are exposed to community violence will suffer from the disorder.

www.medicinenet.com/posttraumatic_stress_disorder/article.htm

caused by reminders of the traumatic events themselves, recurring nightmares about the trauma and/or physiological arousal to anything that resembles the event)

- a persistent avoidance of anything related to the event (includes efforts to avoid places, people, and experiences that remind the suffering person of the trauma and a general numbing of emotional responsiveness)
- a persistent sign of increased arousal (for example, hyperarousal, including sleep problems, irritability, impulsiveness, trouble concentrating, hypervigilance, and exaggerated startle response)

When people dealing with PTSD *acquire anger management skills, deal with their anxiety and fear, improve their communication skills, and use relaxation techniques,* they will gain a sense of mastery over their emotional and physical symptoms.[5]

It would be ideal if parents and caregivers could prevent all trauma from happening to teens, but of course this isn't possible. They *can* have helpful *conversations about the natural consequences of bad choices.* These talks are best received if they are held in a nonthreatening, dispassionate environment, not in the heat of anger or panic. For instance, parents might talk to their teens about drunk driving and share a story about someone they know who was killed or hurt.

5 : ACTION STEPS

For the Counselor

1. Invite Honesty about Emotional Pain

Many trauma victims can't articulate their pain at first because they experience shock and emotional numbness, but sooner or later, they need to open the valve to their emotions and let them flow. Often it isn't smooth or pretty. They may express both sadness and outrage, and they may blame virtually anyone for the event. Don't correct the teen's emotions, but when the time is right, certainly after the emotional explosion subsides, talk about truth, responsibility and blame, and the mysteries of God's ways.

2. Watch for Patterns of PTSD

After a few weeks, if the person continues to suffer from symptoms such as panic attacks, inordinate fears, flashbacks, withdrawal, outbursts of anger, and sleep disturbances, the teen may have PTSD. Contact a professional counselor. PTSD is a serious mental disturbance. If it is treated appropriately, the teen may be freed from the nagging fears that haunt him.

3. There May Be No Answer to "Why?"

Often those who suffer trauma ask, "Why did this happen?" or "Why did God let it happen to me?" Usually there are no simple answers to these questions, and we do people a great disservice by giving them pat answers. Perhaps the most eloquent answer is to simply offer your presence and kindness, and say, "I don't know. All I know is that God is good, but His ways are mysterious."

For the Teen

1. Understand the Nature of the Trauma

- Try to discuss what happened—if you can remember it. The memories will be painful, so try to remember them only in the presence of a counselor or trusted adult.
- Try to be honest about your feelings and events with your counselor.
- Consider joining a support group of survivors of similar trauma.
- Understand that you did not deserve the hurt that happened to you and that you didn't cause it.
- Depending on the nature of the trauma, understand that you may need to erect some boundaries with particular people so that you will not be hurt again.

2. Express Your Feelings

- Express your real feelings. If you have anger at people who caused your trauma, express it. This does not necessarily mean confronting them. There are symbolic ways to express your feelings, such as writing letters that won't necessarily be sent. This can be very powerful.
- If you're angry with God, express that as well. He can handle it.
- If you have grief over a loss experienced through the trauma, express your grief.

3. Know That You Will Heal

- Healing will come with God's help.
- It is important that you engage in a process that will help you heal, either in further individual counseling or in group counseling.

4. Know That You Will Have Victory

- Beyond just healing, you will have victory over the trauma. Begin to consider some of the positive strengths you will have in your life as a result of healing from this trauma.
- Know that you will eventually be able to forgive and this will set you free. This is the ultimate spiritual victory.
- Know that you will be able to be of great comfort to others who experience similar traumas.

The risk of developing PTSD from different types of trauma includes:

natural disaster 4%

witnessing a killing or serious injury 7%

child's life-threatening illness 10%

sudden unexpected death of a family member or friend 14%

shooting or stabbing 15%

serious accident or injury 17%

sexual assault other than rape 24%

severe physical assault 32%

rape 49%

PTSD Alliance

6 BIBLICAL INSIGHTS

God is our refuge and strength, an ever-present help in trouble. Therefore we will not fear, though the earth give way and the mountains fall into the heart of the sea, though its waters roar and foam and the mountains quake with their surging.

Psalm 46:1–3

No matter what happens—natural disasters, violence, accidents, or sexual assault—we can turn to God as our source of strength and help.

The Lord is close to the brokenhearted and saves those who are crushed in spirit.

Psalm 34:18

When we feel devastated and hopeless, God understands our pain and wants to restore our sense of safety and joy.

Jesus wept.

John 11:35

When their brother Lazarus died, Mary and Martha blamed Jesus for not being there to save him. Jesus didn't correct them. He just cried because He cared so deeply for the whole family and felt their loss. In the same way, Jesus weeps when we weep over our losses.

Therefore, since we have a great high priest who has gone through the heavens, Jesus the Son of God, let us hold firmly to the faith we profess. For we do not have a high priest who is unable to sympathize with our weaknesses, but we have one who has been tempted in every way, just as we are—yet was without sin. Let us then approach the throne of grace with confidence, so that we may receive mercy and find grace to help us in our time of need.

Hebrews 4:14–16

We experience loss, rejection, suffering, and heartache, but so did Jesus. Whatever we suffer, He suffered too. He understands our pain and our confusion and He invites us to trust Him with our deepest wounds and most painful feelings.

7 PRAYER STARTER

Jesus, You understand suffering because You suffered incredible losses when You walked the earth. You don't blame us for feeling the pain of traumatic events. You weep with us. Thank You, Lord, for Your care, Your love, and Your purpose for us.

We don't know why this painful event happened, but we trust You to use it in some way to draw this teen into a deeper relationship with You . . .

RECOMMENDED RESOURCES :8

Clark, Chap. *Hurt: Inside the World of Today's Teenagers.* Baker Academic, 2004.

Crabb, Larry. *Shattered Dreams.* Random House, 2002.

Dobson, James C. *When God Doesn't Make Sense.* Tyndale House, 1997.

Hart, Archibald D. *Dark Clouds and Silver Linings.* Focus on the Family Publishing, 1994.

Wright, H. Norman. *The New Guide to Crisis and Trauma Counseling.* Gospel Light, 2003.

Yancey, Philip. *Disappointment with God.* Zondervan, 1997.

_____. *Where Is God When It Hurts?* Zondervan, 2002.

Video Game and Cyber Addiction

1 : PORTRAITS

- Raymond's parents got him a gaming system for his fifteenth birthday. All his friends enjoyed playing, and for a while it seemed like a harmless pastime. After a couple of months, however, Raymond seemed to be obsessed with playing. He had always been a good student, but he missed homework assignments because he played games so long each night. And he began skipping meals because he was in the middle of "important games." When he and his parents got into a heated argument about this, he shouted at them, "You gave it to me. Don't you want me to enjoy it? I'm not hurting anybody!"

- Carl has always been socially awkward, but he seemed to find a niche playing online games with kids around the world. At first, his parents were thrilled that he was connecting with people for a change, but then they began to find him playing all hours of the night. "That's when kids in Japan can play," he protested. Also, they found out he had been gambling on the games, and he had lost more than five hundred dollars. They had no idea where he had gotten that much money.

- Sandra was overweight, shy, and withdrawn. She had very few friends at school and she spent much of each day chatting with people she met through online social networks. She had posted a picture of her beautiful sister as her own, and some good-looking boys in other states expressed interest in her.

2 : DEFINITIONS AND KEY THOUGHTS

- A nationwide survey suggests that approximately 8 percent of teens show signs of behavioral addiction to video games.[1]

- Many teens admit to skimping on chores and homework, lying about how much they play, showing poor performance on tests of homework, and struggling to cut back on video game playing without success.

- According to the Center for On-Line Addiction, the *warning signs for video game addiction* include:

    — playing for increasing amounts of time
    — thinking about gaming during other activities
    — gaming to escape from real-life problems, anxiety, or depression

— lying to friends and family to conceal gaming
— feeling irritable when trying to cut back on gaming

- It is hoped that "video game addiction" will be a *formal diagnostic disorder* in the upcoming revision of the *Diagnostic and Statistical Manual of Mental Disorders* (expected in 2012). Game addiction is defined as *excessive and compulsive use of computer and videogames that results in social and/or emotional problems; despite these problems, the gamer is unable to control this excessive use.*[2]

- *Pathological gamers* play longer hours each day, experience relief from withdrawal symptoms when they play, experience cravings as they anticipate playing, and exhibit more than twice as much aggressive behavior as nonpathological gamers.[3]

- Though statistics on computer and internet addiction are hard to determine, *media usage of eight- to eighteen-year-olds has increased significantly* in the past ten years. In 1999 the average time of media use per day was 6 hours and 19 minutes; in 2009 it was 7 hours and 38 minutes, almost an entire adult workday.[4]

- If you include multitasking between media modems, such as television, music/audio, computer, video games, print, and movies, the total media exposure per day in 2009 was 10 hours and 45 minutes, an increase from 7 hours and 29 minutes in 1999.[5]

ASSESSMENT INTERVIEW 3

1. What do you enjoy about video games or the computer?
2. How much time do you spend doing that each day?
3. How does your playing video games or using the internet affect your schoolwork and your family relationships?
4. What do your parents think about the amount of time you spend at the computer?
5. Have you lied to them about it?
6. Have you tried to cut back? If so, what happened?
7. If you don't change your habits, what are some probable consequences for your future?
8. How can I help you?

WISE COUNSEL 4

Online gaming or *compulsive computer use* may not seem as dangerous as drugs or alcohol, but if there are no boundaries, over time lives can be ruined by these behaviors. Children who play or go online several hours a day have *little time to build friendships, complete homework, or enjoy sports.* Psychologists report that these behaviors can result in twenty-one-years-olds with the *emotional intelligence* of twelve-year-olds. Many teens who struggle with addiction to computer games or online sites have *poor self-esteem and difficulties in relationships.* A *family history of addiction* may also be a contributing factor.[6]

Methods used for recovery from addictions to video games and social networking sites fall between *abstinence* used for drug addictions and *moderation* used for food addictions. Most addicted teens will *continue to use computers* but they need to *scale back their use*, possibly eliminating their involvement in gaming, social networks, or other sites that have caused problems in the past.

Parents who are concerned their teen may be addicted to video games or compulsive online behavior shouldn't dismiss their child's behavior as "just a phase." They need to keep careful records, including:

- logs of when and how long the teen is involved in these behaviors
- problems (relationships, homework, chores, lying, stealing) resulting from the activity
- reaction of the teen to time limits

Parents need to be informed about the *common signs of addiction* related to gaming and online behavior. They include the following:

- *Mood modification*: seeking the feelings of euphoria, excitement, or relief
- *Tolerance*: needing more and more of the behavior to get the same feeling of excitement or relief
- *Withdrawal*: irritability and/or physical effects that occur when the behavior is suddenly reduced or discontinued
- *Relapse*: after a commitment to quit or cut back on the behavior, the teen soon goes back to previous patterns of behavior
- *Deception*: lying to cover up excessive use, loss of money, secret relationships, or stealing
- *Complications*: preoccupation with the behavior causes lower achievement in school, conflicts at home, and withdrawal from normal activities
- *Isolation*: withdrawing to the world of games, social networking sites, or other online behavior and failing to connect with real people; withdrawal becomes self-perpetuating because loneliness is one of the strongest predictors of game addiction among online gamers.
- *Anger and hostility*: withdrawal and conflict create anger but limit conflict resolution skills

Parents can acknowledge the attraction of video games, social networking sites, and other online attractions without condoning addictive behaviors. Open lines of communication. Ask questions, and listen without demanding change. In the context of honest dialogue and understanding, parents can share their concerns and discuss reasonable limits. If the teen resists or refuses to limit the time spent in games or online, it's an indication that there is a real problem.

ACTION STEPS :5

1. Understand the Problem

- Video games and computer use are not inherently bad for you; it's the amount of time and energy you devote to their use that can be detrimental. If playing video games and using the computer are negatively affecting your attendance or grades at school or your relationships with friends, family, teachers, or coaches, you have a problem. The first step toward a solution is admitting that you need help.

2. Be Accountable

- Sign a contract with your counselor, parent, or friend who will help you stop your overuse of video games and the internet and hold you accountable.

3. Replace the Behavior with Other Activities

- Explore possible options for becoming involved in activities outside of the home, such as sports, youth group, music lessons, or art.
- Ask your parents to help you find and get involved with activities that fit your personality and perspective on life.

4. Seek Professional Help

- A professional counselor will help you deal with all aspects of your addictive behavior, including obsessive thinking, self-concept issues, compulsive behaviors, and establishing limits and consequences.

BIBLICAL INSIGHTS :6

But I say, walk by the Spirit, and you will not carry out the desire of the flesh. For the flesh sets its desire against the Spirit, and the Spirit against the flesh; for these are in opposition to one another, so that you may not do the things that you please.

Galatians 5:16–17 NASB

Obsessive thinking and compulsive behaviors are serious problems. They thrive on empty promises that these things will bring relief from the concerns of life and give us the thrills we crave, but they leave us feeling ashamed, empty, and lonely. We can't shake obsessive thinking and compulsive behaviors on our own; we need the power of God's Spirit, the truth of God's Word, and the encouragement of God's family to help us take steps forward every day.

"Everything is permissible for me"—but not everything is beneficial.
"Everything is permissible for me"—but I will not be mastered by anything.

1 Corinthians 6:12

Paul demonstrates clearly that being allowed to do something does not mean it will benefit us. It is not against the law or sinful to play video games or use the computer. However, spending too much time connected to any behavior can breed addiction and mastery—and being mastered by anything other than God and His will for our lives leads only to destruction.

Therefore if you have been raised up with Christ, keep seeking the things above, where Christ is, seated at the right hand of God. Set your mind on the things above, not on the things that are on earth. For you have died and your life is hidden with Christ in God.

Colossians 3:1–3

Escape and thrills seem attractive, but they aren't God's plan for us. He wants us to enjoy life to the fullest, but that involves strong healthy relationships and obedience to His calling. We need to say no to those things that take us down the wrong path, and we need to say yes to God and His purpose for our lives.

Be very careful, then, how you live—not as unwise but as wise, making the most of every opportunity, because the days are evil. Therefore do not be foolish, but understand what the Lord's will is.

Ephesians 5:15–17

Every addict will tell you that the behavior seemed like a good idea at the start. Sooner or later, though, many addicts come to their senses and realize how foolish they've been. At that moment of repentance, they need someone to extend a hand of grace and truth to help them learn to live according to God's will.

7 PRAYER STARTER

Jesus, thank You for the breath You have given us today. Give my young friend wisdom in discerning how to best use her time and the role that technology plays in that. We are so grateful, Lord, that You care about the details of her life, even things like video games and online social networks. Show her how to use these resources wisely and in a way that would honor You—and maybe to avoid using them for a while to be free of the hold they have on her. Technology can be a gift from You if we use it wisely, but, Jesus, You are the only One who can truly satisfy. Set our eyes today on the things that really matter.

RECOMMENDED RESOURCES : 8

Abanes, Richard. *What Every Parent Needs to Know about Video Games.* Harvest House Publishers, 2006.

Bruner, Olivia, and Kurt Bruner. *Playstation Nation.* Center Street, 2006.

Clark, Chap, and Dee Clark. *Disconnected: Parenting Teens in a MySpace World.* Baker Books, 2007.

Covey, Sean. *The 6 Most Important Decisions You'll Ever Make: A Guide for Teens.* Fireside, 2006.

Illian, Jason. *MySpace, My Kids: A Parent's Guide to Protecting Your Kids and Navigating MySpace.com.* Harvest House Publishers, 2000.

Kendall, Peggy. *Connected: Christian Parenting in an Age of IM and MySpace.* Judson Press, 2000.

Kern, Jan. *Eyes Online: Eyes On Life: A Journey Out of Online Obsession.* Standard Publishing, 2008.

Maier, Bill. *HELP! My Child Is Hooked on Video Games.* Focus on the Family Resources, 2006.

Sax, Leonard. *Boys Adrift: The Five Factors Driving the Growing Epidemic of Unmotivated Boys and Underachieving Young Men.* Basic Books, 2008.

According to the Entertainment Software Association (ESA), the average age of a competitive video gamer is about 21, so many are teens.

http://www.pbs.org/ newshour/generation- next/demographic/ gaming_12-22.html

Notes

Introduction

1. Shankar Vedantam, "Social Isolation Growing in U.S., Study Says," *Washington Post*, June 23, 2006, A03, http://www.washingtonpost.com/wp-dyn/content/article/2006/06/22/AR2006062201763.html?referrer=emailarticle.

2. "Poll: Have You Ever Wished You Could Surgically Change Something about Your Body?" *Seventeen*, 2007, http://www.seventeen.com/health-sex-fitness/special/plastic-surgery-poll-0807.

3. "Did You Know?" http://www.dietjokes.co.uk/jokes/053.php.

4. National Eating Disorders Association, "Statistics: Eating Disorders and Their Precursors," 2006, http://www.nationaleatingdisorders.org/uploads/statistics_tmp.pdf.

5. "Hookup Survey Results," *Seventeen*, 2007, http://www.seventeen.com/health-sex-fitness/special/hookup-survey-results-hsp-0406.

6. According to the American Psychiatric Association, "Let's Talk Facts about Common Childhood Disorders," 2005, http://healthyminds.org/multimedia/commonchildhooddisorders.pdf.

7. "Respect Your Mind, Protect Your Body," http://www.idph.state.il.us/public/respect/hiv_fs.htm.

8. According to DivorceMagazine.com, "On U.S. Divorce Statistics," http://www.divorcemag.com/statistics/statsUS.shtml.

9. Kathleen Berger, *The Developing Person: Through the Life Span*, 6th ed. (New York: Worth Publishers, 2005).

10. U.S. Census Bureau, "The Father Factor: Facts of Fatherhood," *National Fatherhood Initiative*; http://www.fatherhood.org/father_factor.asp.

11. According to DivorceMagazine.com, "On U.S. Divorce Statistics," http://www.divorcemag.com/statistics/statsUS.shtml.

12. National Center for Fathering, "Fathering in America Poll," January 1999, http://www.fathers.com/content/index.php?option=com_content&task=view&id=399.

13. "Teen Mania," 2003, http://www.teenmania.org/corporate/index.cfm.

14. Let Us Reason Ministries, "The Church Losing Her Salt," 2005, http://www.letusreason.org/Current30.htm.

15. Quoted in ibid.

Abortion

1. David C. Reardon, *Aborted Women, Silent No More* (Acorn Books, 2002).

2. Jay N. Giedd, et al., "Brain Development during Childhood and Adolescence: A Longitudinal MRI Study," *Nature Neuroscience* 2 (October 1999): 861–63.

Adoption

1. http://www.adoptionissues.org/emotional_issues.html.

Alcoholic and Abusive Parents

1. Action Steps adapted from http://www.4children.org/issues/1997/july_august/fact_sheet_domestic_violence_and_young_children/.

Anxiety and Phobias

1. *Diagnostic and Statistical Manual of Mental Disorders, IV-TR.* (Washington, DC: American Psychological Association), 475–78.

Attention Deficit Hyperactivity Disorder

1. These parameters were approved by the Council of the American Academy of Child and Adolescent Psychiatry on June 5, 1996, *Journal of the American Academy of Child and Adolescent Psychiatry* 36, no. 1 (1997): 138–57.
2. Retrieved from http://www.add.org/articles/parentingteen.html.

Bullying

1. http://www.familyfirstaid.org/bullying.html.
2. http://www.k12.wa.us/SafetyCenter/HarassmentBullying/pubdocs/bullying-factsforteens.pdf.

Cutting

1. Quoted in Shari Roan, "Turning the Hurt Toward the Self," *Los Angeles Times*, December 8, 2008; http://articles.latimes.com/2008/dec/08/health/he-cutting8.
2. Ibid.
3. Ibid.
4. Ibid.
5. Elizabeth Lloyd-Richardson, Nicholas Perrine, Lisa Dierker, and Mary Kelley, "Characteristics and Functions of Non-Suicidal Self-Injury in a Community Sample of Adolescents," *Psychological Medicine* 37 (2007): 1183–92.
6. Amanda Purington and Janis Whitlock, "Self-Injury Fact Sheet," *ACT for Youth Upstate Center of Excellence Research Facts and Findings: A Collaboration of Cornell University, University of Rochester, and New York State Center for School Safety*, 2004, http://www.actforyouth.net/documents/fACTS_Aug04.pdf.
7. Parenting.org: www.parenting.org/cuttingselfinjuryhelp/understanding.asp.
8. Adapted from: Kidshealth.org.

Depression

1. Sources include: "Mental Health: A Report of the U.S. Surgeon General"; U.S. National Library of Medicine; National Institutes of Health; Kidshealth.org.
2. "Bipolar Disorder in Children and Teens," *American Academy of Child and Adolescent Psychiatry*, 2008, http://www.aacap.org/cs/root/facts_for_families/bipolar_disorder_in_children_and_teens.
3. National Mental Health Association, "Adolescent Depression: Helping Depressed Teens," http://smhp.psych.ucla.edu/qf/mood_qt/factsheetd.pdf.

Destructive Dating Relationships

1. Liz Claiborne Inc., "Teen Dating Abuse Survey 2006," (Teenage Research Unlimited, 2006), http://www.loveisnotabuse.com/web/guest/home.
2. Bonnie S. Fisher, Francis T. Cullen, Michael G. Turner, "The Sexual Victimization of College Women," Washington: Department of Justice, National Institute of Justice; publication NCJ 182369, 2000.
3. Quoted in Barbara Whitaker, "Teen Dating: A Mom's Guide," *Good Housekeeping* (July 2006); http://www.goodhousekeeping.com/family/teens/teen-dating-jul06.
4. " 'Sexting' Shockingly Common among Teens," *CBS News*, January 15, 2009, http://www.cbsnews.com/stories/2009/01/15/national/main4723161.shtml.
5. Whitaker, "Teen Dating: A Mom's Guide."
6. Ibid.

Discipline

1. N. B. Mitchell, "What's Your Parenting Style?" http://www.lifeway.com/lwc/article_main_page/0,1703,A=150741&M=50018,00.html.

2. Chap Clark and Dee Clark, *Disconnected: Parenting Teens in a MySpace World* (Grand Rapids: Baker, 2007), 127–29.

3. Ibid., 142.

4. Ibid.

5. Ibid., 143.

Drugs and Alcohol

1. The AntiDrug.com.

Eating Disorders

1. "Frightening Statistics behind Eating Disorders," *Denver Post*, May 11, 2009.

Fatherlessness

1. Childtrends.org.

2. Henry B. Biller and Robert J. Trotter, *The Father Factor: What You Need to Know to Make a Difference* (New York: Pocket Books, 1994).

Forgiveness

1. American Medical Student Association, "Healing through Forgiveness," http://www.amsa.org/healingthehealer/forgiveness.cfm.

2. As cited in Gregg Easterbrook, "Forgiveness Is Good for Your Health," http://www.beliefnet.org.

Gangs and Violence

1. Bureau of Justice Assistance, "Gang and Drug Related Homicide: Baltimore's Successful Enforcement Strategy," 2003.

2. Helpinggangyouth.com, "Gang Facts and Statistics."

3. http://www.ncjrs.gov/spotlight/gangs/summary.html.

4. Adapted from: SixWise.com, "Joining a Gang: How to Help Kids Prevent It, How to Tell if They've Joined One, How to Help Them Out."

God's Will

1. John Piper, "What Is the Will of God and How Do We Know It?" Desiringgod.org, 2004, http://www.desiringgod.org/ResourceLibrary/Sermons/ByTopic/92/621_The_Goodness_of_God_and_the_Guidance_of_Sinners/.

Grief

1. Family Caregiver Alliance, "Grief and Loss," National Center on Caregiving, http://www.caregiver.org/caregiver/jsp/content_node.jsp?nodeid=404.

2. Karen Kersting, "A New Approach to Complicated Grief," *The Monitor* 35, no. 10 (Nov. 10, 2004): 51–55; http://www.apa.org/monitor/nov04/grief.html.

3. Elisabeth Kubler-Ross, *On Death and Dying* (New York: Macmillan, 1969).

Guilt

1. Les Parrott, *Helping the Struggling Adolescent* (Grand Rapids: Zondervan, 1993), 143.

2. R. Zahn et al., "The Neural Basis of Human Social Values: Evidence from Functional MRI," *Cerebral Cortex Advance Access*; http://cercor.oxfordjournals.org/cgi/content/full/bhn080v1.

Inferiority

1. Parrott, *Helping the Struggling Adolescent*, 163.

2. U.S. Department of Education, http://www.ed.gov/parents/academic/help/adolescence/part8.html.

Loneliness

1. Jacqueline V. Lerner, Richard M. Lerner, and Jordan Finkelstein, *Adolescence in America* (ABC-CLIO, 2001), 408–9.

2. Ken Rotenberg and Shelley Hymel, *Loneliness in Childhood and Adolescence* (New York: Cambridge University Press, 2008), 253–55.

3. John Cacioppo et al., "In the Eye of the Beholder: Individual Differences in Perceived Social Isolation Predict Regional Brain Activation to Social Stimuli," *Journal of Cognitive Neuroscience* 21, no.1 (2009): 83–92.

Obesity

1. American Academy of Child and Adolescent Psychiatry, "Obesity in Children and Teens," no. 79, updated June 2008; www.aacap.org/cs/root/facts_for_families/obesity_in_children_and_teens.

2. Marla E. Eisenberg, Dianne Neumark-Sztainer, Jess Haines, and Melanie Wall, "Weight-Teasing and Emotional Well-Being in Adolescents: Longitudinal Finding from Project EAT," *Journal of Adolescent Health* 38 (2006): 675–83.

3. Centers for Disease Control, "Overweight and Obesity," http://www.cdc.gov/obesity/childhood/causes.html.

4. American Academy of Child and Adolescent Psychiatry, "Obesity in Children and Teens."

Obsessions and Compulsions

1. *Diagnostic Statistical Manual of Mental Disorders IV-TR* (Washington, DC: American Psychiatric Association): 462–63.

2. Ibid.

3. Ibid.

4. Southwestern Medical Center, "Obsessive-Compulsive Disorder," http://www.utsouthwestern.edu/patientcare/healthlibrary/obsessive_compulsive_disorder__ocd_/0,,P00737,00.html.

Parent-Adolescent Relationships

1. Kristin A. Moore et al., "Parent-Teen Relationships and Interactions: Far More Positive than Not," *Child Trends Research Brief*, December 2004; http://www.childtrends.org/files/parent_teenRB.pdf.

2. Tiffany Field, Miguel Diego, and Christopher E. Sanders, "Exercise Is Positively Related to Adolescents' Relationships and Academics," *Adolescence* 141, no. 36 (2001): 105–10.

Parents' Divorce

1. Centers for Disease Control, "Cohabitation, Marriage, Divorce, and Remarriage in the United States," *Vital and Health Statistics* 23, no. 22 (July 2002), http://www.cdc.gov/nchs/data/series/sr_23/sr23_022.pdf.

2. Ibid.

3. Susan V. Dahinten, Jennifer D. Shapka, and J. Douglas Willms, "Adolescent Children of Adolescent Mothers: The Impact of Family Functioning on Trajectories of Development," *Journal of Youth and Adolescence* 36 (2007): 195–212.

4. Philip M. Stahl, *Parenting after Divorce: A Guide to Resolving Conflicts and Meeting Your Children's Needs* (Atascadero, CA: Impact, 2000).

5. Thomas Gullotta, Gerald Adams, and Jessica Ramos, *Handbook of Adolescent Behavioral Problems* (New York: Springer, 2008), 35–36.

Peer Pressure

1. Laurence Steinberg and Kathryn C. Monahan, "Age Differences in Resistance to Peer Influence," *Developmental Psychology* 6, no. 43 (2007): 1531–43.

2. Cheryl Hanna, "Sex before Violence: Girls, Dating Violence, and (Perceived) Sexual Autonomy," *Fordham Law Urban Journal*, 2006; http://www.thefreelibrary.com/Sex+before+violence%3a+girls%2c+dating+violence%2c+and+(perceived)+sexual...-a0147746249.

3. "Teen Peer Pressure: Raising a Peer Pressure–Proof Child" (10 June 2009); www.webmd.com/parenting/teen-abuse-cough-medicine-9/teen-peer-pressure-raising-peer-pressure-proof-child?page=2].

Pregnancy

1. "Pregnant Teen Help," www.pregnantteenhelp.org/articles1.html.

Promiscuity and Sexually Transmitted Diseases

1. Bernadine Healy, "Teen Sex and Pregnancy: Part of a Bigger Problem," January 9, 2009; health
.usnews.com/blogs/heart-to-heart/2009/01/09/teen-sex-and-pregnancy-part-of-a-bigger-problem
.html.

2. KidsHealth, "About Sexually Transmitted Diseases," http://www.kidshealth.org/teen/sexual_
health/stds/std.html.

3. Statistics from www.cdc.gov/std/stats08.

4. Jeff Jacobs and Barry H. Garst, "What's the Big Deal? Taking a Look at "in" Issues for Teens
Today," *Camping Magazine*, November/December 2007, http://findarticles.com/p/articles/mi_m1249/
is_6_80/ai_n24216206/?tag=content;col1.

Schoolwork

1. Kristin A. Moore et al., "Parent-Teen Relationships and Interactions: Far More Positive than Not,"
Child Trends Research Brief, December 2004; http://www.childtrends.org/files/parent_teenRB.pdf.

2. Katherine Alimo, Christine M. Olson, and Edward A. Frongillo Jr., "Food Insufficiency and
American School-aged Children's Cognitive, Academic, and Psychosocial Development," *Pediatrics*
108 (2001): 44–53.

3. Tiffany Field, Miguel Diego, and Christopher E. Sanders, "Exercise Is Positively Related to
Adolescents' Relationships and Academics," *Adolescence* 141, no. 36 (2001): 105–10.

4. Denise Hallfors, et al., "Adolescent Depression and Suicide Risk: Association with Sex and
Drug Behavior," *American Journal of Preventive Medicine* 27, no. 3 (2004): 224–31.

Sexual Abuse

1. ACE Study, "Prevalence—Adverse Childhood Experiences"; http://www.cdc.gov/nccdphp/
ace/prevalence.htm.

2. Don Schnure, "Teen Chat Rooms Peer Pressure Statistics," *Family and Marriage Community*, 2008;
http://www.thefreelibrary.com/Teen+Chat+Rooms+Peer+Pressure+Statistics-a01073853029.

3. Dan Allender, *The Wounded Heart: Hope for Adult Victims of Childhood Sexual Abuse* (Nav-
Press, 2008).

Sexual Orientation

1. Gary Schneeberger, "Sexual Orientation Can Be Changed," Focus on the Family Action Center,
http://www.citizenlink.org/CLtopstories/A000010419.cfm.

2. Alison Lobron, "Easy Out," *Boston Globe*, November 11, 2007, http://www.boston.com/
bostonglobe/magazine/articles/2007/11/11/easy_out/?page=1.

3. "APA Revises 'Gay Gene' Theory," May 21, 2009, http://exodusyouth.net.

Spiritual Doubt

1. Henry David Thoreau, *Early Spring in Massachusetts: From the Journals of Henry David Thoreau*
(New York: BiblioBazaar, 2008), 224.

Stress

1. Suniya S. Luthar, "The Culture of Affluence: Psychological Costs of Material Wealth," *NIH
Public Access Author Manuscript* 74, no. 6 (2003): 1581–93.

2. Denise E. LaRue and Judith W. Herrman, "Adolescent Stress through the Eyes of High-Risk
Teens," *Pediatric Nursing* 5, no. 34 (2008): 375–80.

3. American Academy of Child and Adolescent Psychiatry 66 (2005); http://www.aacap.org/cs/
root/facts_for_families/helping_teenagers_with_stress.

Suicide

1. Aurelia Williams, "Teen suicide facts and answers," *Family and Marriage Community*, 2007,
http://www.thefreelibrary.com/Teen+Suicide+Facts+and+Answers-a01073779704.

Trauma

1. www.medterms.com/script/main/art.asp?articlekey=8171.

2. Bob Murray, "What Is Childhood Trauma?" www.upliftprogram.com/facts_childhood_trauma .html.

3. "Helping Your Child or Teen Cope with Trauma," www.medicinenet.com/script/main/art .asp?articlekey=21351.

4. Ibid.

5. American Psychiatric Association, *Diagnostic and Statistical Manual of Mental Disorders* IV, text revision (DSM-IV-TR), 467–68.

Video Game and Cyber Addiction

1. "1 in 12 Teens Addicted to Video Games," April 20, 2009, http://www.psychcentral.com/ news/2009/04/20/1-in-12-teens-addicted-to-video-games/5438.html.

2. Jeroen S. Lemmens, Patti M. Valkenburg, and Johen Peter, "Development and validation of a game addiction scale for adolescents," *Media Psychology* (2009): 77–95.

3. S. M. Grusser, R. Thalemann, and M. D. Griffiths, "Excessive computer game playing: Evidence for addiction and aggression?" *CyberPsychology and Behavior* 2, no. 10 (2007): 290–92.

4. Kaiser Family Foundation, M2: Media in the Lives of 8- to 18-year olds, 2010.

5. Ibid.

6. Amy S. Clark, "Detox for Video Game Addiction? Experts Say Gaming Can Be a Compulsion as Strong as Gambling," www.cbsnews.com/stories/2006/07/03/health/webmd/main1773956.shtml.

24753467R00164

Made in the USA
Lexington, KY
03 August 2013